a *career*
in your *suitcase*

a *career*
in your *suitcase*

THIRD EDITION

JO PARFITT

DISCLAIMER

Who Should Read This Book?

'Work is love made visible.'
Khalil Gibran

Do you want to find work that is based on what you most love to do, that fits your dreams, your lifestyle and your needs and that works wherever you find yourself living?

A *Career in Your Suitcase*, means simply, work that moves when you do. Whether you are moving to another continent or simply another city you may have to uproot your current career to create a new one. If you have had a career break, a country break or simply need a new start, this book is for you.

This book is for anyone who lives or hopes to live in another place and has to start again. If you want to find fulfilling, enjoyable work that is a perfect fit for who you are, where you live and what you want from your life, then this is for you.

You may be about to emigrate, to retire, to return to work, to move elsewhere temporarily or permanently. You may be what is termed an 'accompanying partner' of an expatriate employee and about to move once or many times. You may be about to move alone, as part of a couple, or with a family and want to work in a new location. You may want to run a business from your kitchen table or home office, find part-time, full-time, freelance or contract work. You may want to develop a one-off successful company or you may simply want to find something to do that can be sustained and grown as you move from place to place.

This book has much to offer the global nomad who needs a career with global networks and about which they can stay motivated despite frequent upheaval. Yet it also speaks directly to anyone, anywhere, who has ever wanted to discover, once and for all, what they really really want to do for a living and how to turn that dream into reality.

Praise for *A Career in Your Suitcase*

'A Career In Your Suitcase' is the perfect primer to inform and inspire spouses moving internationally. Jo Parfitt writes from the experience of someone who successfully created a number of concurrent and consecutive portable careers.'
> **Beverly D Roman, Publisher, BR Anchor Publishing**

'Research has shown why it's so important to maintain a professional identity when moving around the world. Jo Parfitt has literally written The Book on how to maintain this identity... full of practical advice and sage guidance, written from the heart by someone who's been there.'
> **Anne P Copeland PhD, Executive Director, The Interchange Institute,**
> ***www.interchangeinstitute.com***

'With A Career In Your Suitcase, Jo Parfitt is giving much-needed attention to a subject of increasing importance: meaningful occupations for expatriate spouses.'
> **Patricia Linderman, Co-author of The Expert Expatriate:**
> **Your Guide to Successful Relocation Abroad**

'In today's global economy, an international career can be built anywhere where electricity and a telephone line are available. In A Career In Your Suitcase readers will find the practical advice and encouragement to help make it happen.'
> **Lya Sorano, CEO, The Oliver/Sorano Group, Inc. *www.lyasorano.com***

'An awesome networker and intrepid traveller, there is nothing that Jo doesn't know about creating, sustaining and growing a portable career whilst moving round the world. Yes, there really is a career in your suitcase and Jo ensures that you unpack it safely.'
> **Gill Cowell, Publisher, The Weekly Telegraph**

'Jo is the perfect example of how a 'trailing spouse' can make the most of her time abroad. She is a brilliant networker and a great believer in giving out advice and help to anyone she meets who need it. In her book she tells readers how they can use their talents and experience to develop profitable and portable careers. She has certainly practised what she preaches and readers will find her common sense approach to developing a career inspiring and thought provoking.'
> **Laurence Rogers, The Brandmakers Company, *www.thebrandmakers.co.uk***

'Jo's passion and real life knowledge of this subject always mean that her talks are well worth listening to. You even come away learning something if your career is thoroughly stuck in one country, without a suitcase in sight.'
> **Christine Searancke, Director, Be Clear Ltd. *www.beclear.co.uk***

'I greatly admire your entrepreneurship. A true role model!'
> **Shari Leslie Segall, Director, Foreign Affairs Ltd. France**

'Heard the talk, read the book and seen the website. As an ex-expat myself, it's all good, helpful, and supportive stuff! Now running my own business, it's still good to top-up information and make new friends. Thanks Jo.'
Susie Clark, Director, Small World Relocation, www.smallworldrelocation.co.uk

'I attended one of the first Career In Your Suitcase workshops at the Global Living Conference in 1998 and it showed me that I could write a book and get it published, even if I was a Trailing Male and no one else thought I could do it.'
Huw Francis, Writer, international business consultant and male expat spouse, www.huwfrancis.com

'Thanks for the wise words – just what the doctor ordered.'
Vera Nicholas-Gervais, www.soulgouls.com, Canada

'Women are encouraged to think outside of the box. Jo Parfitt inspires us to redefine what we need to take out of the box and put into our suitcases. After listening to her portable ideas, travelling light takes on a dare-to-dream 'blue sky' perspective. In essence, all you need to carry are the tools you have accumulated within, thereafter it's all about the re-packaging!'
Connie Moser, RMS Relocation Management Services b.v. Editor, Resource and Development, Amsterdam

'A smart move! The book and complementary website addresses everything and more for spouses on the move. Both informative, practical, personable and supportive, it is a must have tool.'
Hilly van Swol, President of CONSULTus Expatriate Briefings and Intercultural Seminars and author of When Abroad – Do as the Local Children Do

'Having watched Jo in action during one of her Career In Your Suitcase workshops, I wistfully wondered why I couldn't have met her twenty years ago when I first went abroad. Developing my professional life would have gone a lot more smoothly.'
Robin Pascoe, Expatriate Press

'If anyone can write about a career in your suitcase, Jo Parfitt can. Her experience, knowledge and network of global contacts are clearly demonstrated in her A Career in Your Suitcase series... true enlightenment for any mobile individual who aims for eternal blue skies.'
Assunta Mondello, Expatriate Adviser, The American Hour

'While both husband and wife have adjustments to make in an international posting, the accompanying spouse (generally the wife) must build a 'life-between-flights' so to speak. Those women who have had meaningful careers will gain practical knowledge and skills from Jo Parfitt who has lived the life. Her valuable insights provide excellent coping suggestions.'
Carlanne Herzog, MA, Cross-Cultural Coordinator/Trainer Prudential Global Workforce Development Intercultural Services

Contents

Introduction

Since I first conceived this book, back in 1996, in Stavanger, Norway, I have watched the idea of a career in your suitcase evolve, pick up speed and grow into what I consider to be the number one solution to the dual career problem. It has been well over ten years now and many people, from all over the world have inspired me and added to my vision. However, one person in particular has to be held responsible for this book. Back in 1996, Kit Prendergast asked me to tell the members of the professional women's group she chaired about the career I had sustained while I had lived abroad in three different countries. She then encouraged me to develop my knowledge into the first ever Career in Your Suitcase workshop. Kit made me believe I had something to say. She gave value to my experiences.

The input and support of this book's contributors and all the people who have shared their secrets with me over the years have enriched this publication. Rather than take the wisdom and experiences of others and put them into my own writing style, I have instead chosen to publish their work in their own voices. With two men on the team as well as American, British and Canadian contributors, the range of styles is evident.

I would like to thank The Expatriate Archive Centre in The Hague, for allowing me to use material from the transcripts of two digital recordings. Thanks too to The Permits Foundation for their input regarding work permits and to The Trailing Spouse, ORC Worldwide and GMAC for their surveys. The Expatriate Archive Centre, The Trailing Spouse, Career-in-your-suitcase.com and CareerByChoice.com provided many pertinent quotations but the majority came from the mentors and bloggers at ExpatWomen.com and my gratitude goes to Andrea Martins who sourced them for me. Thanks too to Going Global, NetExpat, HR-Sense and Be Clear for their contributions regarding CVs, interviews and presentation skills, respectively. Most of all, I would like to thank Galen Tinder, REA Manager, for his tremendous contribution and advice on every chapter of the second edition of this book and his continued dedication to this, the third, updated, edition. As an American with over 25 years experience in human services, who currently works as a senior manager and career consultant for this book's sponsor, Ricklin-Echikson Associates (REA), Galen's input has been invaluable.

Inevitably, I give huge thanks to my husband, Ian, for making my career in my suitcase possible in the first place. I have immense gratitude to my children, Sam and Josh, for respecting the fact that I often work from home and for always being supportive. But it is my parents, Peter and Jenny Gosling, who have believed in me and shown their pride in even my smallest achievement, since the day I was born. And that has made all the difference.

Jo Parfitt
March 2008

From The Sponsor

In our fast paced and increasingly global economy we take for granted that employees and their partners will relocate across state, provincial, national and continental borders at the behest of their employers and for the enhancement of their careers. While we assume that moving is a fixed and growing feature of contemporary life, it can often be a wrenching experience for the partner and other members of the family. The family pain and disruption of relocation is a primary reason why employees turn down opportunities for new assignments or abandon these assignments before their completion.

REA is a global company that specialises in partner assistance services and is committed to helping employees, partners and families make healthy and productive transitions. We choose our international consultants for their professional expertise in career counselling and their experience handling the unique challenges of relocation. All have lived and worked in foreign countries and are well-versed in the career and life transition challenges.

For the relocating partner, an important ingredient in a positive relocation is finding opportunities to pursue employment and vocational growth. This is true especially of expatriate partners. These men and women often find it particularly difficult to find conventional employment at a time in their lives when they particularly need to maintain their own professional and social identity.

When Jo Parfitt offered REA and me the opportunity to collaborate on the third edition of this book, we were honored and excited by the prospect of bringing our experience and expertise to bear on the employment and vocational challenges facing expatriate partners.

In the last several years we have learned more about the repatriation experience and better appreciated that repatriation can be as jarring and confusing as expatriation. Repatriates are rarely able to return to the job or company they left and may not, for that matter, want to do so. They may be interested in building on their international experience but have as little idea of how to do that as they did about what to do at the beginning of their partner's assignment. There are parts of this book that should be helpful to partners returning to a home that seems foreign to them.

We hope through co-authoring and co-sponsoring the third edition of *A Career In Your Suitcase* that we have made a modest but tangible contribution to the well-being and positive experience of globally mobile families. We also hope that in this way we are contributing to the health and viability of our emerging global society.

Galen Tinder
Senior Consultant and Manager
Ricklin-Echikson Associates Inc. *www.r-e-a.com*

Foreword

International mobility is an important driver and result of the global economy. According to the United Nations, there are almost 200 million international migrants in the world, equivalent to the population of Brazil. This number has more than doubled in the last 25 years. Currently, one in 35 people, or three per cent of the world population, is an international migrant and around half of them are women. I often wonder how they and their families adapt.

A small proportion of international migrants are intra-company transferees, highly skilled men and women who are posted by international employers for three or four years at a time. Dozens of studies over 20 years have shown that it is the policies and practices that apply to the family as a whole that make or break an international assignment. In particular, concerns about dual careers and whether the partner will be able to get a job in the new location, are the major reasons why staff turn down an international assignment.

During my 30 years in international human resources management, I have seen that the partners of international employees face a bewildering array of challenges when they start to think about how they will manage their own career for a life on the move. The best international employers recognise this and offer a range of support. Permits Foundation, of which I am a director, is an employer initiative that advocates a relaxation of work permit regulations for partners of expatriate employees worldwide. But that is only one part of the solution. Career in a Suitcase sets out to show partners what they can do to help themselves.

When Jo asked me to write the foreword, I was delighted to accept. I met Jo in 1998 at the Paris Women on the Move Conference not long after she had published the first edition of Career in a Suitcase. At that time, I was managing Shell's Spouse Employment Centre and Jo's book, with its practical examples of a portable career, immediately became part of my library. What struck me then and what continues to impress me is Jo's authenticity and passion for sharing the ups and downs of a mobile lifestyle. Jo really walks the talk of her own stated mission 'sharing what I know to help others to grow'. Her ability to pull together her own personal experience with case studies, a wealth of resources and advice from other experts in her extensive network, has resulted in a thoroughly insightful, recognisable, believable and useful handbook.

Jo's concept of the portable career is a brilliant solution to the dual career challenge because it opens your mind to a wider range of choices and gives you the 'I can do this too' feeling.

If a portable career is a career in a suitcase, this book must surely be in the essential hand luggage of every traveler on this voyage of discovery and inspiration.

Kathleen van der Wilk-Carlton
Director Permits Foundation

1 a career in your suitcase

'Work is love made visible.'
Khalil Gibran

Introduction - Setting The Scene

Until 1987 I had enjoyed a successful career as a partner in a computer training business. I made my living from teaching and writing and had already published more than ten computer handbooks. But then I got married and my husband was posted to Dubai. Telling me that I would regret it for the rest of my life if I refused to join him, my new husband persuaded me to become what is sometimes rather unflatteringly called a 'trailing spouse'. In this politically correct world the term has become the more anodyne 'accompanying partner'. Yet, it is perhaps the men in our number who have created the most compelling term - that of STUDS, which stands for Spouse Trailing Under Duress Successfully. I'll stick with calling myself an 'accompanying partner'.

In the 20 years that have followed, I have come to agree with my husband. I am glad I made the journey and yes, I would have regretted it for the rest of my life had I stayed behind. During these intervening years, I have developed what I call a *career in my suitcase,* a portable career that moves when I do. A career that is mobile, sustainable and keeps growing despite moving country every few years.

The first ten years were a struggle, in which I did my fair share of door-slamming and sulking. But it was around 1997 that I read Robin Pascoe's '*A Wife's* Guide' and realised, at last, that a) I was not alone and b) I was not mad. In fact I was part of something often called the *Dual Career Issue.* It was around this time that I published the first edition of *A Career in Your Suitcase.*

Ten years ago I began to study the phenomenon. I attended conferences, interviewed countless experts and talked with many women, and men, who shared my interested in portable careers. As a journalist, I was able to learn about this at the coalface and then share what I knew in the best way I knew - by writing about it.

Today, few international corporations remain ignorant of the dual career issue. It is on the agenda of almost every multinational corporation. Sadly though, many organisations find it a bit of a hot potato and offer the same kind of support they always have - with work permits, language and training. But it is impossible to create a one size fits all solution to this dilemma. Few mobile spouses will be able to climb their chosen career ladder, stay in the same field, or even the same company. Few will find it easy to hop from permanent employment to permanent employment. For even if there were work available, other hurdles get in the way, such as a lack of work permits or fluency in a new language. Perhaps your qualifications will not be accepted in a new country? Or maybe your usual career just does not exist in your new location? And then, with the demands of conducting an international relocation and all the domestic duties that entails, not to mention the responsibility of looking after a mobile family, it can be hard to find suitable work that fits round everything else.

If you plan to make just a single move or move within the same country, then thankfully issues such as language barriers, work permits and unrecognised qualifications are unlikely to be a problem. But you may still find it difficult to obtain work similar to before the move. A fisherman would have to find a creative solution if he moved to an inner city. Someone with a shop selling tartan in Scotland may find it hard to establish the same business in the south of England. There are many barriers likely to hinder your progress. I believe that a portable career may be just the solution you have been looking for.

SO WHAT IS A DUAL CAREER ANYWAY?

Many of today's families comprise two working partners, both wanting to pursue a long-term career. They may both want to work because it is the natural next step after higher education, but maybe they simply need the money. With the average house price in the UK set at about ten times the average salary, this is no surprise. Of course, this is one of the reasons why so many choose to emigrate. To move to a better life with a lower cost of living. In 2006, one million British people emigrated permanently. Others move temporarily, on one or more assignments away from their home base. Many go overseas. In 2007, there were estimated to be 200,000 expats working legally in The Netherlands alone. At the same time there are 57,000 in Shanghai, while in the United Arab Emirates foreigners make up over 80 per cent of the entire workforce.

As we become more educated and open to women in skilled and managerial positions, it is likely that an educated, successful man will have an educated and career orientated wife and vice versa. Educated, career orientated people want to work, and must frequently do so in a dual career scenario. Yet it is rare for both partners to receive promotions or opportunities at the same time and in the same location.

According to the 2006 GMAC Global Relocation Trends Survey, which surveyed 180 international companies, 66 per cent of the assignments that had been refused, were rejected because of the spouse's career. ORC Worldwide's 2005 Dual Careers and International Assignments survey was completed by 145,000 people in 254 international organisations, representing almost 12 million people worldwide. It states that 74 per were concerned about the spouse's career with 72 per cent unhappy about the loss of income that would entail.

Yvonne McNulty conducted the 2005 Trailing Spouse Survey, found at *www.thetrailingspouse.com*, and interviewed 264 accompanying partners (91% female / 9% male). A massive 70 per cent believed that an assignment's success has much to do with the spouse's ability to transfer her or his career to the new location.

The apparent ideal of partners taking it in turns with their career is both unlikely and impractical. More often, the balance eventually shifts towards one person's career while the other partner reconciles himself or herself to taking a back seat for a while. Losing the esteem that goes with a professional identity can produce dire and sometimes permanent consequences. So, despite an increasingly global and mobile society, the progress of the career of the accompanying partner still poses a problem.

The Trailing Spouse survey reveals that 79 per cent of respondents were working before the move with 84 per cent are educated to at least bachelor's degree level and yet just 36 per cent found work when they arrive. The 2006 Global Relocation Trends Survey showed that while 59 per cent of spouses were employed before assignment only 8 per cent found work. This is worse than ever.

'Historically, the average gap has been 33%, and the largest previously recorded gap was 39% in the 2005 survey. The data clearly shows that the percentage of partners and spouses employed before an assignment has been increasing since the beginning of this survey, and after the 2002 survey, it has hovered at 50%.'
GMAC Global Relocation Trends Survey 2006

THE IMPACT ON IDENTITY

'It is more stressful to not have work when you want it than to do something you dislike.'
Tom Jackson, author, Guerilla Tactics in the Job Market

An unhappy spouse will impact the move badly. The main reason for spousal unhappiness is the difficulty he or she has in maintaining a professional identity or career. Valerie Scane, an accompanying partner who has lived in the Far East, has researched this phenomenon and believes that this loss can make a female into a 'hollow woman'. Without the security of maybe the job title, the colleagues, the income, the routine and satisfaction that can be derived from a career, you can start to lose sight of who you are. This can be very frightening.

With a loss of identity comes a loss of self-confidence and self-esteem. Enforced idleness can be hard to deal with. Without something 'interesting' to think about, it can be easy to become stressed or depressed.

'Due to my inability to be employed for the first time in my working life I am dependent on another person. I feel trapped and observed all the time. This raises the stress level enormously.'

'My loss of job, loss of self-esteem, and an imbalance in the relationship is very stressful. Prior to this last relocation we were at the same level job wise.'

'By not being able to continue with my career I am made to feel like a second-class citizen... It is a lonely life, and we, the trailing spouse, are left to re-invent ourselves after every relocation. It's exhausting and unrewarding. I regret my life.'
'My self-esteem has taken a beating because I don't feel that I am contributing to our household finances.'

'I had no idea how much my sense of self-worth was tied to my career.'

'I felt that I had given my real "self", and had become less of a person.'

'Companies need to support the spouse in allowing them to further their career. I do not live for my husband, nor do I live for his work, and they just couldn't understand that my work/career was, and is, as important as his. He did not marry a housewife and I will never be one.'

'I was a barrister in Australia who thought it might be fun to take a year to live with my husband in far north Finland. It wasn't. I couldn't work. I was ignored and my whole identity disappeared. We now live apart for 5 days a week - he in far north Finland, me in Helsinki. I am working, but it is not the senior job I had in Australia and this has caused intense bitterness.'

Respondents, 2005 Trailing Spouse Survey

WHAT CAN BE DONE TO HELP?

There is no doubt that traditional, salaried careers are the hardest for the accompanying partner to obtain and retain. Increasingly, companies are realising that self-employment and a portable career offer a viable solution. In addition companies see the benefit of offering partners opportunities for further education and assisting them in finding attractive volunteer roles.

'Of all the issues explored in this study, the dual-career challenge still remains the number one concern for the trailing spouse. There is a critical need for sponsoring organisations to plan and prepare spouses for the intrinsic impact of losing their career or stepping out of the workforce for an extended period of time whilst on assignment. And whilst spousal support programs were viewed as an essential requirement in the expatriate policy by the majority of respondents, too few trailing spouses were actually receiving this level of support from the organisation.'

2005 Trailing Spouse Survey

Despite all the best intentions on the part of both would-be employees and their employers, there are often obstacles to working in foreign lands.

These barriers are:

- Lack of work permit
- Lack of fluency in the host language
- Incompatibility of certification
- Lack of suitable employment
- Cultural differences
- Country nationals having priority
- Mobile spouse's inevitable lack of longer term commitment
- Mobile spouse's lack of transferable skills

The Trailing Spouse survey found that 53 per cent cited work permit restrictions as the major barrier, with language barriers coming in at 11 per cent, qualifications not being recognised at 9 per cent and limited opportunities at 8 per cent, thus, they are, in order.

Reasons for not working abroad according to accompanying partners

1. Work permit restrictions
2. Language barriers
3. Qualifications not recognised
4. Limited opportunities

It appears that the priorities shown by the affected accompanying partners do not quite mirror those demonstrated by the companies offering assistance, though they are certainly on track.

'Most Asian countries we were posted to do not allow wives or dependents of an expat worker to work because they would like positions to be filled by local people, unless one has a very specialised kind of profession that locals cannot do.'
Business administrator, 2005 Trailing Spouse Survey

'I have had two jobs since arriving one not in my field and one part-time as a writer. Locals in both jobs have replaced me because that is the law. I am now working to establish a consulting business where my clients are off Bermuda so I don't need to get involved with work permits. I should have done this long ago.'
Corporate Communications, 2005 Trailing Spouse Survey

'I have had job offers, but the visa issue is the reason it doesn't work out. Very frustrating! Employers are put off by the extra paperwork and the fee even though I've been offering to pay that.'
Journalist, 2005 Trailing Spouse Survey

'I am a psychologist registered in NZ and just moved from Sweden where language AND qualifications were not recognised – a very sharp learning curve for me and a major personal struggle especially as a financially dependent newly-wed too with an MA suddenly reduced to washing undies! Set up LifeLine in Shanghai (anonymous telephone help line) mainly for expats there – lots of stories of loss of identity and the strain that puts on relationships.'
Victoria, New Zealander in India, *www.expatwomen.com*

'To arrive in the States without being sponsored by an employer is a nightmare. The qualifications you get in the UK go for nothing here. I was made to feel inadequate and as if I was discriminated against [...] It was really frustrating and I literally had to beg someone to give me a chance.'
Lizzy, British in America, *www.expatwomen.com*

'If you come placed with a Company from your home country, I have found, especially for women, there to be a 'halo effect'. Companies here think (often correctly): "hey, if they're willing to send her here, she must be a high performance individual." And you get a lot more respect [...] My most important advice for anyone contemplating a move to a foreign country, always try to get placed from your home country. It will save a lot of time and aggravation in attempting to find jobs in your new country. My experience in the Mediterranean is that most high profile executives end up teaching English for a long, long while, or end up in jobs well below their expertise (and very far below their old pay levels). This is not the case in the UK - Ireland - Scandinavian countries.'
**Lisa, British in Italy, *http://burntbythetuscansun.blogspot.com*
and *www.expatwomen.com***

ASSISTANCE OFFERED TO ACCOMPANYING PARTNERS BY THE COMPANY

The Global Relocation Trends Survey shows that 58 per cent of companies offer cross-cultural training to the whole family. The ORC Dual Career Survey shows that this was offered by 64 per cent of companies. Interestingly, ORC shows that the support services generally offered to the spouse is delivered with the following priority:

1. Language training
2. Cultural orientation
3. Work permit assistance
4. Education and training
5. Job search assistance
6. Career counseling
7. CV preparation

'If we accept that organisations cannot and should not simply throw more money at the problem, as such tangibles generally do not provide long-term motivation and are no real compensation for career and income loss, then more needs to be done at the intangible level. Those with careers want to remain in careers for their own intrinsic motivation and satisfaction. And taking into account issues in the housing market, particularly in Europe, two incomes have become a basic fact of life. Initiatives that support career enhancement and the opportunity to pursue job and career opportunities provide the way forward if couples are to accept and remain in an international posting. Recognising this, the survey sees a substantial rise in initiatives taken by employers to offer work permit assistance to spouses/partners and to become involved in lobbying via the Permits Foundation - with some notable success to date.'
ORC Worldwide, Dual Careers and International Assignments Survey 2005

Let's take a look at the spouse's top four reasons for failing to find suitable work overseas first and consider how the lead employee's company may be tackling them.

Work Permits

With work permits being the major issue, let's look at this first.

Many countries provide work visas for the relocated international assignee – but not for the spouse. In fact, spouses are often unaware of the work visa regulations that will prevent them obtaining regular work. Fortunately, this is improving.

One of the key findings of the ORC 2005 survey was that the number of organisations turning their attention to work-permit assistance and lobbying for improvements for relocating working spouses/partners has doubled.

In many countries of the world, the partners of expatriates on assignment are simply not granted a work visa, or labour card. While diplomatic families are sometimes permitted to work through bilateral arrangements, thousands of others are denied the chance to work in their host country or at least face a long complicated process to get a work permit.

In June 2001 The Permits Foundation was launched. This is a body dedicated to promoting access to employment worldwide for the spouses of expatriate executives. Jan Schaapsmeerders, was its founding chairman and CEO of Shell People Services at the time. Gill Gordon, HR director of Schlumberger Limited, currently chairs the foundation.

'It is essential that these men and women feel they can take expatriate posts which offer fair employment prospects to their spouses too. Otherwise, The Permits Foundation believes, fewer people may take up assignments abroad, which lessens the skills base and technology transfer available to both developing and developed countries. We hope the Foundation can help persuade governments worldwide that the spouse of an expatriate employee can also make a useful contribution to the local economy.'
Jan Schaapsmeerders, published in Woman Abroad magazine

Permits is a non-profit corporate initiative and the brainchild of Kathleen van der Wilk-Carlton, who has been invited to write the foreword for this book. In 1995, she was the founding manager of the Shell Spouse Employment Centre, now part of Global Outpost Services. Almost 50 international companies and organisations currently sponsor the Permits Foundation. A board of ten sponsors meets quarterly to review strategy and plans and is actively involved in supporting efforts in particular countries. It is no surprise that the foundation is growing rapidly; lack of work permits is the major barrier to partner employment as we have seen. Being a sponsor is a clear indication that an employer is keen to improve the situation for its employees.

Since its inception, Permits Foundation has developed a clear picture of international best practice and uses this to show countries the gap between where they are now and where they need to be to make their country more attractive to international staff, trade and investment. Specifically, Permits wants legally resident spouses and partners to have an open permission to work during an expatriate assignment. The group has already been successful in promoting change in a number of countries.

> 'The first milestone was the introduction of work authorisation for the spouses of intra-company transferees and treaty traders in the USA in January 2002. We had supported a US coalition of employers and proposed that the legislation was widened to cover all nationalities. Since then we successfully promoted change in The Netherlands, France and Hong Kong, which passed regulations allowing spouses of highly skilled staff to work freely. In the case of the Netherlands and France, this also applies to family members.'
> **Kathleen van der Wilk-Carlton, quoted on www.expatwomen.com**

Currently 17 countries have favourable arrangements for granting work permission to the spouse, partner and sometimes even children of work permit holders. Within Europe, apart from the Netherlands, Belgium, Denmark, Finland, France, Germany, Sweden and the UK allow family members of non-EU citizens to work, with some variations in the criteria and procedure. Outside Europe, the list includes Argentina, Australia, Canada, Hong Kong, Japan, New Zealand, Singapore and USA.

The European Union, which as a basic principal allows free movement for work of its own citizens, has now grown to 27 member states and transition restrictions for citizens of the new member states are gradually being removed. By 2011, free movement for work purposes will be extended to European citizens and family members of all 'EU 25' member states and by 2014 it will also apply to citizens of Bulgaria and Romania.

Towards the end of 2007, The European Commission presented plans for a European "Blue Card" for highly skilled migrants from outside the EU. These proposals also contain provision for spouses to access the employment market.

Plans are now underway at Permits Foundation to develop local networks that will promote change in India, Indonesia, Japan, Malaysia, Russia and China. These countries were selected principally because they are such important destinations for companies right now.

Building on the experience of best practice countries that already allow spouses to work, Permits Foundation aims to show that allowing spouses to work is an integral part of a policy of managed migration that goes hand in hand with attracting trade and investment. This should be perceived as an advantage, rather than a disadvantage, to the host country. Highly skilled staff and their spouses have much to offer local economies.

The Permits website will keep you informed of all the latest developments country by country and is well worth a visit. The website of Fragomen, Del Rey, Bernsen and Loewy PC also provides information on global immigration.

> 'It would be a great help if they could assist with legal and administrative work related to obtaining a work permit.'
> **Respondent, 2005 Trailing Spouse Survey**

Language

Unfamiliarity with the local spoken language can restrict an expatriate's employment options. Everyone spoke English when I lived in Dubai and I never felt the need to learn Arabic. Later on, in Norway, the locals spoke English, and so for day-to-day life there was little need to learn Norwegian. However, many of those who worked in offices found that speaking Norwegian helped integrate them into the company and business culture. In addition, many professions required that expatriate employees be fluent in the native tongue. Learning a language to a level of proficiency can take years – often time that is quite simply not available to the expatriate spouse on a one to three year assignment.

Although lack of work permits is the main reason a career has to be cut short, it is language learning that most companies are happy to provide to spouses. The ORC survey found that it is offered by almost 80 per cent of companies, with work permit information and advice coming in at just over 60 per cent. The Global Relocation Trends survey found that 69 per cent offered language training and 36 per cent work permit help.

'Unfortunately, I needed total fluency in Norwegian in order to be able to work here in my usual profession. I also needed approval from the local education authority for which I would have had to submit all my college and other course work as well as the certificates so they could ascertain whether they were compatible. Although I could have provided the paperwork, I would never have been fluent in the language.'
Kit, American in Norway, www.career-in-your-suitcase.com

Education

Sometimes your qualifications stand for nothing in a new country. This means you may have to further your study to obtain new, acceptable, qualifications or shelve your career. Incompatible licensing and certification can be a huge problem in some professions, particularly healthcare. In some countries a homeopath will also have to possess nursing qualifications, for example.

Some skills just cannot be transferred and retraining will be the only option. A ski instructor would be hard pressed to find vocational satisfaction in Singapore, for example. And although I was able to make and sell date chutney and even a date cookery book in the Middle East, I found little demand for either in Norway where palm trees are rare.

'Any ideas I had about career I left behind the minute I left my main career in the UK but what it has opened up are opportunities, huge opportunities for personal growth and development. I am just finishing off a psychology degree at the moment. I may never be able to use it but it's been very interesting. It is useful to me. I've learned a lot. I has helped me with my family and understanding my kids and all sorts of things.'
Julia, British, The Expatriate Archive, OAC5/3/3

Companies recognise that the provision of careers and study advice and even the finance for study are of great benefit. The ORC survey found that just over 47 per cent of companies offered education or training, just over 32 per cent offered career counseling. The Global Relocation Trends Survey found that 30 per cent offered advice on education and training with 15 per cent offering to reimburse costs.

> '[I wish companies would] give me intensive language training and an amount of money to buy information and specialised help during the relocation.'
> **Respondent, 2005 Trailing Spouse Survey**

Finding Opportunities

Lack of opportunities is cited as another factor that prevents spouses from finding work. But many spouses simply do not know where to look. This is where a careers advisor or a local advisor can be invaluable. The Global Relocation Trends survey found that 19 per cent of companies help with networking, 17 per cent help with job search and fees, while the ORC survey found that just over 32 per cent offered career counselling and almost 37 per cent job search assistance.

> '[I wish companies would] provide assistance on contacts. All I want is fair opportunities, not mere cash.'
>
> 'Educated, professional spouses need to be seen more as an asset, to be marketed to their local economy. I would prefer that my wife's employer spent more effort investigating what I do and using their local connections to make an appropriate match.'
>
> '[I wish companies would] offer career guidance/counseling for spouses unable to work due to legal restrictions of host country.'
>
> '[I wish companies would offer] assistance in finding a suitable job through local and inter-company networking and/or through outplacement companies (headhunters). I would also appreciate administrative and financial aid to continue my education.'
>
> '[I wish companies would] pay for a partner career course and counselor/coach on the spot to help get a picture of the market. Give me intensive language training and an amount of money to buy information and specialised help during the relocation.'
> **Respondents, 2005 Trailing Spouse Survey**

The dual career challenge is one that will not go away in a hurry. Fortunately corporations are finding creative ways to help ease the problem. Some maintain the belief that it is their role to provide a number of services and options that will empower people and give them the tools to help themselves. But for now, let me continue with my story and how A Career in Your Suitcase was born.

My Story

Let's go back now to my arrival in Dubai back in 1987. I was a new wife unaccustomed to idleness. We were living in a fully serviced apartment and it was not many weeks before I tired of sunbathing and small talk around the pool. I found it hard to do what I considered to be 'nothing' all day. My identity, until my marriage, had been tied up with my career. I liked to work, to feel I was achieving something and to be financially independent. I liked the camaraderie of colleagues and the opportunity to keep learning and developing. With no support or inspiration from my husband's employer, I decided to make my own luck and, over the next 20 years on the move, acquired a range of skills that would allow me to create, maintain, pick up and pack my portable career. Despite living in five different countries, in the end I learned how to look inside myself to discover what I most enjoyed doing and how I might adapt my interests and my skills to match them up with opportunities in each location.

During the first decade I made and sold chutney, and taught French, creative writing and computers. I became a journalist, wrote manuals and newsletters and self-published a cookery book. When I noticed how desperate the local expatriates were for books I turned to network marketing and sold Dorling Kindersley books and CD-ROMs. When I heard my dinner guests commending the delicious curry our Indian housekeeper had prepared, I ran a small take away service. I soon realised that problems are simply opportunities in disguise.

When we returned to England for a few years in 1997 with our two children, I noticed that things had changed. People no longer had careers for life back home either. Mothers wanted some work life balance and their frequent domestic relocations meant they wanted portable careers too. By 1998 I had formed Summertime Publishing and published the first edition of *A Career in Your Suitcase*. Since then, not only has that book sold out and been well received all over the world, but its message has inspired thousands of men and women, mobile and non-mobile, and encouraged them to create a career based on their passions. Since the first edition was released I have travelled the world speaking about my own experience and sharing the knowledge I have acquired. Along the way I've also been inspired by other people who have also created careers for their suitcases, and have learned from them.

After seven years back 'home', and a second edition of this book, we moved abroad again, to The Netherlands this time and my career came too, continuing to grow and develop along the way.

This third edition is a culmination of everything I have learned and all the people I've met – not only since the first book came out but from the very beginning, more than 20 years ago, when I inadvertently became involved in what is known as a dual career partnership.

I believe that a successful portable career is possible for anyone. First we must look inside ourselves to find our passions, then we must look outside ourselves to find the opportunities in the locality, and finally we must find a way to blend this together so that we can tailor-make a career that fits our values, aspirations and lifestyle.

A Career in Your Suitcase is there to inspire, inform and support anyone who wants to find work that they love. It's for all those people who, like me, want to continue working despite relocation. It's for everyone who believes that challenges are merely opportunities in disguise and that our world is full of surprises. Take a look at this book, be inspired by its contributors and then move onto its accompanying website *www.career-in-your-suitcase.com* so that your journey may never end.

Ten Steps to a Career in Your Suitcase

1. Consider hiring a coach or career consultant to join you on your journey at any or all stages of the process.

2. Find your passions, values, mission and meaning.

3. Assess your skills, talents, strengths and uniqueness.

4. Discover what you want and need from a career at this stage in your life.

5. Brainstorm the perfect portable career for you.

6. Adjust your career to fit your current location and the opportunities it holds.

7. Do the research and learning you need to prepare for transition and your chosen career.

8. Create the marketing materials you need (CV, website, cards, brochures).

9. Network to meet the people you will need as they become your clients employers, role models and support team

10. Make it happen by setting goals, staying motivated and developing the self-belief and confidence you need.

---

2 *find your passion*

In this chapter I will help you find out who you are and what you would like to do for a living. I'll begin by showing you how I was fortunate enough to turn something I love doing into a portable career that earned me money. Then I will inspire you with ways to find your passion too.

'Your reason and your passion are the rudder and the sails of your seafaring soul.'

Khalil Gibran

In this chapter:

- How I found my passions
- Life without work
- How my passions became portable
- How my career in my suitcase came home
- Why our passions can be hard to find
- Find your passion
- Getting started
- Put your passions on paper
- Ask your friends
- Self assessment tests
- Putting it all together

How I Found My Passions

I firmly believe you can do what you love and earn money from it. I've always believed this – despite the day at school when my careers adviser informed me, at age 14, that writing was not a career option, but just an indulgence! That was when I began my attempts at conforming. And though I had written my first poem at six, my first play at 13, kept a diary since age 11 and penned hundreds of letters, still I shelved my dream.

I loved French though. And for me that included the literature, the language, the people, the country and I found the teacher, Mr Feather, inspiring. It was also the subject in which I received the best marks. So I went to university to study French. I knew I didn't want to be a teacher, nor a translator. Somehow I realised I had to be creative, and so it was during the year I spent abroad in France, teaching English conversation to a group of despondent teenagers, that I found the perfect outlet. I would write a book called *French Tarts*. Not once did it strike me that I couldn't cook. I knew I had a great idea and a great title, and that my pursuit of authentic recipes from real French people would get me a few dinner invitations.

My plan worked. Octopus, the first publisher whom I approached with my idea, snapped it up. I quickly taught myself to type and use a word processor so that I could produce the manuscript. The book came out in English in 1985 and then in French, in France. I put this immense good fortune down to beginner's luck. I had become a writer after all. I was 24 years old. I was doing something I loved and earning money.

Yet, despite getting an agent and deluging her with many other ideas for cookery books, I guess I was let down by the fact that I was neither a trained nor an experienced chef. With hindsight, I realise that my enthusiasm didn't quite match my skill and some of my ideas left a lot to be desired. Anyway, after spending a year churning out synopses while I worked as a temporary word processing secretary, I decided it was time to change direction.

Instead of finding more work as a cookery writer, I found myself teaching word processing – the skill I'd only learned in order to produce the manuscript for *French Tarts*. But I found that I loved the work, particularly when I was required to create typing exercises for the students. I also liked producing the documentation and course handouts.

Surprisingly, the work energised me. I would never have dreamed that my creative soul would enjoy something as technical as word processing – but it did. I found that I enjoyed the lessons, meeting new people and watching the students learn and grow. In my own small way I was changing people's lives for the better. My enthusiasm must have shown because one of my clients asked me to go and work for him, developing some new computer training materials. The idea excited me and so, aged 25, I went freelance and have never looked back.

A few lucky breaks later, I found I had written 15 computer handbooks in plain language for some of England's largest publishers. Within a further two years I was in partnership with two others, running a thriving computer training and writing company.

Then I fell in love with Ian and we decided to get married. The trouble was that my new husband had been 'temporarily' posted to Dubai and refused to cut short his assignment and come home. So I moved abroad.

LIFE WITHOUT WORK

When I arrived in Dubai the day after my wedding, they put a stamp in my passport that read 'not permitted to take up employment'. I was devastated. I had a few writing contracts to complete that I'd brought with me, but would have to spend six weeks waiting for my computer to arrive so I could begin work. Until this moment my work had been my life and my passion. I'd developed few other interests and knew no one in Dubai. With no company support, I had no idea where to look for friends or things to do. Work was all I knew. By then, ironically, I had become quite a good cook, but knew no one to invite for dinner.

Two days before my computer arrived, Ian came home from the office to find me crouched on the floor of our beautiful apartment, ripping a newspaper to shreds and crying my eyes out from sheer frustration. Without work I was a fish out of water.

Of course I could have attended Arabic language classes, or learned to paint in watercolours. I could have joined the gym, or asked my husband to introduce me to the wives of his colleagues and friends. I could have taken advantage of the wonderful swimming pool and tennis courts that went with our apartment. I could have taken a taxi and explored the city. But all I wanted to do was work, and nothing else would do.

I had lost my professional identity. My personal identity too was so intertwined with work that I had forgotten who I was without it. I had no idea that volunteer work or taking classes might have fulfilled me. Being beholden to my husband and his company made me feel impotent, invisible. We had maid service in the apartment, so I had little to do. Shorts and tee-shirts didn't need much ironing. Despite the fact that I soon had a driving licence, I was nervous about taking to the roads alone. I felt like a hollow woman. I didn't feel whole without my computer and some work to do.

Women, returning to work after taking time off to have children find their confidence at a new low. But this is not reserved for mothers. It happens to lots of people after a career gap. Add to this having to live in a strange place, maybe with a new language, unfamiliar customs and unfathomable laws and your confidence can sink still lower. After so many knocks it can be hard to get going again and start looking for work.

'You need guts. You need to have the courage to say "I am going to do this."'
Belinda, Dutch, The Expatriate Archive, OAC5/3/3

'It is like this everywhere, change. Everything is new, so your confidence needs to be very strong just to say "Okay, here I am, wait for me, I am coming." ... I came over here at 24 with my first born son, three month old, and I didn't know where to go, what to do. My husband was flying round the world ... [I thought] Okay, what do I do here? And you just feel you don't really know where to go, what to do, or if you are doing things right.'
Flavia, Italian, The Expatriate Archive, OAC5/3/3

It had always pleased me to have a label. I was a 'writer' and a 'computer trainer'. I was not 'just a wife' and the very idea made me feel hugely uncomfortable. I realised I had a personal need, not only to have a professional identity, but also to earn my own money – however little. I didn't want to have to ask my husband for the money to buy him his own birthday present.

I appreciate that my own case may be extreme; over the years I have mellowed enormously and even taken up a few hobbies – but I am sure I'm not unique. As the surveys cited in the introduction show, up to 80 per cent of spouses want to work overseas and sometimes as few as eight per cent succeed.

'I have only been here for two or three months. My role has changed ... because my wife is here [as the lead employee]. I am now house husband and father ... fundamental change . . so much that it creates a spiritual crisis ... the whole identity has changed from the real one and the new one has not appeared yet ... there is a shift in the whole of the little ground on which I stand. It is giving way and sinking, sinking . . then I ask myself why? Why is this so? Behind this is fear ...Am I able to touch this fear? Am I able to embrace this fear? Or am I avoiding it? Sometimes I find I do avoid it because I don't want to [face] it. So I [focus on] TV, BBC news and so on so that all my projection is on something external and this is perhaps a way to cushion this crisis... .The mental crisis inside is so deep ... then as I come to terms with the gap within, it starts to open up the whole empty space, that I haven't seen [before] and I don't want to look at it.'
Wong, Malaysian in Europe, The Expatriate Archive, OAC5/3/3

HOW MY PASSIONS BECAME PORTABLE

Well, my computer did arrive and I completed my book contracts. But once they were finished, I soon learned that editors found it difficult to liaise with overseas authors. This was before we had email and fax machines and so, reluctantly, I realised I had to go back to the drawing board and create a new career for myself. Today, happily, things are very different for writers.

Ian had promised me that we would only be abroad for six months or so – but the thought of even a few months' sabbatical filled me with horror. I simply had to look for alternative employment.

Despite the stamp in my passport that apparently didn't allow me to work, I discovered that not all hope was lost. In fact, working in Dubai was remarkably easy. Provided you found a local company to sponsor you and supply a labour card, you could do almost anything at all.

Over the next six years in Dubai, and three in Oman, I developed a range of complementary and changing careers that I dipped into when the opportunity arose. Fortunately, I was also happy to discard some career streams when the opportunity disappeared. This ability to reinvent myself and be flexible has been key to my success. Each reinvention has taken place because I first looked inside myself to see which skills, interests and passions most excited me at that time. Next I looked carefully at the local market, to see where the gaps lay, or where I might find the most luck.

If I look inside myself, I see the following key skills, all of which have grown out of my passions:

- Creativity
- Writing
- Teaching
- Helping people to grow
- Flexibility
- Willingness to learn
- Desire for variety
- Being with people
- Communication
- Computer skills
- French
- A love of food and cooking
- Connecting people through informal networking

These core skills have led me to become a journalist, author, a teacher of creative writing, a teacher of French conversation, a copy writer, a publisher and co-author of a cookery book called *Dates*, a copy typist, a curriculum vitae producer, a computer teacher, a trainer of trainers, a computer training centre course developer, a manufacturer of Christmas decorations, a Dorling Kindersley book distributor, a manufacturer and marketer of date chutney, a founder of writers' circles, a keynote speaker, teacher, trainer and a newsletter editor. More recently, I have been editor of a couple of international expat magazines, become a publisher and a publishing consultant.

When I look inside myself, I can also see the values that motivate me and make my professional life work for me. Some people value money, others value fame, free time, flexible hours or variety. Values change over time and it's worth taking a look at yours regularly. If you want to be true to yourself, you need to consider your values as well as your passions. My values, right now, are:

- Sharing
- Supporting
- Making a difference
- Using my passions
- Interacting with people
- A balance of introversion and extroversion
- Being accessible and affordable
- Developing a specialism within a variety of projects

When living abroad, we were lucky enough not to need me to produce a solid second income. This has been a terrific opportunity and has given me permission to do only what I most enjoy. But when your family needs a second income, as ours did on repatriation to the UK for seven years after a decade overseas, your dreams may take a little honing.

> 'Going abroad and moving from one part of the country to another forces you to take a look a why you do things and how you think. You have to look inside yourself and find an inner strength. The people you usually turn to for that strength are not around. No one ever comes to you. You have to go out there and do it yourself. You have to be self-reliant. I feel that all these problems have, in time, turned into my personal strengths. It has been a totally positive experience.'
> Cheryl, American, *www.career-in-your-suitcase.com*

HOW MY CAREER IN MY SUITCASE CAME HOME

When we repatriated I had to earn some money. Overnight I became responsible for paying two sets of school fees and for family holidays. The first project I worked on when we came home was the publication of the first edition of *A Career in Your Suitcase*. I formed Summertime Publishing and, during 1998, launched this title and one called *Forced To Fly*. This took a lot of work and investment, and the returns were relatively small at first – so I decided to develop a range of seminars and workshops on the theme of portable careers. I soon discovered that, on average, about a quarter of delegates would buy a book too. And while these seminars were successful and well received, the marketing response was slow to start with. Along the way, I discovered that those who most wanted me to speak, and whom I most loved addressing, tended to be non-profit associations and international conferences – who had little, if any, budget. If I was to meet my financial target I had to think again.

Once more I looked inside myself, and decided that I had to calculate which among my many careers had the most earning potential. I had to think hard about which of my skills would earn me the most money per hour and for which there was also a market. During my soul searching I realised it was time to take my journalism to UK based magazines and newspapers. I love writing and in order to give me the most satisfaction, I needed to write about subjects that interested me. It became clear that I had picked up a few more skills and passions to add to my list. I could now call myself an expert on expatriate living and portable careers. I began in earnest to look for opportunities. Within a few months I was writing for *Resident Abroad* (later called *FT Expat*), *The Weekly Telegraph*, *Women's Business Magazine* and the *Smart Moves* section of *The Independent on Sunday*.

Journalism was my *job*. Portable career presentations and publishing were my *career*. At first my job funded my career but over time the two merged until I was able to pick and choose my writing projects and my presenting started to earn me money.

When, in 2000, three years after we came home, I was offered the chance to edit a new magazine called *Woman Abroad*, I jumped at the chance. Without a doubt, this position was the culmination of my career experiences to date and it allowed me to exercise all my skills and values at once. I was flying. Sadly, after the tragedy of 9/11, the magazine was forced to fold as living abroad lost its allure for a while. In 2002 I had to go back to the drawing board and this time I emerged as a Book Cook, specialising in editing books for clients and helping them through from pipedream to publication. You can find out more at *www.thebookcooks.com*.

But it was not enough for me to simply help others to produce their books, I had to write my own too, and in 2002, *Grow Your Own Networks* was published as well as a second edition of *Career in Your Suitcase*, followed in 2004 by *Find Your Passion*. Yet I need a balance of introvert and extrovert activities in order to be happy and so this was when I developed a range of writing workshops to add to the career workshops that first began in 1997. My love of travel meant that I took every opportunity to run these courses overseas.

In 2005, we moved abroad again, this time to The Hague, Netherlands, and having been careful to make my business global, many of my clients came too. I continued to be a Book Cook, marketed my workshops locally and, of course, kept on writing my books. In 2006, *Expat Entrepreneurs* was published. In 2007 a second edition of *Find Your Passion* and a new one, *Expat Writer - Release the Book Within* joined the list as well as a second edition of *Dates*.

I had outgrown the Book Cooks and the Career in Your Suitcase brands, and though they continue to exist, in October 2007, I became Expat Rollercoaster, a fitting metaphor for the up and down life, packed with excitement and fear that has become my life since I first went to Dubai in December 1987.

I believe it's my *right* to be able to do what I love for a living. If I want to be energised by my work, to look forward to each morning, to be authentic and enthusiastic, then it is vital that I'm passionate about my work. If we do what we love then our enthusiasm and energy will do our marketing for us. If you take a look back over my long list of specialisms you may be able to spot the 'red threads' that have run through everything I do. I first wrote the list of values that appeared a few pages back five years ago. When I revisit them, it is clear that little has changed. The 'red threads', the common denominators, that have sustained me despite those ups and downs and five moves, remain:

- Sharing
- Supporting
- Making a difference
- Using my passions
- Interacting with people
- A balance of introversion and extroversion
- Being accessible and affordable
- Developing a specialism within a variety of projects

Like many, my values are my passions. I need to incorporate them into my daily life in order to be happy. They are, to me, as vital as fresh air, food and water. It is easy for me now to seem complacent, and to point out exactly where my passions lie. But it was not always like that. It is only now, with the luxury of hindsight that I can look back and see the patterns and the 'red threads' emerge. I believe very strongly that finding your passion is the fundamental first step to creating a portable career that will sustain you from move to move and that will keep you motivated. A career based on your passion, is more likely to earn you money too because if you truly believe in what you do, people will notice and they will believe in you too. And then, of course, they will buy!

WHY OUR PASSIONS CAN BE HARD TO FIND

Back when I was 14 and my school careers adviser told me I couldn't make it as a writer, as I told you earlier, I picked another path. Interestingly, I'm also passionate about French – but if you noticed, it doesn't feature much in my most recent portfolio of careers. As a result, it would be easy to assume that this was never a true passion yet, even as my second choice, its value is now apparent. I love to travel, to meet people of other nationalities, to mix with other cultures and to communicate with them and learn about their food. Not content to be ever the tourist, for me, studying French meant that I also lived in France and had French friends. As a teenager I had many pen friends, and visited them on my own, in Germany and France, each summer. My potential love for expatriate life was written in my stars long before I chose to study French at university.

Sometimes we need to look more closely at the choices we make in order to spot the elements that excite us. Sometimes we are persuaded away from our passions for a variety of reasons I will go on to discuss here.

Between the ages of 11 and 15 I loved drama and took classes in speaking and acting. I was nervous about improvisation and preferred to have a script. Yet, at 15, at a local drama festival, I walked away with five first prizes. I was featured in the local paper and some of my friends made sarcastic comments about my showing off. I quit, never to act again. While there was no doubt that I loved acting and was good at it, I didn't want to lose friends over it. Rather than ostracise myself from my peers, I chose to give up something I enjoyed. Do you recognise this pattern in yourself? Often we suppress our passions because we want to conform. I decided not to flaunt my success and was never picked for the major parts in the school plays. Deeply disappointed, I became convinced I must have lacked talent.

When I was 18, I was picked for an interschool debating competition. I had such a crisis of confidence that I learned a script, when I was supposed to speak from cue cards. We lost. For the next 20 years I was quite sure that I did not belong on a stage at all.

In 1997 we were living in Norway. I'd started to compile notes for the first edition of *A Career in Your Suitcase*. One of the mums from my son's preschool, Kit Prendergast, commented that my story was inspirational and that I should do a short presentation to the business women's network there. Not one to pass up an opportunity or a challenge, I agreed. Then I worried myself silly! I was desperately nervous and, typically, wrote a complete script word for word. On the night, however, I found that people were truly interested and I dared to ad lib a little. The evening was a success and was the catalyst for a three hour workshop that I designed and ran with an American named Elizabeth Douet.

Nine months later we presented our workshop at the *Women on the Move* (now called *Global Living*) conference in Paris. We were to speak in the auditorium to between 100 and 300 people. On a stage, with radio mikes, overhead projectors and sound engineers. I was terrified and suffered with nerves for three months beforehand. Huw Francis, who writes *Chapter Eleven* for this book, was at that seminar. He says my voice trembled the entire time. Nevertheless the adrenalin rush I experienced afterwards was fantastic – and I was hooked.

Today, I have run this seminar and its many permutations all over the world, to thousands of different people. I know I belong on a stage. I prepare cue cards or Powerpoint presentations, but rarely look at them. My passion for being on stage was suppressed for so many years for reasons common to many of us.

Look to your past for clues as to where your passions may once have lain.

Another reason why we lose sight of what we love to do, is that we become rather good at other things. We may not be particularly talented at music, but practise hard because we want to be in the school orchestra with our friends. We develop a competence in an area so we can fit in.

With practice we can be good at almost anything – whether it be music, sport, mathematics or driving – but this does not mean the subject fills us with energy. Sometimes it can be hard to separate the things we love to do and do well, from the things we like to do less, but still do well.

Remember back to when you were at school and had to make choices about the subjects in which you wanted to specialise. If you performed well in many subjects then it may have been difficult to decide where to focus. However, the chances are that you elected to focus on the subjects that gave you the highest grades. Sadly, the subjects we do best in are not always the ones we love most.

You could be really good at maths, for example, and become a successful accounting firm partner only to realise one day that you are neither happy nor energised. As John Clark says in his book *The Money or Your Life*, you can get to the top of your chosen career ladder and suddenly realise that 'you have the ladder against the wrong wall'. Dr Katherine Benziger, in her book *Thriving in Mind,* calls this 'falsification of type'.

This is why it's so important, when you are trying to assess your skills, that you take account of the things you do at work and in your leisure time. Think about the activities that fill you with energy, even if they are not earning you money right now.

Don't expect it to be easy to find your passions. They may have been locked away for many years. You may have to dig deep to revive them. It may take a long time and you may be in for some surprises. But stick with it. The reward is well worth the effort.

Find Your Passion

Ever since the publication of a book by Richard Bolles, *What Color is Your Parachute?*, people have begun to believe work is more than just a salary. Bolles writes both for people who are out of work and for those weary of work lacking in fulfilment and meaning. His book provides readers with the blueprint for a journey of personal and vocational self-discovery.

Bolles recommends that we think of our work as the expression of our mission in life and he supplies us with many inventive exercises to help us identify the nature of this mission.

'I've turned my passion into work by capitalising on France's interesting food and culture backgrounds. Last year, with the help of a colleague, I organised wine tasting weekends in the well-known Bordeaux and Burgundy wine regions in France. I am planning another weekend trip to the Champagne region. France's gourmet offerings – wine, cheeses, local delicacies – allow me to help my students discover the answers to the secrets of French gastronomy. Whether it is a pre-class trip to the local outdoor market to select fresh ingredients for the menu we will prepare, or a more involved weekend trip to a specific region, I enjoy teaching others to experience, understand and appreciate France's culinary offerings.'
Sue Y, British, *www.career-in-your-suitcase.com*

In the following exercises and suggestions you'll find a mixture of activities and inspiration I have picked up over the last 15 years or so. Each has merit. Some ideas are of my own invention, others were inspired by other people.

If you decide you want to explore this topic in more depth then I suggest you refer to my book, entitled *Find Your Passion*, available from *www.amazon.co.uk*.

Getting Started

It is not surprising that many people neglect the difficult task of self-scrutiny. After all, where do you begin? How do you get started? How do you know you're on the right track? And how do you keep yourself accountable for the results? Here are several suggestions to launch you on your own voyage of self-discovery.

BUY A NOTEBOOK

Prepare to do a lot of soul searching, thinking and writing. Buy yourself a large, lined notebook, preferably spiral bound, in which to write your thoughts and exercises. Choose a large one, about A4 or foolscap in size. Try not to succumb to doing this on a computer. If you want to be creative, it's more productive to have a pen in your hand than a keyboard beneath your fingers. Computers use the left, logical, side of your brain. A notebook and pen will use the creative, right side.

MAKE A SPACE

Give yourself permission to make a space in which to explore. This may mean you will have to give up something else in your life to provide time for your voyage of discovery. Ideas will only come to you if you have the space in your head in which to think and the space in your life in which to take action.

Practitioners of *feng shui* recognise the value of clearing clutter from their lives. Space clearing, clutter clearing and life laundry can help you to make the mental space in which to explore your dreams. Try to tidy your workspace at the end of each day, so that each morning you're faced with a clear desk. Put your files and papers behind closed doors and remove mirrors from areas where they reflect clutter.

So, create yourself a mental and physical space to give a positive start to your journey.

MAKE A TEAM

Self-assessment is very effective when you're able to talk with others who can provide perspective, balance and insight. Solitary self-assessments may invite self-delusion and frustration and the 'finding out what you want to find out' syndrome. We all need help in order to see ourselves accurately. Self-assessment is an interactive process. When someone else is there to probe and challenge it stokes our imaginations and self-reflection.

Recruit supporters who can be on your success team. Find people who will give you permission to find out who you are, and who believe in you. You need to be encouraged and praised. If your closest family members are not with you in this, then prepare for a rough, but I hope not unbearable, ride. Best of all, find some friends you know well, who can join you on the journey too, and meet or send emails each to other regularly to keep each other motivated and on track.

If you can't build your own team of supporters, you should seriously consider hiring a coach or careers counsellor. I know from painful experience that I won't go to the gym if I'm alone. It's too easy to let myself down. Involving someone else makes it much easier to make a commitment.

You could always kick off with a Blue Sky Party. I use 'blue sky' to refer to those magical times when we discuss dreams and make plans with someone else. It's a time for brainstorming – or 'random-entry listings' as it is now politically correct to call these sessions. It is a time for ideas. But I also take 'blue sky' to refer to the blue sky that can emerge from the clouds, and the hope that it brings. A summer's day, with a blue sky above, is something many of us, particularly the Northern Europeans, long for. Divide the time you have available by the number of guests you invite and take turns to blue sky with each other.

MAKE A START

Take that first step. Start doing something right now, even if it is only for half an hour. Don't set yourself up for failure. Be realistic and do what will work for you. But start now. Once you begin, and you see patterns and insights emerging, you'll find it hard to stop.

MAKE A COMMITMENT

Promise yourself that you'll do all this. But also tell someone else what you're doing. Make a commitment to someone else – a friend, counsellor or coach – whom you can trust to check up on your progress regularly and with love. Also, make a commitment to yourself that you'll be honest and that you will listen to your inner voice. Often the first thought that pops into your head will be the most authentic. Trust your instincts. We don't mean to lie to ourselves deliberately, but through our efforts to capture what is true we can be influenced by what we would like things to be – as well as by what we think we should be. Try hard to be honest about what you are and how you feel.

MONITOR YOUR PROGRESS

Start that notebook now. Write down your thoughts and your achievements each day under the appropriate date. This will help you keep track of your progress and make it more concrete. All you achieve and the thoughts that come to you each day. Date each entry. When you write things down it will make your progress more real and encouraging.

Put Your Passions on Paper

PASSIONS AND VALUES

In order to assess ourselves we need a structure. We can build this structure around the standards by which we are evaluated when we apply for a job position. Earlier in this chapter, I divided the elements that make up my career-based skills into passions and values. Write each of these words at the top of separate pages of your notebook and, as you have ideas about your passions and values, jot them down on the relevant page.

YOUR LABEL IS SHOWING

We all have an idea of how we appear to others and how this may differ from how we see ourselves. It can be very revealing when we also take a look at how we view others. If we consider a trait in someone else to be negative, then we are likely to disapprove of it in ourselves, and so on.

I did the following exercise at a workshop given by Gail MacIndoe, who contributes to this book. First we each took a partner whom we had not known previously. I had to write down how I think others see me, and then how I had viewed my partner the first time I had set eyes on her. This was daunting but revealing. The disparity was painful. I had to tell Jane that I had thought she was a bit serious and professional and that I had been put off by her wearing blue socks with brown shoes. Jane told me that I'd appeared accessible and friendly but that my dress sense was dull and belied my personality. That brown suit has never left the wardrobe since!

Write down six to ten words describing how you think you look, sound and behave. Now write down six to ten more ways that your friends and relations think you look, sound and behave. Now write down six to ten more words that describe how you feel you're seen in a work context. If you have different words in each list then you have some work to do!

I DO NOT LIKE

Sometimes it can be easier to work out what we do not want than what we do want. So write this list and be honest.

Label a blank page with the words 'I do not like' and write down all the things you do not enjoy doing, or that you feel you're poor at doing. Include all the things you leave until last and that make you yawn when you think of them. For example, I hate doing my year-end accounts and making sales calls. Identify the three things you hate most and consider what their opposites might be - since they may well be the very things you love.

CAREER DRIVERS

We all have different motives for working. Some people want fame, others money, others a quiet life or quality time with the family.

In her book *Transform Yourself*, Ros Taylor says there are nine career drivers, which are the catalysts to get you up in the morning. Taylor provides a detailed questionnaire to help you work out what yours may be.

Think about whether you are more motivated by money, power, spirituality, expertise, creativity, community, autonomy, financial security or status.

'It is never easy re-establishing a career after a move, but I enjoy the social aspect of working, as well as the money. No, it is not easy, but as I said before I am very motivated and like to have some financial independence as well as a professional identity.'
Sue B, British, *www.career-in-your-suitcase.com*

TIME FLIES

Write 'Time Flies' at the top of a piece of paper and write down the things you have ever done when you realised afterwards that time had flown by. While you are gardening or shopping perhaps? In conversation, cooking, typing or driving? Think about it. When time flies so fast that you lose track of it, you must be having fun.

ENERGY SOURCES

It is widely accepted that we expend far less energy doing the things we love than the things we don't. Some people claim that we use an astounding 100 per cent less.

Head a blank page with the words 'energy sources' and write down the things you do that energise you. What makes you feel like you're flying? What makes you want to sing? What makes you happy and puts a spring in your step? Now work with the next list, 'energy vampires', to find out some of your possible energy drainers.

ENERGY VAMPIRES

On this page write down the things you do that make you feel tired. What activities bore you, and rob you of motivation and momentum? Also list the types of people who seem to drain you of energy. Think of them as energy vampires, these tasks and these people that suck life out of you. If types of people don't come to mind, list actual people. Consider whether they are demanding or impatient people, perfectionists or people who can barely get one foot in front of the other. If you can calculate when you feel drained it can help you to see when you're energised. If you feel drained by people who are bossy, then think about working in an environment that allows you to be the boss. If you find it hard to be among needy or weak people, then think about working in a high energy, successful environment. If you feel uncomfortable among charismatic, dynamic people, then perhaps you would feel happier in a nurturing, supportive field.

33

FEAR OF SUCCESS

Contrary to popular belief it is not always a fear of failure that stops us from doing something – it is just as likely to be a fear of success. When I was a five year old, I had to change schools because my family moved house. I have a vivid memory of that first day at my new school when the teacher asked me to stand up and recite the alphabet. I did so, using the adult pronunciation of 'ay, bee, see'. The teacher told me I was wrong and that it should be pronounced phonetically 'ah, buh, kuh', which is the standard teaching method in England. I felt uncomfortable. Children stared at me. The teacher said I was 'too clever' so I was moved up a class, away from my peers. I saw this as a punishment. When I look closely at my life I can see many instances later on where I 'dumbed down' in order to fit in. According to Dr David George, the eminent education expert, England is one of very few countries where it is not cool to be clever. For the remainder of my school life I forced myself to be average, and my grades reflected this. Only since my fortieth birthday have I realised that deep down I may actually be academic.

Recently I have braved talking about this to my English girlfriends, only to find that, so far, each one of them, like me, had feigned being average. I remember when my then 11 year old son said that he was pleased we had chosen him a school that encourages academic competition, because he could not bear to be bullied and called a 'boffin' elsewhere.

Consider the times in your life when you may have sabotaged your success. I sabotaged mine by dumbing down. Think about your motives. Think about the passions you may have suppressed as a result. Write them down.

WHEN SUCCESS WAS EASILY WON

In her book *I Could Do Anything I Wanted if Only I Knew What it Was*, Barbara Sher provides many great exercises. Some of the most revealing have to do with success. Sher too believes that we are blocked more by our fear of success than by our fear of failure.

There will have been times in your past when you did allow yourself to succeed at something. Times when you did not give in to peer pressure or fears. Write a list of these achievements. Remember also to include those that are not work related.

PORTFOLIO PEOPLE

It is accepted that we can work on lots of projects at once, each project drawing on different strengths. When I was in Oman I made date chutney, taught creative writing and wrote as a journalist. Accept that you can do many disparate things. Write down as many things as you can think of that you'd like to do. Don't limit yourself by only writing down the things that you know to be possible right now, or those that might earn you money. Write them all down. Don't stop until you have run out of dreams. Now, from this list, mark which ideas are impractical right now, and which ones are feasible. Be aware that you may be able to do some of these things consecutively, and others concurrently.

DO YOU WANT TO BE ALONE?

Most people tend to think of themselves as either an introvert or an extrovert. In fact, very few people are all one or all the other – most of us are a mixture of both. When I analysed my typical working day I realised that I work best alone, not just by myself in an office, but in a whole building! I like to work from home or a small office, but only when no one else is there either as I do not like being interrupted. Yet I do need daily social input in order to redress the balance a bit. Working alone as I do, I still need time to brainstorm with others, preferably face to face. So I belong to a women's business network and try to diary a few lunch or coffee meetings each month. I also run writing and career workshops and have a busy speaking career, as this gets me among people. As a mentor and consultant, I encourage face-to-face meetings rather than by email or Skype, as I need the energy from being in a room with other people. I also need to get away from my normal environment regularly, and enjoy time at conferences and abroad on speaking and teaching tours to recharge my batteries with concentrated interaction and learning.

Think about your ideal working environment. Do you want to be alone, with people, or a mix of the two? Like me, do you need to do one sort of task completely alone (writing and preparation) and another that allows you to be with people (teaching, speaking and consultancy). Would you like to work with people, but spend your leisure time alone? What's worked for you in the past? What hasn't? Write a description of your ideal work/life balance.

WRITE YOUR DREAM

Imagine what kind of work you might do if you knew you could succeed at it, that would fit with your lifestyle, that you would earn enough money from and for which you would have all the necessary resources and knowledge at your fingertips. In other words, write down your dream job. As you work at this, you may surprise yourself. Perhaps you have several dreams? If so, write them all.

WHEN I GREW UP

Think back to when you were a young child. What did you want to be when you grew up? I wanted to be an actress or a singer! I guess that means I wanted to be on a stage. Perhaps I did realise that dream in an oblique way, since my work now puts me in front of people in various ways. Think about your own childhood aspirations. What did you want to do and be when you grew up? Have you fulfilled any of these hopes, even if only indirectly? Is there more you can do to work towards them now? Write down what you wanted to do when you were young and how these aspirations may still be alive in you.

FAMILY INHERITANCE

Think about your parents and your grandparents. Taking each of them in turn, write down what you think their passions may have been. Now write down what you think their values may have been, and their assets. Which of their passions, skills and characteristics do you think you may have inherited?

I LOVE

Write down absolutely everything you enjoy doing, including those things you do on vacations, in your leisure time, with your family, on your own and at work.

SPEEDWRITING

I am a firm believer in speedwriting as a valuable way to get inside yourself and unlock your secrets. Speedwriting has nothing to do with shorthand. Instead it refers to the method by which you write really fast about whatever is on your mind. For this to work you must use a lined notebook with a spiral binding, so that it is easy for you to move from page to page. Some people call this kind of writing 'stream of consciousness'.

When you write fast like this, your thoughts may be random – but that's fine. Put down each thought as it comes to you and keep on writing until you have no more to say. Let your mind wander. You must not stop writing to think. If your ideas are slow in coming then write down words such as 'words words words' or 'I must write I must write', but do not take your pen off the paper.

Speedwriting feels like magic. You can almost sense that the thoughts go straight from your soul to the page, bypassing your brain. Lose control, don't worry about spelling, grammar or punctuation. Just write.

In her book about speedwriting, called *Writing Down the Bones*, Nathalie Goldberg talks about the process at length. She says that speedwriting allows your subconscious to emerge and is a great way to find out what you really think and want and believe. As a fan of this method I have to agree. Once I was unsure when to run my next series of creative writing classes. I agonised over the day of the week, the time of day and the pricing I would use in a new country. So I speedwrote around my thoughts for about 20 minutes, and miraculously the answer came to me. I would run them on a Thursday morning at 9am. Simple when you know how!

You can speedwrite on any topic you like, of course, and the results can be therapeutic. I even know of several people who formed their own speedwriting group and met monthly to write together and share their experiences. Often it can be very painful to read out loud what you've written. So before you leap into starting a group be careful that you will be among firm friends.

Here are some ideas you could work with, to set you off with speedwriting:

- ❐ The job of my dreams
- ❐ I wish
- ❐ I hate
- ❐ In a perfect world
- ❐ In my teens
- ❐ When I was a child
- ❐ I love
- ❐ If only
- ❐ Next year
- ❐ Work

KEEP A JOURNAL

One of the biggest influences on my life has been a book called *The Artist's Way* by Julia Cameron. I completed this workbook as part of my personal journey of introspection back in 1994, when I was living in Muscat, and my friend Karen recommended it. So impressed was she with it, that Karen would buy several copies every time she went home to England to give to her friends.

This book is particularly designed for people who want to unlock their inner creativity and to discover who they really are. Yet it is not reserved for artists – we all have creativity in our soul. Cameron asks readers to devote 12 weeks to her course, which includes speedwriting a journal for ten minutes every morning. In addition, Cameron provides a chapter on a different subject each week, asks questions and invites you to reflect on that topic for seven days.

Try to write your own journal every morning as close to waking up as you can. You're likely to remember your dreams, which can be most revealing. It is interesting that once you start to anticipate writing down your dreams on waking, your dreams become more vivid and revealing than ever. I recall distinctly a dream I had about eight years ago while I was journalling daily. I saw that I was working in an attic surrounded by the colour turquoise, and that people came to me and I gave them books. Eight years later I have an office upstairs in my house, and it is lined with books. Indeed people do come to me, usually through email, to buy them. I have resisted painting the walls turquoise, but know this to be a colour that for me represents water, creativity, the sea and peace. Funnily enough, if I look at the pictures and cards I have pinned up around my desk, they all contain quite a splash of turquoise!

WRITE YOUR LIFE STORY

Most of us enjoy reading an autobiography. We find them insightful and revealing. So there is every reason for us to write our own in order to find out more about ourselves too.

It is common for career counsellors to ask their clients to begin work by writing their own life story or career review. When we make an effort to see each of our career choices on paper we can begin to understand what motivated us to make each decision. It is not uncommon for the process to take several hours. Once you have identified your own career drivers in this way you are in a strong position. You are back in the driving seat of your new career.

I would always suggest that you write any of this soulsearching stuff longhand – but as memories are wont to return randomly you would be forgiven for using a word processor this time.

Start at the beginning and write about what you loved to do when you were a child, what frightened you, about your friends, your family, your achievements and the things you did at play. Then proceed into your teenage years, your twenties and beyond, right up until the present day. Write about your work, your education, your leisure time, your relationships and why they ended, or why they worked. What made you happy? Write about your successes, your failures, your passions, the things you spent most time with and the things you least liked to do. See if you can spot any of the catalysts that caused certain things to happen in your life, the reasons you had arguments with your friends, the reasons you did well in certain subjects and what made you choose them.

When you've finished, look back and see if any patterns emerge. See if this reflection holds some of the keys to what you loved to do.

In her book *Work with Passion*, Nancy Anderson gives pages of instructions on how to write a highly detailed and insightful autobiography. Her version is likely to extend to 50 pages or more! However, if you feel you need help with this, few books are more thorough than hers. For example, Nancy asks you to begin your autobiography by writing about your grandparents.

YOUR MENTAL PHOTOGRAPH ALBUM

Dr Phil McGraw is the psychologist doctor who began his life in the spotlight as a regular on the Oprah Winfrey show. He has written several useful books to help you understand yourself and your family better. His two books *Life Strategies* and *Self Matters* can be very helpful in a general way.

Dr Phil asks us to identify our Defining Moments, the moments in our lives that shaped us forever. The moments that we can remember clearly with all of our senses. I can remember distinctly how it felt that day the teacher told me I was too clever for her class. I can see the disdain on her face, feel the warm September day outside the classroom, remember how cold I suddenly became and how very saddened. This was a defining moment for me that shaped my life. Yet on a happier note, I recall the evening launch party for our date cookery book in Oman. The room smelled of incense and spice, the guests wore a mixture of eau de nil traditional Omani dress and Western clothes. We ate miniature date and nut cutlets and dates stuffed with ricotta cheese and pine nuts and drank cardamom flavoured Arabic coffee. Outside the window of the Pearl restaurant at the Al Bustan Palace hotel, we could see the sea away through the palm trees. This time I knew I loved the exoticism and opportunity of life abroad and I also knew I could succeed.

Look out for your Defining Moments in your life and career. Sometimes they will be times that made you feel terrific, sometimes they made you sad and sometimes they will have filled you with so much energy that you could almost feel your ego disappear. You were at one with the world.

Take a look at your mental photograph album now, seek out the snapshots that stay clear in your mind and work out what they tell you about yourself today.

WRITE YOUR MISSION STATEMENT

Over the last few years I have been fortunate to attend a workshop entitled 'Write Your Own Mission Statement', given by inspirational Danish holistic management expert Helen Eriksen. An actor at heart, Helen's workshop is a lesson in how to forget convention and follow our instincts to be different. She teaches how we can free our 'inner originals', claiming as Jung did that 'we are born original and die as copies'.

'When we know where we are going we approach everything differently,' explains Helen. 'We tend to act reactively when we don't know what we want and end up simply going wherever the wind blows. Often we find ourselves landed on a shore where we do not belong at all. Conversely, proactive people are conscious of where they want to go and why and then set their sails accordingly.'

Helen shows us how to find out what our core values are by examining our achievements, both personal and professional, and then working out which of our values motivated us to be successful. Values such as 'transforming', 'sharing', 'learning', 'dreaming' or 'communicating' may come to mind.

When you have written down your successes and the values that inspired them, you might notice that some values are not as important to you as they used to be – and that you have acquired others which don't appear on your early lists.

Select about three of these values and see if you can put them into a sentence. That sentence can be your mission statement.

I last participated in Helen's workshop in January 2002, just before I embarked on the project of rewriting the second edition of this book. My core values that day were 'enthusiasm', 'creation' and 'sharing'. The mission statement I produced became 'to use my enthusiasm to create things that I may share with people who want to do what they love for a living'. Now it's your turn. Today, as we begin 2008 I have honed my mission to simply 'sharing what I know to help others to grow'.

ASK YOUR FRIENDS

Several years ago, Canadian Donna Messer, then in her forties, left her job as a teacher for a new career that embodied her skills and her passions. When she looked in the mirror she saw only education and experience. She had no idea what she wanted to do, nor what she could do aside from teach. So she asked three of her friends what they saw when they looked at her.

'You make things look nice,' said the first friend, referring to the wonderful decorations Donna would make out of next to nothing to dress up the village hall or her home.

'You make things taste good,' said the second, reminded of the great food Donna would concoct from a random selection of ingredients and spices, and serve to the entire football team when they arrived on an impromptu visit.

'You bring people together,' said the third friend, as she recalled the way Donna could organise disparate people into a team and marshal their combined resources to create a successful project.

Thus inspired, Donna went on to create a company called Orange Crate, which sold original combinations of herbs and spices, packed into neat wooden boxes. She also created her team of associates from among the farmers in her community, who felt they could not yet contribute to the business, but who offered invaluable help with duties such as driving, deliveries and book keeping.

Orange Crate began with a small loan from a local bank and ten years later was sold to a group of three companies that joined forces to buy it.

'They were a food company, a media company and a financial institution, so we must have done something right!' recalls Donna.

Donna no longer runs Orange Crate. She now travels the world speaking to large groups, conferences and corporations, inspiring them in turn, with her stories of resourcefulness and networking. Since 2000 she has also been editor of the magazine *Business Woman Canada*. She shares her secrets at *www.connectuscanada.com*.

SELF-ASSESSMENT TESTS

There are a number of self-assessment tests available on the market and many can be completed online. Some are free of charge. Such an objective overview of your talents can be insightful, though you may find that some seem complicated and others trite. You may find some discrepancies, but in general they have huge value and are great fun, particularly if you get a few friends together and do one each before comparing notes.

Gail MacIndoe is a behavioural and values analyst and uses a number of time-tested and cross cultural validated assessment tests to help her clients gain an insight into their behaviour, attitudes and values. She believes that such tests may provide:

- an increased understanding of self
- an increased understanding of others
- understanding of your motivations
- insight into how your behaviour affects and communicates with others
- awareness of your natural strengths and weaknesses
- understanding of what motivates your decisions
- insight into your causes of conflict

MYERS-BRIGGS TYPE INDICATOR

There are many personality assessment tools available, and few are better known than the Myers-Briggs Type Indicator (MBTI). According to Jung's typology all people can be classified using three criteria:

1. **Extroversion - Introversion**
   This first criterion defines the source and direction of energy expression for a person. The extrovert has a source and direction of energy expression mainly in the external world, while the introvert has a source of energy mainly in the internal world.

2. **Sensing - Intuition**
   The second criterion defines the method of information perception by a person. Sensing means that a person believes mainly information he receives directly from the external world. Intuition means that a person believes mainly information he receives from the internal or imaginative world.

3. **Thinking - Feeling**
   The third criterion defines how the person processes information. Thinking means that a person makes a decision mainly through logic. Feeling means that, as a rule, he makes a decision based on emotion.

Then Isobel Myers-Briggs added a fourth criterion:

4. **Judging - Perceiving**
   The final criterion defines how a person implements the information he has processed. Judging means that a person organises all his life events and acts strictly according to his plans. Perceiving means that he is inclined to improvise and seek alternatives.

The different combinations of the criteria determine a 'type', such as ISTJ *Introvert Sensing Thinking Judging* or ENFP *Extrovert INtuitive Feeling Perceiving*.

There are 16 types, each one having a four letter name (or formula) according to the combination of criteria.

For a certain person a type formula and quantitative measure of expression of each criterion (strength of the preference) can be determined using the Type inventory. Then the corresponding type description can be represented.

BEHAVIOURAL STYLE ANALYSIS ASSESSMENT

The Behavioural Style Analysis assessment (DISC) is based on the work of Dr William Moulton Marston. By means of personalised reports, respondents have the opportunity to increase their knowledge of themselves and how they interact with others, resulting in increased effectiveness and productivity.

THE PERSONAL INTEREST, ATTITUDES & VALUES ASSESSMENT

The Personal Interests, Attitudes and Values assessment (PIAV) is based on Eduard Spanger's book *Types of Men* and measures the relative prominence of six basic attitudes, interest or motives in personality. This assessment is widely used to provide insights into the motivation of a given individual. Attitudes and values help to initiate one's actions and are sometimes called the hidden motivators because they are not always readily observed. The PIAV report identifies these motivating factors and attitudes.

THE CAREER TACTICS ASSESSMENT

This questionnaire can be completed online in just a few minutes and is designed to help people think more systematically about the specific strategies they have used in their career.

Although management capabilities and professional and technical expertise are clearly major factors underpinning a person's effectiveness and future progress, in themselves they may not be sufficient. Career success and failure is not simply an outcome of talent. Critical to success and failure is the deployment of one's personal time and effort in responding to the realities of human nature and organisational life.

Career Tactics highlights this dimension: which tactics have you made most and least use of in the personal advancement of your career? What are the gains for deploying these tactics in the future; what are the potential risks?

FALSIFICATION OF TYPE

Dr Katherine Benziger, whom I mentioned earlier in this chapter, has created a unique profiling tool, which focuses on natural competences and Falsification of Type called the BTSA Assessment. This can be accessed at *www.benziger.org.*

PSYCHOGEOMETRICS

In her book *Transform Yourself*, author and TV psychologist Ros Taylor describes a number of personality testing tools, including the Psycho-geometrics tool developed by Dr Sue Dellinger. This tool invites you to look at a number of shapes and decide which one best represents you. The results are most revealing.

For example, if you see yourself as a squiggle, you are likely to be creative, witty and messy. If you choose a triangle, you may be focused, decisive and athletic.

DO YOUR OWN ASSESSMENTS

The DISC, PIAV and Career Tactics assessments can be completed online via various independent consultants.

The MBTI can be completed at numerous websites including *www.knowyourtype.com* and also in the book Please Understand Me by David Keirsey, which explains additional assessment methods.

You can find more at *www.career-in-your-suitcase.com*.

ASK A PROFESSIONAL

These days any good careers counselor or coach will have access to a variety of self-assessment tools. Many will have been trained in the application of these tests and conduct them at the start of a program as a matter of course.

Putting It All Together

This has been a demanding chapter, involving lots of honest introspection from you. By no means does it contain all the exercises and lists you can work with – and we're constantly adding new ones to *www.career-in-your-suitcase.com*.

Details of all the books and websites mentioned here can be found in the Resources section of this book.

We have not touched on turning your passions and skills into a career yet. This chapter has focused on looking inside yourself. It is only once you have found out what you most enjoy doing and where your passions lie that you can begin to create your perfect portable career.

In the following chapter you will start to assess your skills, to find out what you can do, and where you have talent.

'Should one work to live or live to work? The majority do not want to simply get by because they have to work. Once passion is brought into the equation work does not feel like work at all. It becomes more enjoyable and one is usually more productive and stimulated resulting in greater achievements and performance.'
Carol, American, *http://delhi4cats.wordpress.com* and *www.expatwomen.com*

'I think the key to success is to be working on something you ab-so-lute-ly love doing or feel very passionately about it would be very difficult to stay focused and housebound doing something that you didn't believe in.'
Victoria, New Zealander in India, *www.expatwomen.com*

---

3 *what can you do?*

Now that I have got you thinking about your passions and what really matters to you, it is time to start thinking not so much about who you are, but about what you can do. With thanks to REA for their lists of skills.

'Whatever you are, be a good one.'
Abraham Lincoln

In this chapter:

- Your calling
- What is a perfect portable career?
- What can you do?
- New perspectives

Your Calling

Finding our passions, which we can also think of as 'callings', or the work we were born to do, is a challenge. Converting these passions into a career requires ingenuity and persistence. To unearth our passions we need to look inside ourselves. When we seek to translate what we love into work, then we need to look outside ourselves.

First, we need to look inside ourselves, and unearth our passions. We have covered that in *Chapter Two*. Next, here, we look further inside ourselves to analyse our skills and find out what we are good at. Next we need to brainstorm a bit about the best kind of career and finally we need to adapt that 'dream' to the market. We then look at the location and environment where we're living, whether temporarily or permanently, and consider whether we want to work locally with the people and resources in our community, or beyond our community through computers and other modern technologies. We want to notice and investigate all the opportunities immediately around us, while also exploring the possibilities that lie beyond that. But let's begin by taking a look at the portable career, which is, after all, our goal, to see which kinds of jobs fit the bill.

What is a Perfect Portable Career?

A career that you can put in your suitcase and take with you anywhere in the world is a portable career. But we want you to find the perfect portable career, not just any career. If it is not a perfect fit for you then it will not be easy for you to sustain it through additional moves or a return home. The elements that make that career qualify as *portable* are as follows:

- It is easy to transport, with no heavy equipment to ship
- You do not need a warehouse of stock, that may be hard to sell, and even more difficult to pack and take with you
- It is based on your passions, the things you love to do
- It uses your top favourite skills and talents
- It can operate in more than one location
- It is flexible enough to be adaptable to new opportunities and markets
- It allows you to build a global network that is not lost when you move
- It fulfils your needs
- It fits round your other commitments
- It provides the objectives you require – financial, fame, making a difference, or whatever
- It motivates you so much that you can keep going regardless of new moves
- It can be set up quickly in a new location
- It is sustainable despite moves
- It continues to grow
- It makes you happy

Here are some examples of portable careers that may fulfil the above objectives.

TEACHING

Teaching is maybe a softer skill than you realise. If you can teach one thing, the chances are you can teach another. I taught computers in England, French conversation in Dubai, creative writing in Oman and how to create a portable career in Norway. Along with teaching, comes training and running workshops. Take a presentation skills course and you will be able to run workshops for adults on subjects in which you specialise without a teaching qualification.

You can teach online too. Online tutors or e-tutors guide students through an Internet learning experience. If you have a teaching background, why not create courses that can be delivered electronically via email, online tutorials or audio/video conferencing, as well as telephone conference calls.

'In Japan I taught businessmen, school children and even a three year old. The businessmen paid best but the children were better students, they were less tired and more relaxed. In Italy, Milan, I taught at a language school, which was well paid, easy work with motivated students. I also taught in four companies, which was interesting but the classes were larger. In Thailand it was terrific fun but such hard work. Here I decided to teach on a voluntary basis to help deprived individuals to better themselves. Social interaction was as important as teaching. I could choose what I taught too. In Belgium I taught three retired ladies who had decided to expand their horizons despite being over 70. This was very challenging, I needed lots of patience as their memories were poor.'
Fiona, British in many countries, *www.career-in-your-suitcase.com*

VIRTUAL ASSISTANCE

All businesses need some administrative support, yet we don't all have the time, skills or inclination to do it ourselves. Administrative duties include maybe, accounts, maintaining a database, upkeep of a website, sending newsletters, invoicing and copy typing. A virtual assistant offers a combination of services that can be done from anywhere in the world from a computer. I know several people who use a VA to answer their telephone and respond to email. I use one to work on my database, another to upload items to my websites and have used them in the past to send my newsletters too.

COACHING

Life coaching, business coaching and career coaching can be conducted from almost anywhere there are people looking to develop themselves. Many coaches operate face to face with clients, but now that there is Skype, email and webconferencing, many coaches operate remotely. You need training and qualifications to be a good coach, of course but you are able to study for this by distance learning.

NETWORK MARKETING

Companies like Tupperware, Avon, Forever Living and Usborne Books all operate in this way. You become a distributor, buy a start up pack at a favourable price, you may even receive some training and then you work at selling the product. Many network marketers sell directly to the public by hosting parties in people's homes. But you can also make money by recruiting others to work in your team. You are responsible for motivating your team and in return you get to earn a percentage of their income. This can be very rewarding, and, providing you choose a product about which you are passionate, and a company that allows you to operate in the appropriate countries you stand to grow a very lucrative business.

Network marketing can be a perfect choice if you want to maintain flexible work patterns. Your success depends on the quality and reputation of the product (always check this out) plus your own natural people and organisational skills.

I was a Dorling Kindersley Family Learning distributor in two different countries and found it to be hugely lucrative, as well as a good way to meet people and make friends. I picked the product because the countries I was living in had a shortage of good quality English books at the time and the market was ripe for the picking. Although I did my best to assure that my operations were legal, when in Oman, I discovered that a local bookstore was not happy with what I was doing and put a stop to it. Not all network marketing companies have licences to trade in every country, so do make sure that you check up before you barge on in, as I did.

'Many network marketing schemes such as this [Cabouchon] give their distributors no set monthly targets. You sell products at the usual retail price but you buy them from the manufacturer at discount. The discount increases as you sell more products. Cabouchon is a good choice of party plan product because jewellery is relatively easy to post. It is also quite affordable. By inviting people to host parties in their homes you help to add to the social scene. Generally expatriates have a bit of spare cash too.'
Pauline, British in Norway, *www.career-in-your-suitcase.com*

ONLINE TRADING

If you enjoy investing in the money markets then you may enjoy trading both for yourself and even for clients. You could also organise investment clubs, teach others how to trade and offer an advice service maybe, while making money for yourself with your own investments.

THERAPY, COUNSELING, HAIRDRESSING OR BEAUTY

Once you have trained in a skill such as reflexology, acupuncture, psychotherapy, beauty, hairdressing, colour and style analysis or similar there is a good chance that this could become a portable career. While you cannot take clients with you when you move, you can take your skills and, with a good marketing strategy, you can find new clients fast in a new location. You do need to check that your qualifications are recognised in the new country though and that you will not be restricted by lack of language skills. Being a therapist can be a very portable career, however, it is usually dependent on you having a local client base. And a local client base takes time to build and cannot move with you. However, if you keep in touch with your clients and friends and have a global network, there is a good chance that some clients and referrers will be around in a new location. However, the best way to keep your business alive despite postings is to have another string to your bow. Maybe you write a book on your specialism, which you can continue to sell online regardless of where you live? Or perhaps you could also become a network marketing distributor selling a product that complements your work? An aromatherapist could also sell essential oils. A beauty therapist could sell make up. A massage therapist could sell aloe vera products and so on. You will find that there are a range of products suitable to complement most businesses.

> 'In Norway most of my clients came from my husband's company. Women hate having to change their hairdresser when they move. At least with me being English they knew I would understand what they wanted.'
> Pauline, British in Norway, *www.career-in-your-suitcase.com*

WRITING

Being a journalist can be a good source of income wherever you go. If there are no English language publications locally then now is the time to expand your horizons and write for international publications, airline magazines, papers in your home country and expat magazines and websites. Be an author and write books if you that appeals to you. But if you prefer to write short sharp pieces, consider writing public relations material, website content, brochure copy and so on. If you can write, then maybe you can edit and proofread too. Create information products such as ebooks and you can sell those online and the customer can download them immediately, so there is no shipping involved. While you can make a career from writing non-fiction, creative writing, poetry and fiction also make great portable careers.

GRAPHIC DESIGN

Learn to use the graphic design software used by printers and publishers of marketing and other material and you will never be short of work. Create business cards, company brands, layout books and articles, brochures and other things. Learn to use digital image software and not only can you work with photographs but you will find yourself in demand teaching others this skill too.

WEBSITE DESIGN AND MAINTENANCE

Few businesses do not have a web presence. Learn how to use the software, to upload material, and register with the search engines and you will be kept very busy. If you have an eye for design, or can work with a designer, then your websites will have the edge.

ONLINE SELLING

You can sell goods online without ever having to hold the stock yourself. So, design a compelling website, take orders and collect the money and then pass those orders onto suppliers who are responsible for the packing and shipping. Products sold on the Amazon Marketplace are sold by this same 'drop ship' method. Only those things you buy direct from Amazon are shipped by Amazon themselves. Selling any product online by this method allows you to make money in your sleep.

Ebay is an example of an international online marketplace, making it a perfect business to operate from any country. Ebay has sister sites in many countries. In fact, you can sell all manner of things through Amazon Marketplace too.

ART OR PHOTOGRAPHY

If you are an artist, photographer or sculptor, for example, you can do your art wherever you live and sell it to local clients. Create a website and sell to the rest of the world. You can teach your skill to others too, if that appeals. Many artists turn their work into greetings cards, calendars, coasters and other souvenirs. With a bit of research you may be able to take your art to a new level.

WANT TO KNOW MORE?

A selection of indepth reports on some of the careers mentioned above are available from *www.career-in-your-suitcase.com*. You are also invited to share your own career ideas, so please pay us a visit.

For more inspiration on which career to choose, please take a look at 'Sixty Brilliant Ideas' at *www.career-in-your-suitcase.com* and at the back of this book.

What Can You Do?

So far in this book we have talked a lot about finding your passion and working out what really matters to you. Along the way you may have come to realise not only your *passions* but also the things you can *do*. However, for some readers, you may have reached this stage clearer about what you *love* and how you like to feel, but less sure about what you *can actually do*.

Now, is the time that we can assess your skills. The things you *do*. The practical things, like delegating, managing people, even woodwork or cooking. These are all skills. You may even have developed a talent for some of these skills, and if you are really lucky you may be passionate about them too. Let's take a look at what you can do more closely.

There are three kinds of skills:

1. Hard
2. Soft
3. Personal

ASSESS YOUR SKILLS

When you apply for a job, you will probably be evaluated on the basis of your so-called technical or hard skills. These are talents that can be learned through formal education, on the job training or volunteer experience. Hard skills include computer programming, car repair, and the mastery of surgical procedures. Technical skills often constitute the bare minimum that an employer looks for in a candidate. It would take a small booklet in itself to list all of the technical skills that people use in the workplace, but here are a number to help get you going.

TECHNICAL / HARD SKILLS

As you go down the list place a tick in front of the skills you enjoy using. To enjoy using a skill means that you are proficient at it and gain satisfaction from it. The skills don't have to be ones you are presently using in your professional life.

❑ Automobile maintenance
❑ Fundraising
❑ Record keeping
❑ Computer skills
❑ Operating a cash register
❑ Machine and manual skills
❑ Desktop publishing
❑ Financial analysis
❑ Scientific knowledge
❑ Writing and editing
❑ Accounting/bookkeeping
❑ Forecasting
❑ Creative use of materials/artistic
❑ Surveying

❑ Mental health counselling
❑ Laboratory procedures
❑ Repairing
❑ Drafting
❑ Landscaping/gardening
❑ Using tools
❑ Running factory equipment
❑ Providing medical care
❑ Training and teaching
❑ Inventory management
❑ Proofreading
❑ Designing
❑ Operating machinery
❑ Testing equipment

Write down any technical skills you have that were missing from the list, here:

FUNCTIONAL / SOFT SKILLS

The second category of skills is designated as functional, soft, or transferable. Transferable talents can be adapted from one profession to another. These functional skills are often rooted in innate aptitudes that can be nurtured and polished through training and they represent the second level of employer evaluation. Functional skills can be broken down into three categories, depending on whether they are used in relationship to *people*, *objects* or things, or *data* and ideas. All three categories are mixed together in this list. Once again, place a tick in front of the skills you have and enjoy using.

- ☐ Delegating
- ☐ Negotiation
- ☐ Event/programme coordinating
- ☐ Advising/persuading
- ☐ Public speaking
- ☐ Clerical
- ☐ Researching
- ☐ Manual skills/mechanical knowhow
- ☐ Categorising and comparing
- ☐ Planning/prioritising
- ☐ Administration
- ☐ Resolving conflict
- ☐ Written communication
- ☐ Teaching/training
- ☐ Buying/selling
- ☐ Recruiting
- ☐ Diagnosing
- ☐ Organising/synthesising data
- ☐ Evaluating/decision making
- ☐ Measuring and calculating
- ☐ Laying out processes
- ☐ Summarising
- ☐ Oral communication

- ☐ Analysing
- ☐ Running meetings
- ☐ Supervising/managing
- ☐ Investigating
- ☐ Computing and numerical skills
- ☐ Improving/adapting
- ☐ Building/constructing
- ☐ Organising committees
- ☐ Problem solving
- ☐ Implementing change
- ☐ Motivating and persuading
- ☐ Interpreting
- ☐ Planning/goal setting
- ☐ Organising/managing projects
- ☐ Promoting
- ☐ Computing/calculating
- ☐ Editing
- ☐ Artistic creativity
- ☐ Gathering information
- ☐ Maintaining systems
- ☐ Team building
- ☐ Keeping track of details & monitoring

Write down any more that apply to you and that were missing from the list, here:

PERSONAL SKILLS AND QUALITIES

Third, everybody brings personal skills and qualities to their work, such as the knack for getting along with people, leadership capacities and persistence. Employers look for these qualities to a greater or lesser extent, depending in some measure on the nature of the work. They can be an important factor in tipping the balance in favour of a candidate who is otherwise on a par with the other applicants. In fact, those with several outstanding and valuable personal characteristics are sometimes given the nod over other candidates who possess superior technical abilities.

Tick those in the list that you feel best describe your personal skills and qualities.

- ❏ Friendly personality
- ❏ Enthusiastic
- ❏ Takes initiative
- ❏ Tactful and supportive of others
- ❏ Exceeds what is required
- ❏ Well organised
- ❏ Responsive to the views of others
- ❏ High personal standards
- ❏ Careful
- ❏ Perceptive about people
- ❏ Follows rules
- ❏ Follows instructions
- ❏ Flexible

- ❏ Logical
- ❏ Willing to take risks
- ❏ Accepts criticism
- ❏ Reliable
- ❏ Persistent
- ❏ Accepts change
- ❏ Cooperates/collaborates with others
- ❏ Willing to take on new challenges
- ❏ Leads others
- ❏ Good appearance
- ❏ Adapts to any situation
- ❏ Responds well to emergencies

Write down any more that apply to you and that were missing from the list, here:

55

The next step is to review the three lists of skills and abilities and choose the five most important from each.

1. Take a piece of paper for each set of skills: hard; soft; personal.

2. Select your top five skills from each of the three lists and write each set on one sheet of paper. You will now have three sheets, with five skills on each.

3. Now, take another sheet of paper for each job you've held. At the top of the page indicate the position you held and the company you worked for. A sample sheet is available on the next page. If you're entering the job market for the first time make use of significant school, community and volunteer experiences. Then, for each position or experience, answer the following:

    •   Describe the responsibilities and tasks you performed.
    •   Which of these did you perform the best and enjoy the most?
    •   Which tasks and responsibilities did you like the least? Which were the most difficult to carry out?
    •   What aspects of the work environment were conducive to your doing your best work?
    •   What aspects of the environment were unpleasant or 'de-motivating'?

4. After you have answered these questions for at least three of your past jobs, locate a good sized surface and make three rows of sheets.

5. In the top row lay out the three ticklists of your top five skills and talents. Beneath this lay out your work experience sheets, with your most recent position on the right.

6. Compare the lists. Do your ticked items represent preferences that have been constant through all or most of your career? If these are recent preferences, how did they evolve or get brought to the fore? Do you see any 'red threads'? Compare your three top-five lists with your work duties and responsibilities. How close a match do you find? If ten or more of your top 15 preferences find expression in your current or most recent work, then you and your career are probably a good match. It may not be so clear, however, if two or three of your preferences are particularly critical but are not represented in your current work. If there is a significant gap between your top 15 preferences and your present work, it would be interesting to know if the gap was less pronounced in any of your previous jobs. If you find this is the case, does that fact tell you anything useful about how you're evolving professionally?

Job _____

Company _____

What aspects of the work environment were conducive to your doing your best work?

_____

_____

What aspects of the environment were unpleasant or 'de-motivating'?

_____

_____

Tasks / responsibilities	What I enjoyed about this	How well I performed this	What I disliked about this	What I found difficult

Do you know of a vocation, perhaps one you have considered entering, that carries responsibilities more closely aligned with your top preferences? If so, then this profession certainly bears further investigation. There are three principal ways to do this. First, read about it. A good place to start is the *Occupational Outlook Handbook* published by the US Department of Labor. Second, talk with people in your field of interest. Third, perhaps you can even observe one of these people performing the job during part of their workday.

Practicalities, for better or worse, do come into play at this point. As you measure your skills in relation to what potential professions call for, and begin to home in on new possibilities, you must also factor in what is possible. If you are a 46-year-old accountant and want to become a knee surgeon, you obviously need to consider whether it will be possible for you to spend six to eight years and many thousands of dollars in training. No matter what field you enter, you want to consider the current and projected job market for your next vocation.

New Perspectives

'Thus the task is not so much to see what no one yet has seen but to think what nobody yet has thought about that which everybody sees,'

Arthur Schopenhauer, 1788-860

Schopenhauer wrote the original definition of 'build a better mousetrap' more than 150 years ago, and it remains one of the best ways to describe originality, innovation ... and success.

A portable career requires constant introspection and reinvention - becoming too attached to what you've already 'been' and already 'seen' may be the biggest obstacle to your international career success. There are many inspiring stories in this book of non-traditional approaches to career management. Moving abroad is the perfect time to 'think outside the box'. Prepare to see this box from a new perspective: imagine, just for a second, that perhaps you built that box yourself, climbed in, and nailed the lid down from the inside. With a little critical self analysis, you'll be amazed to discover how many of the obstacles to your successful career development you are placing there yourself, perhaps though self-limiting beliefs about what constitutes a career, where to look for opportunities - and where your own talents lie.

ALTERNATE PATHS

The Chinese believe that while all the paths of your destiny are laid out with your birth, different ones are revealed to you at separate times in your life. The challenge for all of us is to recognise the opportunities being offered. Deepak Chopra calls this 'Synchrodestiny'.

'Very often we fall into ruts in our lives; we maintain the same routines and act in the same manner predictably day after day after day. We set our minds on a certain course of action, and simply proceed. How can miracles happen if we march mindlessly, unthinking and unaware, through our lives? Coincidences are like road flares, calling our attention to something important in our lives, glimpses of what goes on beyond everyday distractions. We can choose to ignore those flares and hurry on, or we can pay attention to them and live out the miracle that is waiting for us,' he writes.

Some doors close, and others in turn open again, and that is how you can view your life abroad, your career path and skills set: as a journey, packed with jewels, treasures, opportunities and adventure around every corner.

'In Chinese, the characters for Challenge and Opportunity are the same. It really makes you think.'
Lisa, British in Italy, *http://burntbythetuscansun.blogspot.com*
and *www.expatwomen.com*

4 *create your career*

Once you've decided what you most enjoy doing, the next step is to select a career, or careers, that will make the most of your passion – and to consider how you'll make it work in your current location. With thanks to REA for the 'What is Important to You' exercise.

'The best advice to give the young is "Find out what you like doing best and get someone to pay for you to do it."'
Katherine Whitehorn

In this chapter:
- Recycling
- Start at the beginning
- Time for some new skills?
- Manage your expectations
- Getting ideas
- Think laterally
- Listen to people
- Career drivers
- What suits you?
- What is important to you?
- Keep your eyes open
- Look on the Internet
- Volunteer
- Blue sky
- Career options
- Entrepreneurs
- Effortless entrepreneurship
- Teamwork
- Working virtually
- Multi Level Marketing
- A woman's world?

Recycling

Before you can make a decision about a new career, you need to think about recycling your skills. When I was at school, we had a campaign to raise student and parent awareness of environmental issues. The slogan was 'recycle, return, re-use'. Be aware that in every location you may have to recycle, return or re-use some of your skills and interests. You may not always need to change careers completely, but you will probably be called upon to make creative adjustments.

'Our education trains us to get a job. It is as if you are on a train and then the moment you can't find a job it is like you have to suddenly jump out of the train. All society is moving in one direction and you got your job, you got your degree, you got your CV and only then can you get your career. A career means there is a well-defined track, but when you leave the one you are on, you do not know what to do next. We have to rethink our identity, our role, everything. When you come off the track you can't just stand there. But there is nothing crafted out there ready, designed for us, to fit in … the concept of work, of career, you have to redefine it all again.' (Paraphrased from original.)
Wong, Malaysian in Europe, The Expatriate Archive, OAC5/3/3

RECYCLE

In Dubai I taught word-processing, but when I moved four hours down the road to Muscat I found that there was little demand for this skill. So I recycled my talent and taught desktop publishing instead. To hypothesise with a more fanciful example, had I sand-skied in the Middle East, I could have recycled this into snow skiing in Norway. My point is this: be prepared to adapt and modify some of your skills so that they fit the needs and the market you find in each location. Realise that in some countries you may need to secure local certifications for activities that are unregulated in the country from which you came. Flexibility and ingenuity are the keys to success.

'While I have had a prestigious career as an American diplomat as well as having held senior executive positions in corporate industry, these kinds of positions are not filled by foreign women in Saudi Arabia. As a result I have had to look for other challenges and opportunities where I can maximise the use of my skills and expertise, which ultimately resulted in the establishment of my own business, Global Watchers Arabia. However even in spite of opening my own business, due to the culture and customs of the male-dominated Kingdom, many times I have had to take the back seat in discussions and negotiations rather than the forefront, which I had routinely done prior to locating to the Kingdom.'
Carol, American, *http://delhi4cats.wordpress.com* and *www.expatwomen.com*

RETURN

Some skills and passions are just not made for a given location. For example, dates were hard to come by in Norway in 1996, so there was naturally little demand for my date cookery books. In the Middle East I was able to find English language journalism work with local publications. But I was out of luck in Stavanger, where there was no commercial English language newspaper or magazine at the time. Sometimes you have to return skills to your suitcase until you need them for a new time, a new place, or a new circumstance.

'... then you move on and you're back to square one and you're back to the struggle. I worked. I was senior manager in the health service ... and then moved out to Oman. I offered to write a ten-year health strategy for the government but they did not want me to. I was willing to do it for nothing. It was my area of expertise ... I retrained as teaching English as a foreign language ... I worked in the Shell school and the British Council and I got some interesting private clients and it was great fun... .I had just got it all nicely set up and low and behold we're posted ... back to the UK and I thought right, what am I going to do now? So I decided to retrain as a therapist ... Did that. Did all my post-qualification client work, started doing some training, eventually got taken into a private group practice where we had a contract with the local hospital and police service so it just meant that I'd got myself beautifully set up. I was teaching three days a week, working in a GP practice one day a week and private practice one day a week and got moved here... same thing. The system's so difference... none of the qualifications are registered.'
Julia, British in The Netherlands, The Expatriate Archive, OAC5/3/3

RE-USE

Some skills transfer more easily than others from place to place. There are few dates in Norway and few snowy slopes in the Middle East. But people who want to learn the English language are nearly everywhere. So teachers of English as a foreign language can usually find work wherever they go. And while date cooking had limited portability, I was always able to teach creative writing. Take a hard look at your skills and evaluate their portability. If few of them are transferable, then think about what additional skills you may need to learn.

'Coming away forced me to think about diversifying. It made me push myself to the limit. You know, it is so easy for people in this situation to focus on the negatives and think about the qualifications or the language they do not have. Coming here made me see what I really was able to do.'
Kit, American in Norway, www.career-in-your-suitcase.com

START AT THE BEGINNING

One way to consider which of your skills may be recycled, returned or re-used is to do what is called a SWOT analysis on yourself and on your present situation. Performing a ruthless assessment of our Strengths, Weaknesses, Opportunities and Threats is always revealing, and very often provides us with key answers. While some of this has already been covered *Chapter Three* it is worth taking another look at yourself from the perspective of the SWOT analysis.

Ask yourself some soul-searching questions:

- What am I good at?
- What are my strengths?
- What are my weaker areas, where I possibly need improvement?
- What do I like doing?
- Why am/was I in my present/previous line of work?
- Do I honestly enjoy what I have been doing in my career to date?
- What was my passion when I was a child?
- What stage am I at in my life?
- What are the obstacles I can foresee to developing a (new or different) career for myself at this point in time?
- What are the opportunities offered by the present situation?
- Can I now relocate/travel more easily now (for instance, than when the kids were younger)?
- What kind of work would I prefer: how much of a commitment do I want?
- Can I work on a contract/interim/consulting basis?
- What skills do I need to update in order to stay current?
- How have my personal and family obligations changed over the years?
- What do I consider the ideal career?
- Whom do I consider my role models, and why?

Really try to pry the lid off that 'box', the one that was the 'old you' and get outside it. There are many paths, and you just might discover a brand new you. Don't be afraid to ask for help. Often your partner's company will offer some form of career counseling assistance, and the Internet is an excellent source of career and study information. Barbara Sher, bestselling author of *I Could Do Anything I Wanted If I Only Knew What it Was*, advises, 'Failure to achieve our career ambitions does not result from a lousy attitude; rather from isolation.' You can't be expected to have all the answers at your fingertips. Go out and find them.

Time For Some New Skills?

There are specific personality traits that are considered highly desirable in adapting to working and living overseas. They include:

- Empathy: also emotional intelligence
- Respect: the ability to value difference
- Interest: in local culture
- Background: language skills, having lived abroad before
- Tolerance (or perhaps 'tolerance for ambiguity')
- Flexibility: do you see the big picture or live strictly by the rules?
- Initiative: achievement-oriented and independent
- Attitude: open mindedness to being exposed to other cultures, race and religion
- Sociability
- Positive self image
- Team spirit: being able to work with and fit into the culture of the local team

Using this list as a guideline, which areas do you think you may need to work on? Language skills? How good is your knowledge of the local culture, market, economy, political situation, really? If this matters to your business idea, then maybe you need to find out more. Do you have personal development skills such as the ability to coach, mentor, work successfully in teams? How is your sense of self?

Now you've identified your own needs: where do you go to fill the gaps? Check out local colleges and universities, community organisations or women's groups, distance learning opportunities. Offer to trade skills with your contacts, acquaintances, friends and neighbours. In the words of one experienced expatriate partner: 'As an expatriate spouse you have been given the gift of time – how you use it is up to you.'

LEARN NEW SKILLS

If you really feel that there are few opportunities that interest you in your current location, and you are not interested in telecommuting, then this may be the time to learn new skills.

One time when I was moving to a new country, I signed up for a correspondence course before leaving; that way I knew I would have something lined up to do when I arrived. In Muscat I taught a course on short story writing and in Stavanger I taught copy writing. Ultimately, that short story course I had done by correspondence led me to teach short story writing, and the copy writing led me to copy writing work; so both helped me with my career and kept me occupied. Even while I was not actively working or looking for work, I felt that I was moving forward.

Learning new skills by correspondence, teleclass or at a local college is a great way to feel usefully occupied. Especially if you study a subject or skill that's in line with your career goal.

'My husband is a career diplomat and we have spent the last 27 years moving around the world. I have developed my own career as an educator and have had dream jobs that I've had to leave for the next international relocation. The last position I loved and had to leave was as the education and youth officer at the US Department of State. There I helped our American diplomatic families navigate all the issues they faced with international moves and the education and successful transitions of their children. I never would have wanted to leave that position, but when my husband received an ambassadorial appointment to Oman (our second tour here), I packed up once again and moved overseas.

'Only this time I did something different. I was tired of leaving behind work I loved and did not want my Rolodex to grow cold. I wanted to build a business that I could do for the next 20 years. Therefore, I started laying the groundwork in advance, and launched my own international educational consulting business last year. Before leaving the States, I earned the right credentials to become a Certified Educational Planner, and used my State Department experience to become accepted as a full professional member of the best professional organizations in the US for my field the Independent Educational Consultants Association and the National Association of College Admissions Counselors. I am working from my home office here in Oman and have clients in various countries around the world. My portfolio includes choosing an international school, boarding schools, working with children with learning differences as well as those who are gifted and talented (and many times children are both), transition and TCK issues, and lastly, one-on-one counseling for students who want help with the complex college admissions process for American universities. I have done site visits on almost 250 American boarding schools and universities in the States and Europe, so my advice carries the weight of experience. I also do public speaking on a wide variety of topics related to education and internationally mobile youth.

'I am pleased with the way many things have gone for me, but I still need inspiration and motivation for what often seems like an uphill climb. I'm taking additional advanced educational consulting classes online through UCLA that have been wonderful.'
Rebecca (Becky), American in Oman, *www.rebeccagrappo.com*

MANAGE YOUR EXPECTATIONS

It's unlikely that you'll be able to move smoothly from place to place without needing to rethink what you will do professionally. Uninformed and unrealistic expectations are one of our greatest sources of discontent. So manage your expectations appropriately. Don't assume that your transition to another culture will be easy. Anticipate challenges and even temporary setbacks. The better you prepare beforehand the more easily you'll make the move into your new environment. Find out what opportunities may be available to somebody with your talents, skills and training. Through a buddy or mentor, try to discover what kind of work – paid or volunteer – other people in your position are doing. Also check on whether there are places to study, and check the availability of affordable childcare, good Internet connections and reliable transportation. If you know what to expect, you won't be setting yourself up for disappointment.

It is worth adding here that any time you spend on research and planning will not be wasted. Find out in advance whether your brilliant idea is viable in your new location if at all, anywhere. Plan it out, imagine that you have the career of your dreams and live with it for a few days. See if you still consider it to be ideal after a few days. It's always wise to look at your idea from all angles and do thorough investigation before spending any money.

'If you don't like what you are doing, where you are, or if you can't get a job where you are, you also know that it wont last and you'll have another chance in another country.

'Finding a job in Nigeria when everyone had said it was impossible [was my greatest moment]. I was, at the time, the only expatriate wife in full-time employment.'
Els, Dutch in Oman, *www.career-in-your-suitcase.com*

Getting Ideas

There is no denying that it can be soul-destroying to have spent years training for one career only to find that you simply cannot practise it in your new environment. I am afraid that you are going to have to be flexible about things. Sure, you trained to be a nurse and that is what you want to do, that is what you are good at and where your passion lies. But if the language barrier is insurmountable, you may have to be flexible about things. Maybe you could offer English language classes to pregnant women? Or you could offer to go in and visit new mothers in their homes soon after the birth? Perhaps you could write a handbook on common childhood ailments, or run first aid classes?

Where there are problems there are also opportunities. If you are flexible and open to change then you may just stumble upon a new career that is more fun and rewarding than you thought it might be.

'I took a part-time position as an admin assistant to get my foot in the door at a hotel management company here in downtown Denver and within 4 weeks I had been promoted to Corporate Accountant. I busted my backside but I had to prove a point. The owner of the company loves me, he knows that I am proving that point and he gets a full day's work out of me.'
Lizzy, British in America, *www.expatwomen.com*

THINK LATERALLY

I write a lot about a Canadian called Donna Messer. You will meet her in *Chapters Three, Four and Five*. This inspiring lady established a thriving business called Orange Crate, selling herbs and spices in neat packages, all because her friends told her she made things look pretty and taste nice, if you remember. This is a fine example of lateral thinking. Some people think creatively by nature, but others are not so adept. One of the best ways to come up with innovative ideas is talking informally with other people. If your own thinking hits a brick wall, get together with some people to 'blue sky', or brainstorm activities you love. The purpose of these sessions is to extrapolate possibilities from your known interests and talents. This tool was mentioned in *Chapter Two*.

If you don't have access to a group of people with whom you feel comfortable enough to do this, then hire a career adviser or coach to help you. If this is not possible either, then use some of the tools suggested in the last chapter to open your mind to creative thinking.

'In pottery, there will always be clay wherever you go in the world. There will always be things you can do if you apply yourself. You can take courses when possible and subscribe to international magazines. So many careers are open to the artist. You can teach, you can become a tour guide of artistic areas and even charge more because of that expertise. You can write about your work or local traditions. Of course you can produce your art and sell it too, and most expatriate locations have several annual craft fayres, it is a marvellous career. My father says that you can never have too much education, and by that he means that knowledge and experience are totally portable. My kiln may not fit in my suitcase but my knowledge weighs nothing.'
Cheryl, American in Vietnam, *www.career-in-your-suitcase.com*

TAKE ADVANTAGE OF LOCAL OPPORTUNITIES

Through networks, the Internet, friends and professional associations, keep yourself informed of upcoming conferences, workshops, seminars and professional development possibilities. These gatherings also offer superb opportunities for making new contacts, for both present and future use. Try to assess the merits of women-only versus more general events; there is a great deal to be said for both.

MIND MAPPING

Described in Tony Buzan's books *Use Your Head* and *The Mind Map*, mind mapping is a playful but serious way to get your creative juices flowing. Begin by writing down in the middle of a blank piece of paper a couple of words that describe one of your passions. Now think of all the permutations of this word or phrase, and write them down on a line that radiates from the centre of the page. As you come up with ideas related to others already there, link them up, in the fashion of an 'organogram'. An example of a mind map that I produced around my own passions can be found on the next page.

Buzan recommends that you use colours and illustrations to bring your mind maps to life; you can see examples at *www.mind-map.com*.

Produce a mind map for each of your passions and see what ideas flow out of these exercises.

Once you've created several mind maps, start a new one with the words 'my career' in the centre and, using your best ideas, see what feasible possibilities are revealed.

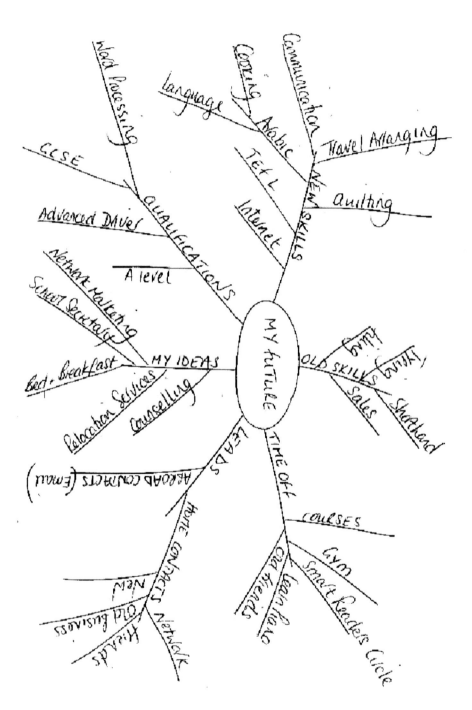

25 CAREER IDEAS

I have used this exercise many times with my students, and it always comes up with up to 25 separate job ideas.

Take a look at the following grid and copy it onto a sheet of paper, or fill in the one provided below. Write down a list of five things that you love to do. These will comprise the main subject areas and should be nouns – such as cookery, art, sailing and computers. Now write down another list of the five things you enjoy and do well. These words should be doing words, or gerunds, that end in *ing*.

Now insert each of the five things that you love to do into the five spaces at the top of the vertical columns, under the heading 'I love'.

Then write down each of the things you do well, into the five spaces at the left hand side of the horizontal columns, beside the heading 'I am good at'.

Finally, you need to pair up the words on the vertical axis with the words on the horizontal axis. If you look at the filled in example on the next page you'll get an idea of how your grid should look. You will have 25 pairs of words that should inspire you towards a possible career.

I love➡ ⬇I am good at					

In the example here you'll see 'cooking art'. If you think laterally then this leads to possibilities like food styling, painting still life food, designing cookery book covers, cake decorating and many other options.

I love➡ ⬇I am good at	ART	COOKERY	SAILING	COMPUTERS	GARDENING
COOKING	Cooking art	Cooking cookery	Cooking sailing	Cooking computers	Cooking gardening
ORGANISING	Organising art	Organising cookery	Organising sailing	Organising computers	Organising gardening
MARKETING	Marketing art	Marketing cookery	Marketing sailing	Marketing computers	Marketing gardening
DRAWING	Drawing art	Drawing cookery	Drawing sailing	Drawing computers	Drawing gardening
ACCOUNTING	Accounting art	Accounting cookery	Accounting sailing	Accounting computers	Accounting gardening

LISTEN TO PEOPLE

One of the best ways of finding out what goods and services people in a given area need and want is to go out among the local community. Chat with people who have been around for a while to find out what problems they are complaining about. In my village in England people were always wishing they could find reliable babysitters, gardeners, house cleaners and window cleaners. Here in The Netherlands people moan about not speaking Dutch, not understanding the administration procedures nor language, finding good schools and so on. While you may have no desire to babysit, garden or clean, yourself you might like to manage a team of other people to do such jobs. Problems are opportunities in disguise, so find out what gaps exist in the local market and see if you might be able to fill them.

Of course, a newcomer may not be immediately privy to such information so think about kick starting the process by attending networking meetings, social events and civic gatherings. You can also read the local paper if you speak the language to see what people are doing, what advertisements are posted and what people are asking for in the 'wanted' sections.

Go to the library and see what is being advertised on the notice boards, and which local amenities have placed their brochures there. You may notice a service that seems to be missing in this community that you'd taken for granted elsewhere.

It was only when I realised that people, including myself, were moaning about not having a portable career, and not knowing how to create their own career on the move, that I came up with the idea for *A Career in Your Suitcase*.

'Somebody asked me to go out with them because they were a foreigner here and always buying the wrong thing. Spending money, coming home with the wrong thing and then not having the courage to go back and tell the shop.'
Belinda, Dutch and now in Holland, The Expatriate Archive, OAC5/3/3

CAREER DRIVERS

Before you begin a business venture, it's a good idea to ask yourself *why* you're interested in the new project. Sometimes it can be easy to embark on something new as a knee-jerk reaction to the negatives of your past freelance or corporate career. Starting something new simply as a way of running away from previous issues is no recipe for success. You may find that the old problems were actually your problems and just come with you! Back in *Chapter Two* I told you that it can be valuable to write your life story as a way of finding your career drivers. Let's consider now what some of those career drivers might be.

YOUR MOTIVES

Rather than running away from the dissatisfying aspects of your previous career, look instead at the positive reasons that drive you towards your new choice. A business based on providing what you do want rather than merely avoiding what you don't want has a much better chance of success.

YOUR TALENTS

Running your own business is likely to allow you to utilise almost all of your talents at once; it's also likely that you will have to develop some more. In the corporate world you would probably have been able to call on the resources of your colleagues with, for example, IT, administration, purchasing or marketing issues. In your own business, you will have to be expert in every aspect.

AUTONOMY

Many people feel a rush of adrenalin when they move from being an employee to being an employer or entrepreneur. It becomes your role to produce the business cards and stationery, choose the furniture, write a catchy slogan or design a company logo. Consider whether you can maintain this enthusiasm throughout each area of your business. Bear in mind that while you no longer have one single boss, you now in fact have many. Your customers will soon tell you what to do.

FLEXIBLE INCOME

Few people would fail to be motivated by the prospect of making unlimited amounts of money – but of course this can go in either direction when you are self-employed. While the sky may indeed be the limit, you may also have to come to terms with earning nothing at all. Fortunately, with today's sophisticated information technology available and affordable, many business costs can be kept to a minimum.

ACCOUNTABILITY

At the end of the day, you have no one to answer to and no one to blame but yourself. If you have failed to do something then you need to be brutally honest with yourself and correct the situation immediately.

LIFESTYLE

This can be a double-edged sword. On one hand, you're not bound by company-determined starting times and schedules. On the other hand, you'll tend to decide your own hours based on the needs of the business. These needs often acquire a life of their own. Like the broomsticks in 'The Sorcerer's Apprentice' in the Disney movie *Fantasia* – they keep multiplying. When you have your own business, sometimes it seems that everywhere you turn there's a 'broomstick' (ie a problem that has a life of its own and quickly multiplies into other problems).

This can create difficulties for both you and your family. Many people complain that their spouse is married to the business, since she seems to be more attentive to its needs than to the spouse's. And the child of one entrepreneur announced one night that she'd like to be one of Daddy's clients, 'Because he's always with the clients and then I'd get to see him more often'.

The more successful your business, the more its needs and demands on your time can grow. You will need to institute policies much like those you find in a larger organisation. For instance, you might declare yourself off limits to family until a specified time, but also make a commitment to keep the business off limits after that time. You may need to refuse to answer the phone at a certain hour, letting the calls go to voice mail no matter how seemingly important. You might have to turn off your mobile phone or turn on its voice mail feature. You may need to force yourself to take lunch hours, small breaks and even holidays (even if just for a long weekend); no one's going to give them to you but yourself.

You're likely to get the most family support if you commit to reasonably predictable rules and guidelines that give them reliable access to you. They will resent you and the business less, and they'll be more likely to respect your business time if they know they will have access to you soon after.

WHAT SUITS YOU?

Before you can decide exactly which career or career areas most appeal to you, think seriously about your objectives. Think too about the unique contribution you, and only you, have to offer. Everyone is different and there will be certain things that you do better than other people. Your own values, passions, goals and skills will combine to become your unique contribution. When you are considering this, think too about what you want in return.

Do you want money or fame? Do you want both? Is it important for you to have time for your family, that the school holidays are kept free and that you have time to show your guests the local sights when they visit? Do you have the space and the discipline to work from home? Would you rather work with people in a formal office or through an informal office share? Is it important for you to use all your skills and passions, or would you be happy just using a few of them? Do you want still to have time for yourself and your hobbies? Do you want to work from nine to five, five days a week? Do you want a busy office or do you prefer to work alone? Do you want a management position, to work in a team? Which job would match your values and passions? Do you crave variety or routine?

At a more practical level, do you want to be dealing with tax and Value Added Tax (VAT) returns? Do you want to employ staff formally and be responsible for their tax and benefits? Your goal may be to earn just enough to keep you away from having to pay any tax at all, or enough to keep you away from paying high level tax. In England, certainly, if you form a Limited Company you need also to employ an accountant and have your books audited. So think seriously about how large or small you want your business to be.

And how about the work conditions? You may know of a job you think you'll love. But are you willing to work the 70-hour weeks it takes to be successful in it, or to commit three out of every four weeks to the necessary travel?

WHAT IS IMPORTANT TO YOU?

In *Chapter Two* you obtained a clearer picture of what you love (passion) and in *Chapter Three* you discovered what you could do (skills and talents). Now, it is time to take a look at what matters. You need to know what matters to you and the things you need to obtain from your chosen career. These things are so important to your wellbeing that without them you could not consider a position, even if it is based on your passions and uses your top skills. For example, if you love to dance and your top talent is performing in public then you may think that a job in an international dance troupe is heaven sent. Only, if you really hate working at night, long distance travel or long periods away from your family, then this really would not be such a good idea.

Think of the list below as your 'job filters'. Once you have compiled a list of the things you cannot live without then run any potential job ideas through your list to check that it matches your values too.

Tick the values below that are important enough to form the basis of your decision to accept a job offer or start a business.

- ☐ Frequent interaction with others
- ☐ Opportunity for personal growth
- ☐ High financial reward
- ☐ Being in charge
- ☐ Challenged to expand professional competence
- ☐ Constant variety
- ☐ See a tangible result or final product
- ☐ Contribute to the well being of others
- ☐ Use analytical and problem solving skills
- ☐ Well-defined and routine responsibilities
- ☐ Freedom from rules and procedures
- ☐ Recognition of achievements by others
- ☐ Authority to make final decision
- ☐ Work that requires solitary concentration
- ☐ Mental challenge and stimulation
- ☐ Always something new and different
- ☐ Job security
- ☐ Opportunity to influence the ideas and values of others
- ☐ Low level of stress
- ☐ A stable work schedule
- ☐ No spillover of work into personal and family life
- ☐ Freedom (from measurement relative to others)
- ☐ Ability to move physically from place to place
- ☐ A short (no longer than 30 minutes) commute
- ☐ Plenty of opportunity for advancement
- ☐ Build friendships and attachments with colleagues
- ☐ Opportunities for dealing with differences and conflicts
- ☐ Work with a spiritual (not religious, necessarily) dimension
- ☐ Environment that fosters close relationships
- ☐ Competitive environment
- ☐ Always know what to expect in your day

Write down any more that apply to you and that were missing from the list, here:

The second step in this exercise is to identify the five most important items from those you ticked.

Most important:

1. _____

2. _____

3. _____

4. _____

5. _____

After doing this, review the entire list again and select the five values that are least important to your professional satisfaction.

Least important:

1. _____

2. _____

3. _____

4. _____

5. _____

Again, there are no magic formulas, but here is a guideline: if an offered job features any fewer than four of your most important values, or any more than one of your least important then you need to think long and hard about accepting it.

KEEP YOUR EYES OPEN

It's important that you don't set your mind on only one option and close it to other possibilities. New ideas, while initially daunting, can also be energising. Try not to keep your eyes so firmly on your chosen path that you miss other opportunities. If, like me, you believe in synchronicity and that most things happen for a reason, be alert to life's happy accidents.

In Muscat several years ago, we were sitting outside having dinner with a group of friends one evening. It was dark and the slim date palm trees were silhouetted against a navy blue sky.

'I wish someone would write a cookery book about dates,' said Susie.

'I have written a cookery book before,' I joined in, 'and I'm sure I know enough about publishing to be able to self publish this time.'

'With my food science knowledge and love of cookery I'm sure I could create some great recipes,' said Sue.

'I already have some great recipes,' added Susie.

Nine months later *Dates* was produced and published by Sue and myself, with contributions from Susie. It sold 4,500 copies in the first year.

So every time a business idea pops into your head write it down, think about it, mind map it, and whatever you do don't forget about it!

If you hear someone say, 'I wish we had ... here,' then log that idea too.

> 'I am registered with the consultancy bureau of the university here. Every two to three months they have people that are going to Malaysia for a business trip or people from the foreign office who are going to work there. They call me to give lessons in our language ... usually 20 to 30 hours or so.'
> Zohra, Malaysian in Holland, The Expatriate Archive, OAC5/3/3

LOOK ON THE INTERNET

Many country or city focused websites advertise local job opportunities. If none of these options interests you, then check the names of the local companies that are advertising. Not only will this give you an idea of where you can look for work, but it will also tell you which businesses are popular. You may be able to find your own creative niche, originate an innovative pricing structure, or target a different kind of client.

If you subscribe to *www.going-there.com* you'll find that local job opportunities are advertised on their website.

There is a whole section on job-hunting on the Internet in *Chapter Six*.

VOLUNTEER

It's always worth considering voluntary work, particularly if it is in line with your career goals. A future employer will always be pleased to see that you have undertaken voluntary work, especially when it is consistent with your objectives. Moreover, volunteer work can often give you additional insight into a specific field and introduce you to contacts who can give you valuable advice about how to pursue your interests. It will add to your suitcase of skills in dealing with people, working with teams, organising, administration and other areas. There is no reason why something that begins as a voluntary project can't eventually grow into a paid work opportunity.

Working without pay often makes business sense. There are many different forms of payment, as countless global nomads have discovered. Volunteer work can offer satisfaction and rewards that are at least as valuable as monetary compensation. Besides the moral benefit in helping others, volunteerism in foreign countries offers another bonus. It can be excellent cultural adjustment therapy.

'Service work, like volunteering a few hours a week at a children's hospital or just helping someone in need, is much more important to our mental health than we think,' reports Dr Kirsten Thogersen, a psychotherapist based in Beijing. 'One of the reasons expatriates often suffer when they move is because they feel disconnected from their surroundings,' says Dr Thogersen. 'To be connected with someone else by giving them some of your time and energy is the best possible protection against depression and other psychological reactions experienced by expatriates.'

Says expatriate spouse expert Robin Pascoe, 'Many expatriate women's organisations in foreign countries organise welfare committees to allow members to channel energy, money and resources into local causes in a way that won't overwhelm them. Frontline volunteering is not for everyone.'

You are also likely to make lasting friendships with host country nationals through volunteer work, in a way that is unlikely in paid employment, and you're much more likely to have to use the local language in your work.

BLUE SKY

From the moment you picked up this book you have shown your interest in finding the perfect portable career. The blue sky featured on the book's cover is no accident. We all need to dream and to find the blue sky of open possibilities.

A dream is more likely to come true when you give it voice and write it down. When you first have a dream you create it in your mind; when you write it down you give it life; and every time you talk about it you give it more power. So as you share your dreams with friends and others whom you trust, the idea grows, problems are addressed and solutions found. At each stage your blue sky dream takes on a more concrete shape and fills out with the particular steps to be taken and tasks to be addressed that will translate the dream from the sky to its real, earthly incarnation.

Remember that you can go from 'blue sky' to 'the sky's the limit'.

Career Options

There are many different ways in which you can put your skills and passions together. No longer is it the norm for you to have one lifelong career and the list of options can be as long as your list of ideas.

CONCURRENT CAREERS

Many people pursue two or more careers simultaneously. One career may be a full time job while the other occupies evenings or weekends. Or a person may have two or more part time careers, with each job expressing a vocational interest or passion. These jobs may complement one another or be in entirely unrelated fields. It's not uncommon for a board level director to work for separate companies on different days of the week, some which may be voluntary.

Whenever I run my career in your suitcase workshops I can guarantee that someone always asks this question:

'It's all very well, this idea of finding a career based on your passion. I need to work and earn money and what I do right now is not based on my passion, so how can I start this great new career and put bread on the table?'

I understand this issue completely. In 1997 we moved back to England after ten years abroad and I had to earn proper money for the family. Determined not to compromise my belief in working with passion I decided that I would have to run two types of jobs concurrently. I would do the work I termed 'job' because they brought in the most money and I would make time for the work I called 'career' too. For me, as I mentioned in my introduction to this book, the thing that earned most money was journalism. And though I love to write, churning out articles week after week and constantly coming up with new ideas under pressure and to deadline was not all fun. I set myself a target of eight articles a month and then spent the rest of my time building my career in your suitcase business. Over time, as my business grew, I could earn more money from my 'career' and could slacken off on the 'job'. Eventually, I was in a position, as I am today, to follow my 'career' alone.

PORTFOLIO CAREERS

Similarly, the portfolio career takes the concurrent career one step further and is increasingly popular as people take on a variety of different jobs, rather than just one. Some people choose to take on one or more better-paying jobs to fund their career ambitions. Rather as an artist contains many samples of work in one portfolio, this kind of career appeals to those who enjoy a varied work life, based on a combination of activities.

The career portfolio may contain some careers that are related or have a common theme, and others that do not. They can include an assortment of child rearing, part time paid employment, volunteer work, community activities and hobbies. This combo-career offers a mix of activities that satisfies a person's need for fulfilment, purpose and variety. When I lived in Muscat, Oman, I had a portfolio of careers. I taught desktop publishing and creative writing, ran a CV writing service, did some journalism, sold books via a party plan scheme, made and sold date chutney, ran a take away service for my Indian maid and even made Christmas tree decorations to sell at festive bazaars. That kept me busy, and the variety of so many different projects at once was exhilarating.

TEMPORARY CAREERS

Consider having a temporary career, even if it lasts for quite some time, which can tide you over while you wait or prepare for a more permanent career. These professional interludes can be a source of fulfilment and identity.

Temporary placements may offer the recently transferred spouse an ideal opportunity. Such assignments are found not only in industrial and secretarial settings. In fact more than 30 per cent of current temporary placements are made in the professional, medical and technical/computer sectors. Temporary placements can be ideal for relocating spouses because they allow flexibility in hours, number of days a week and duration of assignment. They can also present an ongoing variety of experiences. In fact, some people work on a virtually permanent basis for temporary agencies. Others are rewarded for their superior ability and performance, and subsequently hired as full time employees. At the very least, temping presents us with opportunities for networking.

Find out where such contract work may be advertised locally or online. There are several freelance websites out there and those, like *www.smarterwork.com* and *www.elance.com* that specialise in contract work. Company schemes such as *www.partnerjob.com* advertise short-term vacancies for member companies as do local bulletin boards and networks.

JOB SHARING

In a job sharing arrangement, two people collaborate to perform the duties of a single, usually full time, position. Some companies hire new employees who are looking for part time work into positions they can share with another employee. And if a job is not advertised as a job share you can always ask.

TELECOMMUTING

Many companies now attract desirable employees with telecommuting arrangements that allow them to perform many, most or all of their duties from their home office. The telecommuter may work at home several days a week, or alternate between a week at home and a week in the office. In this way many employees find themselves spending their workweek in another country or city. Companies tend to be reluctant to employ people who work away from their colleagues full time for fear that they may grow too detached from the organisation.

It's worth noting that human nature causes us to crave community, and that anyone who embarks on a virtual telecommuting career may find themselves unhappy with the resulting level of isolation. Nevertheless, for some, this is a perfect solution.

FLEXITIME

This is a boon to mothers and fathers who want to be home when their children go to school, or ready to greet them at the other end of the day. Flexitime is also an attractive option for people who want to arrange their hours around what would be an otherwise unbearable commute. Some flexitimers may put in a standard five day, 40 hour workweek, but shift the hours during which they work towards the earlier or later part of the day.

Others may work flexitime yet also have a reduced workweek – so that they are effectively able to spread out three or four days' work over the five-day week.

COMPRESSED WORKWEEK

Another popular option is compressing the 40-hour week into four or even three days. A number of US hospitals pay nurses for a 40-hour week to work three 12-hour days. Federal and state governments in the USA also offer this arrangement to some of their employees. Some couples with children work three-day compressed schedules so that there is only one day a week when both parents are out of the house.

PRO-RATED CONTRACTS

In some countries, such as Norway, it's normal for an employee to negotiate pro-rated pay for a reduced working week. Some employees are able to work a four-day week, others do this during term time only. Employers are becoming increasingly flexible about this kind of arrangement in order to retain key staff, particularly mothers returning to work.

SELF-EMPLOYMENT

In the last decade we have also seen the rise of a new kind of entrepreneur, the self-employed company of one – the sole trader. It's interesting to note that an increasing number of women choose to work for themselves rather than advance their careers into management in large companies.

It appears that women opt for self-employment because they crave the risk and independence it provides. There is no doubt that working for yourself allows you to create the career that suits you, with the hours, environment and personnel you choose. It's common for entrepreneurs to develop consulting businesses in areas of specialisation they've honed through their work with previous employers. Others capitalise on speciality markets perfect for the small company, such as catering, party/event planning and website design.

There are different kinds of self-employment, and many people who work for themselves work alone, or with a team of similarly freelance associates, rather than building a staff. Whether you fancy being freelance, an entrepreneur, or a small business owner, self-employment can be highly portable.

ENTREPRENEURS

These are simply people who work for themselves. The word 'entrepreneur' may sound daunting but it's really just an umbrella term that refers to someone who is self-employed, freelance, an independent consultant or a small business owner, even someone who runs a kitchen table business. Depending on the amount of control, investment of time, budget, marketing effort, risk, innovation or the number of staff, you may consider your own case to be closer to the 'freelance' end of the spectrum than 'small business owner'. However, all these descriptions can also be applied to entrepreneurs.

An entrepreneur is someone who likes to be in control, enjoys an element of risk, is flexible, loves to solve problems and is quick thinking. But a successful entrepreneur finds ways of replicating his or her business and making money from that without necessarily doing all the work. In his book *The Emyth*, Michael Gerber explains how a successful entrepreneur needs to wear three hats – he needs to actually *do* the work, to *manage* the business and the administration that entails and to be *entrepreneurial*, creative and inventive. This can be a tall order for some people, while others thrive on the challenge.

WHAT DO ENTREPRENEURS DO?

In simple terms an entrepreneur is likely to be either selling a range of related products or services into one target market, or selling one main product into a range of markets. He may sell from business to business (B to B), from business to institution (B to I) or from business to consumer (B to C). The readers of this book may like to consider a fourth option, that of expatriate to expatriate (E to E). My own workshops and books are a case in point. I specialise in portable careers and teaching people to write about their overseas experiences. Clearly, my market is expatriates.

However, while marketing to the expatriate community may seem like the most sensible option, be aware that the market is not only a niche market, but also a moving target. You have to be very clear about your product and your marketing efforts here. Additional typical entrepreneur choices include purchasing an existing franchise operation or signing up with a multilevel marketing company. These options are all discussed in more detail later in this chapter.

WOULD YOU MAKE IT AS AN ENTREPRENEUR?

Before you take the plunge into working for yourself, it's important to know all the forms that this business can take. Each form has particular advantages and disadvantages for individuals with varying personalities, skills, and life and family situations. It is worth asking yourself the following questions:

- Do you truly believe in the business you are entering?
- Has this business passed its peak?
- How well does this business fit in with the rest of your life?
- Do you have a unique selling proposition?
- Do you have any experience in this business?
- Can you afford to get into this business?
- How easily can you get out of this business if it were to fail?

For more information on being an entrepreneur please read my book *Expat Entrepreneur* or go to *www.expatentrepreneurs.com*.

STARTING A BUSINESS FROM SCRATCH

This is perhaps the most adventurous of the options. Starting from your own idea (or a variation on others' ideas), you plan and execute your own entrepreneurial venture. In essence, you do everything yourself – generating the business idea, researching the marketplace, checking the competition, determining the form of ownership, formulating a business plan, obtaining funding and doing the finances.

BUYING AN EXISTING BUSINESS

This is often a good option for entrepreneurs who don't want to go through all the hassles and procedures involved in starting a business from scratch. With this option, however, it's important to research and identify exactly what you're buying. You must carefully assess the financial health of the business (often with the help of an accountant). Interview the current owner thoroughly and talk to customers, employees (if any) and suppliers. You must also speak to the current owner about staying on to help you as you take over the operation. And of course, in return for the privilege of buying an existing business, you may also have to invest more cash than if you were starting your own. You need to value the business accurately and to negotiate skilfully for a purchase price and terms that are fair to both you and the current owner.

BUYING A FRANCHISE

There are thousands of franchise options that provide a business model and certain tangible assets along with a known name. Many internationally known food outlets, like McDonald's and Kentucky Fried Chicken, are franchises but there are others out there that offer services such as carpet cleaning and colour consultancy. The costs of buying into an established franchise can sometimes be high, and franchisees are put through a rigorous screening process. The price also depends on how well known the brand is already and how much training and assistance you will receive along the way. Franchises can require long hours in order to make the anticipated earnings. With these levels of financial and personal commitment, make sure that you select a franchiser that is committed to franchisee support and success.

Buying a franchise seems to have many advantages. After all, who wouldn't want to buy into an operation that has instant name recognition, protected territories, time-tested operational procedures and marketing methods and guaranteed profits, all at a reasonable price? The problem, of course, is finding a franchise like this in a very glutted market full of hype and exaggeration. And even if you find the 'perfect' franchise, franchising itself may not suit your personality or satisfy the reasons why you wanted to start your own business in the first place.

BECOMING A CONSULTANT OR
INDEPENDENT CONTRACTOR

This option is often the best for people who have a specific expertise that can be sold to individuals and companies. It has the advantage of low capital outlay, scheduling flexibility, variety and autonomy. But you also need to be realistic about the downside or challenge of consulting – the lean periods, the need to sell yourself constantly and the intermittent (or frequent) feelings of isolation.

TYPICAL TRAITS OF SUCCESSFUL ENTREPRENEURS

Because entrepreneurism has experienced such a boom, it's been the subject of a great deal of study in the popular and business press as well as academia. Numerous studies have been conducted on the traits that make a successful businessperson. Here are some of the most frequently cited:

Competitiveness and drive
Most entrepreneurs score high in these areas. They want to win over others or exceed their own standards for success.

Action orientation
Many people have great ideas for a business, but end their careers in the same jobs where they started. A good idea is usually a prerequisite for a successful business – but even more important is acting on that idea. You must be willing not just to formulate an action plan; you must then stick to it despite the obstacles and setbacks.

Risk tolerance
Successful entrepreneurs do not avoid risk, but they don't take unnecessary risks either. They have at least a moderate tolerance for risk. They know when they are beyond the boundaries of their risk comfort level and they carefully assess the degree of financial and personal risk they are willing to take on. People with very little tolerance for risk often deviate from their plan at the first sign that they may lose a dollar or two in the short term.

Assess your risk quotient. Think about whether you have risked your own or others' money in the past. Consider whether that risk made you feel comfortable or uncomfortable. Of course, if your partner has a lucrative, secure position, you may find that your risk quotient is higher than if you're the sole source of income – or if your steady income is needed to help meet household expenses.

Strong goal orientation

Are you the kind of person who cannot envisage stopping once you have set a goal for yourself? Or are you the kind of person who is more likely to say, 'I just want to enjoy life and have a relatively stress free existence'? What goals have you achieved in the past and how have you achieved them? See if you can identify what motivated you then, so that you can use the same trick this time.

Ability to make decisions

As an entrepreneur, you'll be responsible for making all the decisions for your business. You won't have the luxury of assembling a task force or committee to study the matter and whom you can subsequently blame if the decision has poor results. You will need to act fairly quickly. If a decision needs to be researched, you'll do it yourself, not refer it to the Research Department. You must be willing to determine the proper time frame for the decision according to its importance and possess the flexibility to change a decision or course of action if it isn't working.

Emotional resilience

You must be willing to see setbacks as learning opportunities, not reflections on your worth as a person. Thomas Edison tried several hundred substances before he finally settled on tungsten as the right element for a light bulb filament. If he'd considered himself a failure after the tenth attempt (or even the fiftieth) he never would have invented the electric light bulb. You also need to realise that a typical salesman needs to go through nine rejections before he or she gets an acceptance. As an entrepreneur, you will need to be able to withstand this kind of rejection.

Some sales skills and experience

You may offer the best service or product, but if you are not reasonably adept at selling it, you will never get to deliver it. This doesn't mean you must have a 20-year record of sales success. I'd be no good at selling something I do not believe in, but when I am passionate about a product, my enthusiasm easily persuades others to buy. You need to ensure you'll be effective at selling the product or service you plan to work with.

Preference for creativity over bureaucracy

When problems arise, do you find comfort in the rules and regulations of organisational life? Or do you find them an impediment? Most entrepreneurs enjoy and need to find creative new approaches to finding and delivering business. If you're the kind of person who is always consulting the company's procedure manual, beware!

Optimism

This is perhaps one of the key attributes of a successful businessperson. Psychologist Martin Seligman has studied optimism and found it to be a learnable trait. His book *Learned Optimism* will show you his secrets.

Optimistic thinking can make the difference between success and failure in any new venture, especially one with so many obstacles and problems as the launch of a new business. Optimists think that failure is caused by something that can be changed, while pessimists take personal blame for any failure, attributing it to a character defect they are helpless to alter.

Positive thinking is not the same as optimism and neither is happiness, but somehow they are all connected. If you want to put some more positivity into your life and work think back to your last year of education. Think about the things you enjoyed doing then, but that you no longer do now. Try to put at least one of those things back into your life. Try to give yourself ten minutes of 'me time' each day. And when you go to bed at night, think of three things you are grateful for.

'My mother always says that a vacation is just a change of work. I have always made a point of visiting all potteries and galleries wherever we have been on holiday. I also take lots of courses for up to two weeks at a time. They are really inspiring.' Cheryl, American in Vietnam, *www.career-in-your-suitcase.com*

EFFORTLESS ENTREPRENEURSHIP

If you know you're likely to be on the move again fairly shortly, and that no business you choose is worth the investment it would take to make it a big success in one location, then maybe you should think about starting a more modest concern. One that will conserve your sanity and your professional identity and also give you the flexibility you need.

Think about starting small and then growing the business organically, sharing costs, bartering skills and making your venture work for you.

TEAMWORK

We all have strengths and weaknesses, so why not consider working in a team with a selection of other people? First, identify people whose area of expertise complements yours but with whom you share a common passion or purpose. I know I am great at having ideas, talking to people, teaching, networking and writing but marketing, administration and filing are not in my list of favourite things to do. I believe it is better to focus on your strengths rather than expend energy trying to improve on you're the things you do well. If you put your best efforts into the things you do best and you work with someone with complementary skills you have a better chance of more success in less time. Even if each team member contributes only what he or she does best, together you can cover every aspect of the business from marketing to production.

The other advantage of having a team is that you can spur each other on, you can have someone to share ideas with and you will not need to work alone. When Sue Valentine and I decided to write the cookery book, *Dates*, I focused on writing, editing, desktop publishing and production while Sue focused on the photographs, the properties of dates and finding a sponsor and publisher. We shared writing the recipes between us. Separately, we would work on our specialist areas, then we would set deadlines and meet up to discuss progress. As a result, we stuck to our original plan and the book took nine months to complete from start to finish. Today, writing a book alone, I know I allow myself to procrastinate terribly. If you have a partner or partners in your project you are accountable to someone and that can make all the difference.

> 'I met Irene at a professional conference in Paris. We liked each other instantly. Irene came to one of my cooking classes, I enjoyed one of her walks with Shopping Plus. We found that we both had something to offer each other. We also both had the same type of relaxed working style. We pooled our joined experiences and started "French for a Day".'
> **Sue Y, British and Irene, French, in Paris, *www.career-in-your-suitcase.com***

A PART-TIME TEAM

The owner of a small business, especially a home based one or a consulting practice, can feel very isolated. There are no more coffee breaks or lunches in the company cafeteria with 'the gang'. The consultant can go from engagement to engagement, never developing close or lasting relationships. One antidote to this is to join a breakfast group or other support group for small business owners or consultants, a local networking group, or a forum or trade association. These people can empathise with and understand your problems and concerns in a way that your clients and even your family can't. You may also be able to participate in forums and chat groups on the Web. These might not provide the face-to-face contact you crave, but they have the advantage of being instantly accessible at almost any hour of the day. You could even start your own breakfast club or online forum. A mastermind group will allow you to ask each other for ideas and solutions. Joining a virtual network, such as Ecademy (*www.ecademy.com*) offers this kind of benefit and with hundreds of thousands of members all over the world and countless forums it is a boon to the sole trader. Their Blackstar membership offers the benefits of a mastermind group too.

Business owners and consultants also often complain about a lack of feedback. If you have created your informal support team you will always have a source of ideas, advice and feedback.

BARTER SKILLS

If you don't want to form an association with others and don't want to pay staff, but do need help with certain aspects of your business, consider bartering your skills.

As I've said, I work alone. However I often feel the need for some blue sky and brainstorming myself, so I meet with certain friends over lunch or coffee so that we can bounce ideas off each other.

I have one graphic designer friend who needs some furniture storing. So I am helping her with her removals, and she will produce illustrations for one of my projects. Another friend has bartered life-coaching sessions for me in exchange for my copy editing skills.

> 'When I decided to write 'Gardening in Oman and The Gulf' I had to learn to use a word processor. Expatriate life is full of talented women who are not working full time and a friend taught me how, for free. Another friend taught me how to take photographs. Sometimes we bartered skills, sometimes I paid nothing, sometimes I just paid less than the going rate.'
> Anne, British, in Oman, *www.career-in-your-suitcase.com*

FIND ASSOCIATES

If you know people who do the same kind of work as you, consider making them 'associates'. Without the bureaucracy that comes with hiring staff, you can simply pass some of it over to a trusted third party. This will enable you to take on a greater volume of work without the risk of being overwhelmed by more than you can handle. Clients will be happy with the final product or service as long as you guarantee a uniform high quality.

In the past I have worked with associates and used a finder's fee/commission arrangement. In this way, if my associate passes business to me, I pay her 15% of what I earn and vice versa.

Two advantages of forming associations like this are that your business will appear larger than it actually is, and you may be able to find ways to share marketing and publicity costs with others.

When I returned to the UK in 1997 I wanted to find work as a bit of an expat expert, helping people solve their career problems. But, back home, I was no longer in the 'expat bubble' and felt isolated and unknown. So, I decided to form a group called Words That Work and invited fellow expat experts to pay me a very small fee, I think it was £50, to form a group of six of us and share a brochure, website and letterhead. I made no profit from this idea, but what I did receive was a place in a glossy brochure and the knowledge that when my associates handed out the brochure they would also be promoting me.

JOIN AN ESTABLISHED COMPANY AS A FREELANCE

If you don't want to tackle the paperwork that goes with forming your own company, seek out an established organisation to which you can make a contribution, and determine its willingness to provide you with a work permit or visa. Sometimes you may have to pay them for this service, but the fee will often be less than you would pay to start up a business and obtain your own premises, as is the prerequisite in some countries. Often a deal like this will also provide you with an office address and even a desk.

When I was in the Middle East, I formed this sort of arrangement with a recruitment agency. The deal was that I provided them with a computer training department and curriculum vitae writing service that they branded as their own. In return, I used their office and advertised under their name. I paid them a percentage of all my earnings and the arrangement was profitable for both parties.

'It is hard to work legally in Oman without a local sponsor. It is illegal to advertise or knowingly make money without one. When I was offered the chance to do some food hygiene training for a local company I knew I needed to be legally able to work. So, I approached the British Council, knowing that training is one of their objectives and asked them for their sponsorship as a consultant. We agreed that I would make myself available to any of their clients and they would organise my work visa. I did pay them an annual fee but it was worth it. Where there is a will there is a way.'
Sue V, British in Oman, *www.career-in-your-suitcase.com*

WORK VIRTUALLY

Consider setting up a business that allows you to work by computer or telephone from home, anywhere in the world. Website design, coaching, writing, editing, marketing, market research, accounts, virtual assistance, teaching and many other businesses can be successfully run on this basis. Some companies, particularly those requiring people to run a telephone based enquiry service or telesales office, recruit freelance staff to work from home.

In addition, many careers are becoming Internet based. You can now mentor, coach, teach or provide therapy by email or webcam, using a service such as Skype. You can also conduct teleseminars or video conferences from wherever you live and talk to huge numbers of students based all over the world. While nothing can beat personal contact, there are lots of opportunities for teleworking.

In fact, running a business from your computer, thanks to the marvels of broadband and the Internet, means that you can create a virtual business that is also a global business. And when your clients are global you can take them with you. I will be writing more about establishing a mobile client base in *Chapter Five*, Networking.

Some elements of my business are now global and virtual. I speak with clients all over the world, using my webcam and Skype and have face to face meetings. I run occasional teleclasses and, because I have an international client base and keep in touch with them through an email newsletter, my publishing clients are based worldwide too. Every now and again we talk with Skype, but in between we use email to send documents back and forth between each other. I live in Holland but my virtual assistant, Tracey lives in Philadelphia and my designer, Graham, in Peterborough, England. And, thanks to my global network, when I arrived here in Holland, instead of being invisible as I was when I moved back to the UK in 1997, plenty of people already knew me and greeted me like an old friend.

The disadvantage, however, of working virtually and from home is that you may find yourself starved of human contact. If you are an introvert and happy with your own company (not me!) then this may be perfect for you, but for me, needing to be with people on a daily basis is important for my happiness. The only way I can cope with extended periods alone is to make time in my diary to see at least one other person, face to face, every day. Running workshops and making an effort to meet consultancy clients personally whenever possible is of great help. Some people believe that we only get energy from being in the same room with someone and that email conversations, Internet chats and video links are not the same. Consider your own needs before you decide to work virtually.

> 'When we lived in Sweden, I worked from home, online for an American organisation that provided their clients with "outsourced" expat support.'
> Victoria, New Zealander now in India, *www.expatwomen.com*

A WOMAN'S WORLD?

As the world shifts to a truly global economy, new kinds of leadership are required. And while this book is not designed specifically for women, the chances are, that since most expatriate accompanying partners are women, the majority of this book's readers will also be female. It is worth focusing now on the innate qualities that females can bring to the workplace.

Experts agree that women's focus on relationships, comfort with direct communication and diversity, refusal to compartmentalise skills, talents and lives, innate scepticism of hierarchy and, most importantly, desire to lead from the middle (not from the top) are all key attributes required by tomorrow's leaders.

The talents, experiences, attitudes and skills that women bring with them are precisely those needed in the evolving post-industrial economy, according to Sally Helgesen, author of *The Female Advantage*. She feels that this confluence of abilities and required leadership capacities is creating unprecedented opportunities for women to play a vital role in leading transformational change in organisations and communities. Women are better at seeing the human side, quicker to cut through competitive distinctions of hierarchy and ranking, and impatient with cumbersome protocols.

Bestselling author Esther Wachs Book, who wrote *Why the Best Man For the Job is a Woman,* defines 'new paradigm leaders' as those who combine many of the managerial talents traditionally attributed to men with many of the stereotypically 'weaker' female skills. In detailed interviews with 14 of the top female managers in the USA, Book concluded that new paradigm leaders achieve success for three main reasons:

1. Self assurance compels new paradigm leaders to stay motivated and take risks;
2. An obsession with customer service helps them anticipate market changes; and
3. New paradigm leaders use 'feminine' traits to their advantage.

Book suggests the 'new paradigm leader' learns to take risks, anticipates change, uses her feminine qualities, can articulate her vision, stay focused, connect, take action, get to know her customers and learn to fight back. Skills such of these can all be effectively utilised in the successful reinvention and re-packaging of your own skills set in an international environment.

5 networking

Networking is not about handing out business cards, it is rather about building relationships and making friends. With thanks to REA for the details on informational interviews.

> *'It's not what you know but who you know that makes your business grow.'*
>
> Donna Messer

In this chapter:

- The hidden job market
- Building your network
- Networking etiquette
- Where to network?
- Global or local?
- Connecting
- Passion, presents and persistence
- Create your own network
- Breakfast clubs
- Men and networks
- Employees need networks too
- Informational interviews
- Fear of networking
- Elevator pitches
- Follow up
- Building rapport
- Learn to present

Dr Anne Copeland, director of The Interchange Institute in Brookline MA, has conducted a series of studies into the happiness of accompanying partners. Copeland has discovered that it's not the women who maintain close contact with their friends and family back home who adjust best, nor is it those who have a strong family unit with them on assignment. It's the women who make new friendships who adjust most easily to their new environments. And the way we make friends is by networking.

'Research has shown that women with strong social networks are usually physically and emotionally healthier than those who are isolated,' she says. 'But when a woman moves half way round the world she is hit triply hard. Firstly, she needs the support of friends more than ever because of all the changes she encounters. Secondly, she's now far away from those who know her best. And thirdly, she faces language and cultural barriers to making new friends.'

When you're trying to build a business as well as a social life, nothing can kick start your career better than networking. In a new location, you can start networking straight away, if not before you arrive, by making contact with people to whom you have been referred by your contacts in the previous location.

Statistics say that 65 to 75 per cent of jobs are found through networking rather than through things like recruitment agencies, advertised vacancies and Internet postings.

We like people who are like us. We buy from people we like. How are we ever going to let people find out whether they are like us or they are like us if we don't get out there and network? And no, networking is not about handing out business cards, it is about being nice to people and making friends. Read on to find out more.

The Hidden Job Market

Did you know that even advertised vacancies are often filled by networkers, before or while the advertisement appears? Indeed, 50 and 80 per cent of the positions that interest you will be filled at the 'hidden' level?

Quite simply these jobs are snatched up by people who are no better qualified than you, but who are better connected. People get these jobs by networking or by being part of an already existing network. Networking gives you the best chance of knowing the right person in the right place at the right time. Studies of networking have demonstrated that this 'right person' is rarely a close friend – or even a friend at all. She's more likely to be the acquaintance of a friend, or the friend of an acquaintance. So your chances of getting your desired position increase in proportion to the number of people you know and their networks.

Over the years I have come across countless examples of people who found a job in the hidden job market. One of my friends, newly arrived in Dubai, found herself a job as a secretary for an airline company simply by chatting to someone at a drinks party. I started working for an employment agency, writing CVs, because my husband had told someone he'd met in a bar that his wife had arrived in town and was looking for work. I am about to run a writing workshop for a large ferry company because I met someone who worked there at a wine tasting event. And I found a publisher because I got chatting to the man sitting next to me on a ten-minute train ride. He was that publisher.

My commissions at *The Independent* came about because one of the members of our local writing circle did some sub editing for them. At least two of the career consultants hired by Ricklin-Echikson Associates were recruited as the result of an email I received when I was editor at *Woman Abroad* magazine asking if I could recommend anyone suitable.

A FOUR STAGE EVENT

The hidden job market has four stages. The first one is when there is no vacancy. The second is when a need arises for extra staff. The third stage is when it's agreed that a new recruit is required and informal enquiries are made. The fourth stage is when the vacancy is made public and advertised in the normal way. Most openings will be filled while the vacancy is at stage two or three. The more people you know and who know you may be available for work the more likely you are that when that job comes up, you will be first in line.

Building Your Network

Networking builds a web of contacts and associations.

Like a spider, you cannot build your whole web instantly. It begins with the people you know - relatives, close friends, casual acquaintances and people you haven't seen for some time. Don't forget to include people you see regularly and those you must make a special effort to reach.

You can network with all of these people:

- Neighbours (past and present)
- Friends
- Business colleagues and co-workers (past and present)
- Social acquaintances (golf, tennis and other sports/recreation players, social club members, members of the community met through social or civic activities)
- Professional acquaintances (people with whom you have interacted in present or past jobs)
- Former classmates, teachers and college alumni
- Relatives
- Priests, ministers, rabbis and other religious leaders
- Members of any religious organisation to which you belong
- People in your town and area with whom you have a friendly relationship (local business owner, bank tellers, your estate agent)

Then, once you have established your own first level network, you will discover that the people who belong in other people's networks find their way into yours. Like an elastic band your network can always expand to fit in more people.

But how do you find you way into the networks that belong to your networks? You ask. You ask a specific question based on your need. I am sure you are used to doing this in your daily life. You need a plumber but you are new in town and know very few people, but you are desperate and so you ask the only person you do know, the lady on the reception desk at the school where your children go. She has been there a few years and has no difficulty giving you a few names and numbers. Easily, her network becomes yours.

NETWORKING ETIQUETTE

Mention the word 'networking' and many people raise their eyes to the ceiling as they conjure up pictures of brash, assertive types, thrusting business cards into the palms of complete strangers. Believe me it should not be like that, particularly if it's to produce the desired outcome. I've learned to call the subject of this chapter 'relationship building', 'connecting' or simply 'making new friends'. Networking is simply a method of forming professional relationships and exchanging information with people with whom you share vocational and professional interests.

Donna Messer built her business out of networking. A regular on the international speakers' circuit at conferences and for huge corporations, her businesses, Connect Us Canada and Business Tree, simply facilitate connections between people and businesses. Donna has a training suite at her offices in Ontario. She starts many of her presentations with the words 'Hello, my name is Donna Messer, how may I help you?' Because helping is what she does so well.

'Networking is not about handing out business cards,' she says. 'If you build the relationship first, get to know someone, and they like you, then they will *ask* you for your card. That's much better.'

Donna believes that the secret of good relationship building is to give presents. And she doesn't mean presents that cost money. The nicest present you can give someone is simply the name of someone else who might be able to help them. For the newcomer to a community, the name of a recruitment agency, someone who has lived and worked in the community, or a cheap stationer may be the most welcome gift of all.

When you give someone something they need, even if it is just the number of plumber as seen in the example earlier, you are giving them a *present*. The recipient of the phone number feels pleased with the outcome, as pleased as if she had received a real present tied up with a big ribbon. The person who gave the gift feels of value too and at the same time, a relationship starts to form between the giver and receiver of the gift. They start to like each other. We do business with people we like and so the giving and receiving of a simple phone number may have far reaching benefits.

The more you give, the more you receive. But it's not that easy. Do not expect that if you give a 'present' to one person they will give you one right back. No, it's not like that. You give randomly and receive randomly. Thomas Power, founder of Ecademy, mentioned earlier in this book, has calculated that he has to give 98 presents in order to receive two back in return. However, those presents he receives are of such value that it makes it all worthwhile. This is the law of karma and paying it forward. Good networkers give and give and give and reap the rewards.

WHERE TO NETWORK?

Of course we don't need to join a professional organisation in order to start networking. It's just as easy to make friends in the school playground or supermarket queue. But sometimes we need a little help.

For those like me who want to work while they are abroad, the best kind of networking starts with getting to know people. In time those people become friends and a handful of them become soulmates. Finally, if you're as passionate about your business as you are about making friends, then those friends become your clients too.

> 'I make my own business cards and spread the word. I join professional and other groups and network as much as I can.'
> Kitty, American in Norway, *www.career-in-your-suitcase.com*

Clubs

All over the world the American Women's Clubs thrive on helping newcomers to make friends – and while many of their meetings do involve cups of coffee and sticky cakes, they provide a service that is second to none. Many have offshoot groups for working women, local history or travel. The umbrella organisation, the Federation of American Women's Clubs Overseas (FAWCO), is now in its 80th year and the number of associate member groups is growing.

I remember, back in the early nineties that living in Dubai with two young children and an oft-absent husband made the days seemed endless. It was then that I joined a group called Mother to Mother. Back then I didn't class this volunteer group as a network, but that's exactly what it was, of course. The monthly coffee mornings became a lifeline to me. There were lots of toys for the children and the chance for some adult conversation for me. But this group offered much more besides. There was a library of child related books and videos available, as well as offshoot groups that concentrated on, say, breastfeeding or twins, and a series of grown-ups only events. I soon found myself editing the monthly newsletter, which led me to make new friends with those involved in editorial, events or photocopying.

But it also led me to perfect my desktop publishing skills. When the children were off my hands I found myself teaching desktop publishing. The added value of such an organisation was clear.

In 1996 when my family moved to Stavanger in Norway I experienced the benefits of networks within a day of arriving. My husband was working for Schlumberger, a large oilfield services provider, and their spouses' association (SSA) is run on a wholly voluntary basis by the spouses themselves. There are now over 60 chapters worldwide. The Shell Global Outpost network has its own association, which currently has a similar number of offices.

It was January. Ian had gone to work and I was alone in our temporary apartment with the boys. Snow was falling outside the vast windows. Coming from the Middle East we were not equipped with snowsuits and boots so we couldn't venture out to play. With only Cartoon Network for company, the day ahead looked bleak, until Ian would return with the company car and we could go and hunt for schools, somewhere to live and fur lined clothing. Then I received a phone call from Maureen who introduced herself as my appointed welcomer from the SSA. The next day she visited me in person, armed with flowers and a welcome basket. Inside I found a local street map, newsletters from various local networks and information about pre-schools. I also had the luxury of a real live adult to bombard with questions about living in the land of the trolls. Importantly, I also received an invitation and the offer of a lift to the next SSA coffee morning. Despite having already spent ten years with Schlumberger in two different countries, this was the first time I'd ever been able to meet up with the wives of other employees. It was only a matter of time before I found myself working as their newsletter editor, and ultimately arranging seminars.

Despite the poor quality of Norwegian coffee I was determined to make my first outing to the local FAWCO club too. It was there that I received the extra gifts I needed to make my life more contented. Within five minutes I had the number of a babysitter and discovered how good Norwegian pastries were. I also received a calendar of events for the year ahead and found out how to advertise in their monthly newsletter the creative writing classes I hoped to run. My first course was soon fully booked.

Professional Networks

My professional life has always been important to me, of course, and so I also joined a group for working women that called itself Women's International Network (WIN). Nevertheless I don't mind admitting that it took me almost five months to pluck up the courage to go along. When I arrived I could not have met a nicer, more helpful bunch of people. Here I was able to attend a series of fascinating seminars, meet women who shared my passion for maintaining a portable career, and learn new skills. In the true spirit of karma, I was soon giving my time back to the group producing the newsletter. I also met Elizabeth Douet, who helped me with the first *Career in Your*

Suitcase and its associated seminar, joined a group that taught me how to present, and found more students for my creative writing classes.

When I returned to England in 1997 I had a tough time repatriating my career, but it was harder still to repatriate my identity. After nine months of feeling I did not belong, I decided to start a women's professional network of my own. Four years later, I was still on the committee of Women Connecting Women (WcW) with a database of 200 regulars. Find out how I set it up later in this chapter.

Now, in the Netherlands becoming a board member of Connecting Women was the first thing on my agenda. In fact I was their speaker at my very first meeting. Six months later I grabbed the opportunity to be on the board. This was a wise decision and helped me to make firmer friends and a stronger network. It also gave the opportunity to stand up and speak at the monthly meetings about my role as workshop co-ordinator, which raised my profile in the local community. By volunteering to do something that benefited my business directly was a bonus. For while organising the promotion of the group's workshops I can promote my own.

> 'For the first month I could not cope. I could not face going out because I couldn't communicate in Norwegian. I sat at home and read most of the time. It was so demoralising. After visiting a couple of shops I was exhausted and had to come home again. The Petroleum Wives Club and the Women's International Network (WIN) became my lifeline. I soon took on board positions for both. I also took any substitute teaching I could find at the International School. It took six months to settle down.'
> **Penny, British in Norway,** *www.career-in-your-suitcase.com*

The Internet

This is another source of new friends. Find sites that appeal to you whether they focus on your specialist area, your hobby, where you are living, or are more general in focus. Many will have chat groups you can join, or electronic newsletters (ezines) such as the one connected with this book that I call *The Inspirer*. Both will be a source of contacts and inspiration.

Take a look at a website, find out the contact details of the organisers, or click through to the sites of those who are featured there, and get in touch.

Sites such as *www.expatexchange.com*, *www.expatwomen.com* and *www.paguro.net* help you to connect with other expatriates in your new location even before you arrive. Try *www.newcomersCcub.com* to find out about existing networking groups too.

Of course, there are plenty of networks out there that exist solely online. Ecademy (*www.ecademy.com*) has hundreds of thousands of members worldwide and realtime meetings too. Members can post their profile, join forums and search for and connect with other Ecademists. LinkedIn (*www.linkedin.com*) is a similar idea. Here, you do not make connections with strangers right away, instead, you find someone in your network who is the first link in the chain of 'six degrees of separation' and who can help you reach that person.

'I have found online networking to be an excellent tool - especially the site *www.linkedin.com*. This is a professional networking site and the more information one is willing to share about themselves the better results received. Through LinkedIn networking I was contacted by an international American firm to assist with a detailed marketing research project in Saudi Arabia, which in turn led to additional contacts and opportunities.'
Carol, American in Saudi Arabia, *http://delhi4cats.wordpress.com*

Publications

Several years ago, when I was living in Norway, I subscribed to *Writers News* magazine. One day I spotted a small feature about a lady called Bobby Meyer, who had started an enterprising new publication called *Dual Career Network*. I was so inspired by her initiative that I got in touch. On my next trip home to England we met up and Bobby and I have been firm friends ever since. She helped to proof read the first version of *A Career In Your Suitcase*, wrote a chapter for it and later joined with me to create a website. We've run seminars together and continue to connect with each other and scratch each other's backs as often as we can.

If you see an article that appeals to you in a magazine, newspaper or even on a website, ask the editor to connect you with the author. The editor will be delighted to get some feedback and know that the articles are of interest. Magazines such as *Transitions Abroad, American in Britain* and *Bonjour* tend to be written by and for expatriates. If you want to make new friends, try contacting the people who write or feature in these and other similar magazines.

Remember, you can write to magazines and websites requesting that people contact you to help you with your research. This can be very productive.

And why not write to authors too? One of my closest friends met me that way. She read a copy of the second edition of *Career in Your Suitcase* when in Australia, found my phone number in the book and gave me a call. Soon she was in London and attending my first ever Release the Book Within seminar. It was Jacinta Noonan who invited me to speak at that first Connecting Women event in The Hague, because, guess what, she was living in the Netherlands. Jacinta and I developed and ran a workshop called Find Your Passion together as a result of that phone call. She has now moved to Singapore, and guess what? We plan to run our workshop over there very soon.

GLOBAL OR LOCAL?

I believe that for a portable career to be sustainable and productive that you should develop both local and global networks.

Global Networks

A global network can be established in two ways:

- Connecting with people when you are overseas and adding them to your database.
- Connecting with people you have not met previously through the Internet or publications and adding them to your database.

Now that you have these global connections in your database – and just a name, email address and record of where they live is enough – you need to keep in touch with them virtually, in other words by email.

It is no good meeting someone once, taking their details and then never contacting them again. If you do this you will forget each other. You need to keep each other in your 'top of mind awareness'.

It is said that you do not buy from someone until you have 'touched' them six times. So, in order to 'touch' someone you could maybe, send them an email, a card, or give then a phone call now and again. I simply do not have the time to connect with the thousands in my database individually, so I find the easiest method of 'touching' is to send them my monthly email newsletter, *The Inspirer*. Even if they do not read the newsletter itself, they get to see my name pop up in their inbox, which is of great value. Of course, I do not add people to my database at random. I always ask them first. Here are the ways I add people to my list:

- I invite workshop and keynote attendees to give me their contact details if they want to receive notes afterwards and sign up to *The Inspirer* at the same time.
- I have a sign up box on my websites.
- I have a line in my email signature inviting people to sign up and receive a free gift.
- I make sure that my newsletter is of value, and fill it with inspiring words, tips, news and connections.
- I mention *The Inspirer* in all my publications.
- I suggest that all those who contact me for any reason might like to sign up to *The Inspirer* too.
- I have a website (three actually!)
- I give articles to websites and publications that are read by my target market. I do not charge for the piece if I am able to promote myself a little at the end of the article.

Of course, you do not need to issue a newsletter in order to stay in touch with your network. You may prefer a more personal approach, contacting people individually. I attempt to do both.

It is only by establishing a global network that you can have a global presence and a reputation all over the world. Then, when you are next on the move the chances are you will know someone when you arrive.

> 'I have always maintained all my contacts and networked like crazy. In fact the only reason I found a job in BP was because I met up with an old friend who mentioned a rumour that EDS [my former employer when I had lived in Houston] were putting together a proposal with BP in Stavanger. I made sure I was at the first meeting. In fact, as my old company, Britoil, were bought by BP, I had a hunch that I would know someone at that meeting. Not only did I know three people round that table, but one of them later showed me a photograph in his office of his team from 20 years earlier. I was in that photograph.'
> Alice, British in Norway, *www.career-in-your-suitcase.com*

Local Networks

As I said earlier, I need to be with people regularly and cannot work alone all the time. It is important to me that I have a reputation in the location in which I live and so I work hard to establish a local network too.

Being on the board of Connecting Women has really helped here. I need a local network in order to ensure that enough people know about my regular workshops and sign up to them and to have customers for my books.

Here are some of the ways that I achieve this:

- I attend meetings of local networks, both social and professional.
- I belong to a local business club.
- I write for local magazines and websites, ensuring my name and contact details appear at the end.
- I offer to speak at local club meetings and events, often for free.
- I take a table at newcomers' and other events where there will be lots of expats present.
- I place my books for sale in suitable outlets and leave my flyers and adverts in places frequented by expats.
- I offer everyone the chance to sign up to *The Inspirer*.
- I give prizes based on my business (like free books or places on my workshops) to raffles.
- I have business cards, a bookmark with my details on and a free tips book to give people so that they have something to take away that will remind them of me.
- Whenever I speak I suggest people sign up to receive the notes and *The Inspirer* as before and make a separate list for those who live locally. Then I can send then specific information pertaining to where I am living details of a play, perhaps, a visiting speaker or special event.

Growing a local database takes a little effort but is well worth it. If you want to grow your business where you are living you need to ensure people know about you and that they tell their friends, so you need to make it easy for them to do that.

> 'I put out a newsletter called Paris Gourmet every three months that also lists cooking classes and weekend gastronomy tips. I also network within the many English-speaking interest and study groups in Paris.'
> Sue Y, English in France, www.career-in-your-suitcase.com

Breakfast Clubs

If you prefer the idea of making networking part of your routine and timetabling it for a set day and time every week, then you may like to try joining a breakfast club. Business Networking International *www.bni.com* (BNI) has been around for more than 20 years and now has chapters in 40 countries worldwide. Members pay an annual fee and are then obliged to attend weekly meetings, which are designed to help you to gain referrals for yourself and find them for others too. New kid on the block, Business Referral Exchange *www.brxnet.co.uk* (BRX – earlier BRE), has been going for a decade and has chapters all over the UK. Like BNI, it works on similar principles to BNI. If this kind of networking appeals to you, then you would do well to visit both clubs as a guest first of all.

In their book, *Building a Business on Bacon and Eggs*, authors, Stephen Harvard Davis, Andy Lopata and Terence P O'Halloran, have grown their own businesses through the breakfast club and believe that it holds the key to business success, whether you attend or lead the meetings. Adhering to a set agenda, members all have their chance to share with the group, ask for advice and promote their businesses. Further, they all gain valuable experience in speaking in front of a group.

'Networking is about sharing our individual resources,' they write. This is what makes the business networking format so successful – groups of business skills are brought together for the benefit of all. Members are expected to give to the group and know it is their giving that will make it succeed.'

Men and Networks

Dr Copeland's research proved without doubt that local friendships are of vital importance on overseas assignment, particularly for the accompanying partner. Women are largely conditioned to accept that coffee mornings are part of life. Although women who don't have children comment that they feel uneasy in this environment, men feel even less comfortable. It can be difficult for a man to feel relaxed in such a group, particularly if he's the only male in sight. Many of these great organisations, such as Petroleum Wives, The British Society, American Women's Clubs and so on are non-profit and run by volunteers. Not only are these clubs the traditional bastion of females, but not all men will be happy to run bake sales or serve teas. Ask a man to run the local Boy Scouts or junior football club and he's likely to be much more at ease.

'Many of the problems men encounter are not dissimilar to those experienced by women,' says expatriate Australian Leonie Elphinstone, who conducted a survey into the male accompanying partner. 'What makes the difference is that men are brought up to be the breadwinners and when things go wrong they find they have further to fall.'

While men need to make new friends on location as much as women, they appear to feel happiest when their involvement is not too far removed from their 'comfort zone'. Often the local squash club or playing in a local band will be the best place for them.

Fortunately, the number of groups available to men is growing. Not only is there a network called STUDS (Spouses Trailing Under Duress Successfully), which is mentioned a few times in this book, but other groups are being established too.

Employees Need Networks Too

Networks are vital for business, which is why people like Donna Messer find themselves talking about how and why to network to large multinational corporations. You can have the best product in the world, but if you want to maximise sales potential you need to be seen by your clients. Relationship building is key to this. What is called 'The Old School Tie Network' is a frequent source of business for men, as is the golf course. Professional associations are also of value. A growing number of companies encourage networking among their own employees; Sony Semiconductors runs monthly networking lunches with a visiting speaker. With the retention of key staff a major objective for the employer, it makes sense to facilitate relationship building and true friendships between colleagues. This influences staff motivation and morale, and ultimately the bottom line.

CONNECTING

It is said that most people have a personal network of 250. As mentioned earlier, each of those contacts will, in turn, have his or her own contacts. Ask your contacts to connect you. See if they too have a newsletter and see if you can agree to promote each other. The best networkers, as I said earlier, like to give presents – and giving a connection or tip is a great gift. Whenever I'm told about a great seminar, new book, or exciting conference I email the information to any of my contacts I think may be interested. Sometimes this generates new and beneficial relationships between contacts of mine who were previously unknown to one another. The strength of your network depends on the connections made between your contacts.

Alternatively you may simply want to introduce two people to each other because you know they will benefit from knowing each other. It is always best for the introduction to be effected by the mutual friend, or connector. You will soon discover that some people are much better at connecting you with others. In fact, they offer to connect you before you have even asked.

It is worth nurturing these valuable people. In his book, *The Tipping Point*, author Malcolm Gladwell calls these people 'mavens'.

It is always best for the future of a relationship if you start off with being connected by a mutual friend. In this way, your initial conversation is not a *cold* call. Instead it begins in a much *warmer* place. If you can be introduced to someone at a party or network event that is wonderful, but many such connections are initiated online. When I make Internet connections for my friends I tend to send an email to both the people I want to introduce, and say something along the lines of 'Jane meet Sue, Sue meet Jane. Jane is an interior designer who has worked on some of the great stately homes of England. Sue works at Highview House and is looking to turn it into an hotel'.

When Donna Messer attends a networking event, she's less concerned with meeting new people herself than with finding out about the people who are there and connecting them. She'll introduce herself to person A, often by discussing the high and low points of the buffet, and then ask that person about himself or herself.

She will then bring person B into the conversation and then introduce B to A before leaving them together. Meanwhile, she moves on to do the same with persons C and D. Over time, she will have connected so many people, who are grateful to her, that when she next comes over to chat they will ask her for her card!

Donna tells a story of when she was talking to a group of high school students about networking. On entering the room she said she was going to be their fairy godmother and make their dreams come true. One boy told her that he wanted to fly. Fortunately, he was not interested in growing wings – he wanted a pilot's licence. When Donna asked his classmates if any of them could help, several put up their hands and made suggestions. Finally, one boy disclosed that his uncle was a farmer and had invited him to learn to fly a plane that summer and help him with spraying the crops. He had no personal desire to fly planes or spray crops. This second boy was in fact the first boy's best friend. They'd never discussed flying, so neither boy had any idea how much they could have helped each other out. If you want to know something, achieve something, or connect with someone it pays to ask. It's sad how many people fall short of their highest aspirations for want of simply asking.

KARMA

I mentioned karma a little earlier. Let's go into it in more detail now. The law is, simply, 'give and you will receive'. It can be difficult to keep the faith with karma, when you start to count up that you have given out 25 contacts to the people you have met, and only received three in return. But the whole point of karma is that you need not expect to receive directly from those to whom you have given, nor on the same day, nor in the same circumstances. Instead, imagine that all your gifts are invested in a huge universal bank, and that your returns will be given out at random.

I remember once that I became disillusioned with karma and decided to stop being so nice. I stopped connecting people and I stopped answering people's questions and being nice to them for free. Not only did I soon start to dislike myself, but I also noticed that the karmic pool had stopped paying me those dividends. As soon as I went back to giving, the rewards flooded back in.

PASSION, PRESENTS AND PERSISTENCE

Here we are again, back with my favourite word. Passion can make all the difference to networking. I even run a networking seminar called 'Passion, Presents and Persistence'. I expect you are beginning to understand how the name came about! I've talked about presents already, but it pays to repeat myself here, as I believe that presents are an aspect of networking that people easily forget about.

Passion

Remember that we want to stop being aware of how many business cards still linger untouched in our jacket pocket. We want to make friends. And there is no better way to make a friend than to talk about something not related to business.

When you meet someone new it's tempting to talk about what you do for a living first of all. But consider what a difference it would make if you asked, instead, what they like to do with their time off, who their heroes are or where they buy their shoes. When you are with your real friends you don't spend all the time talking about work, do you? Build new relationships by leaving work until last. Once you've found out more about someone as a human being rather than a service provider, you will find that the work talk comes naturally, and that business cards will be exchanged when the time is right.

Remember, that people like people who are like then and do business with people they like. Have you ever noticed how you tend to like people who like the same things as you? Maybe even those who share your passions? This is why people often end up doing business with those they meet on the golf course, at amateur dramatic clubs and so on.

Presents

You can invest in a new relationship by giving. Give connections, give answers, give help, give support, give tips, give a free gift, a memorable promotional item, the copy of a useful article, the name of a website, the list is endless. Listen to what people say and consider what gifts you could give them as they talk. If they are complaining that they need a language teacher, make them a recommendation. If they say they need clients, tell them about networking groups and so on. Find out what they are passionate about and offer presents based on that passion. So, if someone says they love climbing, tell them about a mountain climbing society, magazine or enthusiast they might like to meet. Presents, particularly when they relate to passion, can be the greatest gifts of all – and they cost nothing.

Persistence

If you attend a networking event or club only once or twice you are unlikely to make friends or business contacts, nor are you likely to sign up new clients. Friendship and trust are built up over time. Many people attend just one meeting at Connecting Women and then never return. No one should expect to get lucky the first time they go along. Over time, as friendships form and you are seen to be dependable, people will begin to trust you and want to do business with you. Remember that while the attendees may not directly be of use to your business, they may well have contacts who could be. Don't give up. Be persistent. Remember that people buy when they have 'touched' you six times, so try to go to six meetings. It is hard to create a relationship with someone when you only meet them once. The more you attend a meeting the more faces will become familiar and soon you will feel you belong. Sadly, you are unlikely to feel you belong at your very first meeting.

In the four years that I attended Women Connecting Women in England, I can claim to have bought magnetic insoles from Jill, who sells magnotherapy products, been colour-me-beautifulled by Carolyn, bought make-up from Jane, found Fiona to edit my books and Nadine to design my marketing materials and seen countless members on my writing courses. I have also been inspired by the stories of so many of the members that I have written articles about them and given them much-needed publicity. The list is much longer, but you get the idea.

How To Create A Network

Before I learned how profitable existing networks could be, I had inadvertently been creating my own wherever I had been living. Writing was my passion back then and I needed to be around other creative people in order to feel fulfilled. When I arrived in Dubai I decided to set up a Writers' Circle. Getting started only involved writing a simple notice, asking people who might be interested to give me a call, and pinning this up on a few noticeboards. We held monthly meetings in each other's homes, kept things informal, charged nothing, took it in turns to make a cake and made great friends. As often happens with networks, those friends too became my soulmates, and ultimately clients – because as soon as I decided to offer a short creative writing course they all signed up.

After creating a Writers' Circle in Dubai, I went on to create one in Muscat and then in Stavanger – but by the time we repatriated to England in 1997 I felt I had moved on. I was now more interested in business. So I set up the women's business group, which, as I mentioned earlier, now calls itself Women Connecting Women. In four years it went from strength to strength, and while I only ran it myself for the first year, I still could not bear to miss a single meeting.

Here in the Netherlands I have not started a group because The Hague is a pretty switched on place and writing circles and professional networks are already in existence. However, when I first arrived, and was feeling a little demotivated and lonely I formed a small group of six people and we called ourselves The Kick Arse Club. We met monthly to inspire and motivate each other and give each other feedback on our ideas. Once we were all up and running the group came to a natural close.

CREATING A NETWORK

Start off by determining the group's focus and target market. When I formed Women Connecting Women I decided that I wanted to create a place where women would feel supported, make friends, learn, develop their careers and their sense of self, and that would be affordable. I wanted to appeal to women who work for themselves, who want to return to work, or who are already employed.

I decided to hire a room in a local arts centre and placed a few small announcements in the local press and on the radio, stating that a new group was starting and that people were invited to attend the inaugural meeting. I organised a photographer from the local paper and press-ganged all my friends to come along and swell the numbers this first time. I promised I wouldn't expect them to attend again unless they wanted to. We had 50 at that first meeting, and from my friends I found three people who would talk for a few minutes about the value of networking at that meeting.

Next we held a discussion on how everyone wanted to proceed and chose to hold monthly meetings on a weekday evening. For the first year we had about 13 regulars, the next year this became about 20, and ultimately most meetings were attended by 30 or more. Each year we changed the committee, one person was responsible for sending out press releases regarding the next meeting, and another for writing a meeting report that we circulated to everyone on the mailing list.

Although the group has evolved over time, we later found a local sponsor who paid for the design of our annual programme, another who printed it, and another who gave us free use of the restaurant adjoining his public house for our meetings. We charged an annual fee for membership, which entitled members to attend all the meetings, advertise their business at the meetings, receive a printed newsletter – and obtain discounts for extraordinary events, for purchases at participating retail outlets and for a host of other benefits. It's worth mentioning that not all groups operate this way. Some groups charge a separate fee for individual meetings, some provide coffee, and others provide wine and even food. It's not uncommon for attendees to be obliged to pay for annual membership after attending two or three meetings.

After a short introduction by the current coordinator, or her representative, attendees were invited to share information about books, websites or businesses they would like to recommend and three people were given five minutes to talk about their business. Next we invited someone to speak to us who received a small gift and travel expenses. The meeting closed with half an hour or so of informal networking – or 'chatting', if you prefer.

Women Connecting Women was commended for its informal nature, and for the way it supported and inspired women to get on in the workplace.

Informational Interviews

It can give your job hunt a real boost if you decide to take networking up a level and into the realms of informational interviewing. This is when you organise an informal meeting with someone, not to ask him or her for a job, but to gather information about the company, your contact's specialist field or career.

When you know no one in your current circle of contacts who can help you directly, ask if someone you do know can refer you to someone who can. If you are still unable to identify a suitable person to interview, then you will have to use the local business directories and make a few preliminary telephone calls. A personal connection is always a godsend, however, so try to get in that way if at all possible.

An informational interview will usually begin with a telephone call – though these days it may be acceptable, and certainly less daunting, to begin with an email. Such a meeting will usually be brief and is designed so that you can find out more about the area of work that interests you. Most of the people you choose to talk to will feel fairly flattered that you considered them knowledgeable about their field, and will be happy to talk to you for half an hour or so.

Use this time to ask about opportunities in general, not necessarily with that specific company, and to see if you can obtain the names of some more people you could contact. You should always dress for such a meeting as if you were going to an interview, and take along your CV just in case. You never know, you may be offered a job there after all.

Eight tips for informational interviews

The eight parts of an informational interview or networking meeting usually follow each other in order, though there may naturally be some overlapping and blending.

1) **Introduction:** Although you have already spoken to your contact by phone, it's always appropriate to introduce yourself.
Example: 'Hello, I am Susan Holland. I have been in computer training for seven years. Jack Travers, Vice President of First Line Bank, suggested that I speak with you. Thank you for seeing me.'

2) **Reason for Meeting:** Why did you choose this person? What interests do you have in common?
Example: 'When I spoke with Jack Travers last week, he mentioned that you have been involved in computer training since its inception 15 years ago. He also said you have a particular interest in training hearing-impaired clients. I had been training hearing impaired people for about three years in London before moving.'

3) **Depressurising:** Set a comfortable tone for the conversation by dispelling the possibility that you have unrealistic expectations or a hidden agenda.
Example: 'Jack in no way said you knew of any openings, but did say you would be an excellent person to speak with about the growth and future of training in the Minneapolis area.'

4) **Agenda:** State specifically what you want to talk about. Share information you have that may be of interest to your contact.
Example: 'I gather, from talking with Jack, that we share a common interest in computer training trends over the next five years. I am interested in knowing how these trends are shaping up in this part of the country. During my last six months in Texas, I participated in a long-term planning group and we found ...'

5) **Personal Presentation:** At this juncture, or at another point in the meeting if it fits better, elaborate on who you are, your background, career objective, your competencies and evidence of these competencies. You should cover these items in three to five minutes.
Example: 'I grew up in Birmingham and became interested in computers while attending Warwick University. After getting my BA in Information Systems ...'

6) **Discuss Questions:** This should make up the bulk of the meeting, during which you ask the questions you came to cover, setting the tone and direction of the meeting. It is

essential to have these questions prepared in advance. They should be designed to encourage the other person to speak about his or her career. There are several questions 'Susan' can ask:

  a) Jack Travers mentioned that you have been in the field with a variety of organisations for more than 20 years. How did you get started in the training profession?
  b) What sort of changes have you seen in the field over the last ten years?
  c) What are the qualifications you think a successful trainer needs today?
  d) What are the greatest challenges you face in the field today?
  e) Where do you think we will see the growth in the profession?
  f) Are there any particular associations or professional organisations you would recommend to expand my network in this area?

7) Referrals: Be alert throughout the meeting for opportunities to discuss other people in the field and to elicit referrals. If these opportunities don't materialise, ask for referrals before concluding the session.
  Example: 'Our discussion has been very valuable. Do you know of any other people in the field who I should speak to?'

8) Conclusion: As the meeting ends, thank the person for her time and interest, refer in a sentence or two to a highlight of the talk, obtain the person's mailing address if you do not already have it and ask if you may stay in contact.
  Example: 'I would like to stay in touch and I will certainly let you know if I find out anything more about companies that specialise exclusively in training the hearing impaired.'

Fear of Networking

People who are naturally outgoing may feel more comfortable with networking than their more reserved counterparts, but this does not necessarily mean that they're better at it. Introverts usually have valuable gifts on which they can capitalise – the capacity to listen attentively, ask thoughtful questions and execute thorough follow-up.

And networking gets easier once you take the plunge. Like other mentally and emotionally challenging tasks, it resembles the lift-off of a rocket. It takes the most energy at the beginning – making your first couple of telephone calls and setting out on your first meeting or two. As you gather momentum, it gets easier. Before every contact remind yourself that networking is the standard way of doing business and finding employment in much of the Western world.

Still, however much you know you need to network, it can be a daunting prospect. Do you remember, I told you how long it took me to pluck up courage to attend that first WIN networking meeting in Stavanger? And I would say I'm fairly extrovert. Going up to complete strangers is difficult, but usually more so when you expect to be tongue-tied. It's normal to feel nervous talking to new people, even if they are just other mothers in the school playground. Going along to a coffee morning full of strangers or attending a new class can be daunting. Even so, I'll wager that most people feel less scared at the thought of a playground or a watercolour class than something that brands itself as a professional network. Believe me, it's all a question of perception. Believe me, too, that there is little difference between them.

You join a network because you want to meet people with whom you have something in common, or who can teach you something. You join a network because you feel you may have something to offer the members. There is no difference between joining the school parent teachers' association and a professional network. If anything, at a professional network you're likely to meet far more people with whom you have something in common.

I know that my greatest fear is not the walking into a room filled with strangers, but that I will walk into the room alone and no one will talk to me. Mind you, once I arrive it only takes one person to exchange a few words with me, or to tell me where to find the coffee, and I feel much better. Perhaps you could persuade a friend to accompany you on your first visit? This might allay your fears of loneliness. However, you should not fall into the trap of spending the whole evening with your friend, and missing out on meeting new people – otherwise you will feel just as daunted the next time you attend.

Make contact with the meeting coordinator beforehand and ask her to make herself known to you when you arrive. This will make you feel welcome, and will give you the purpose of finding a familiar name in the crowd. You could even ask your contact to introduce you to someone as soon as you arrive.

When you attend this kind of event, begin introducing yourself to some people you may know vaguely, reminding yourself that they were strangers once. If you stand around waiting for your nervousness to evaporate, you may only grow more scared still. Take it from untold numbers of the formerly networking phobic – the fear of networking is far worse than the networking itself. So the sooner you swing into action the sooner you'll feel better. By the time you leave you will float out of the doors on a cloud of exhilaration.

Attending a conference alone can be even more daunting, but remember that earlier in this chapter I told you about Donna Messer, and how she spends her time introducing other people. She also makes a point of arriving early, finding out where the cloakrooms are located and tasting the food. In this way, she can approach a stranger and engage in welcome small talk – rather than embarking on a lecture about what she does for a living.

Of course, you will find that all the people in the room will be more than happy to talk about themselves – so if you do find yourself faced with no one talk to, you can confidently approach a stranger and ask them why they came, what they do, or if it's their first time too.

When you read Gail MacIndoe's section on building rapport you will learn about mirroring body language. Next time you find yourself alone at a function, glance around the room and take a moment to mirror the stance of someone else who looks alone, and then catch her eye. It could result in her coming over to talk to you.

Will Kintish is a networking expert based in the UK who runs Kintish *www.kintish.co.uk*. I attended one of his workshops at a Professional Speakers Association conference *www.professionalspeakers.org*. He recommends that it is best to make a beeline for someone else who is standing alone, and to introduce yourself to them. However, if everyone appears to already be in conversation look out for those who are in 'open groups' and there is a gap in the circle of those who are chatting, leaving a space for you to slip into the conversation. Groups of two, where both parties look deep in conversation can be the hardest to penetrate.

Andy Lopata, runs Andy Lopata *www.lopata.co.uk* and speaks and writes about networking strategy. In his book, *'And Death Came Third'*, he recommends that the best way to make conversation with a stranger is to ask open questions, that is those that do not expect a simple 'yes' or 'no' answer and to listen more than you talk.

'The key to good conversation is listening effectively and if you are listening effectively, you ask the right questions,' he writes. 'As questions that show that you are listening, questions based on what the other person has just said and questions that are likely to draw out the conversation. Ask them to tell you more.

Believe it or not, sometimes the simplest methods can be the most effective. Only yesterday, I found myself at a social gathering where the only people I knew were the host and hostess. As I stood there scanning the faces of everyone else in the room I saw how they all seemed deep in conversation with people they clearly knew well. As I pondered how to break into a conversation someone thrust his right hand at me.

'I'm Dave,' he said.

'I'm Jo,' I replied.

'Where do you live?' he asked.

I told him. 'And you?' I asked.

'Oh I flew over from England,' he said.

114

The conversation began as hardly the most interesting I have had, but we had begun to talk. Neither of us felt awkward or threatened. Over the course of the next few minutes we discovered that we both shared a passion for theatre, that Dave was a communications expert and I moved on to offer to connect him with a friend of mine, who was also in his field and looking to combine theatre and corporate communication. We soon swapped cards.

As we talked I made a mental note to write about this today. Not all opening lines need a complicated script as you can see.

ELEVATOR PITCHES

Inevitably, during my conversation with Dave, he asked me what I did for a living?

'I'm a writer,' I said. 'And I teach others to do it too.'

This way of describing what you do in such a way that the other person is likely to want to know more, is called the *elevator pitch*. The term came about to describe how you might tell someone what you do when asked in an elevator and you only have the time it takes to reach the next floor to answer in a compelling way.

While the pitch I used yesterday neither described every aspect of my work, it did not mention that I specialise in portable careers for example, it did pique Dave's interest enough for him to say:

'Oh! What sort of writing?'

'Portable careers, mainly. I help expat accompanying partners to find a career in their suitcase.'

'A career in a suitcase? What's that?'

... and so on. You see. The best kind of elevator pitches are so compelling that the stranger in the lift would prefer to miss his floor and stay talking to you than to leave you not knowing.

It is important that your own elevator pitch is short. But it is also important that you are clear about your target market. The reason for this is that you want the person who is asking you to identify right away whether he may need your services, or just as importantly, he may know someone else who does. If possible create a pitch that clearly shows the benefits of your business too.

My own elevator pitch lacks a little imagination, I admit, but it has been designed to ensure that the person to whom I am talking keeps wanting to know more. When you are talking to a group, giving a workshop or presentation for example, there will be no opportunity to take questions. In this case you may need to work a little harder at your pitch, in order to make it memorable. When I am in this situation I tend to tailor what I say to the audience. So, if I were speaking to expatriates I may say something like:

'I inspire and empower accompanying expat partners, like you, to create a portable career based on your passions.'

Yet, if I were speaking at an HR conference I may say:

'I write and speak about how to solve the dual career challenge without it costing a fortune.'

The ultimate goal is that upon hearing your pitch the person asks, "How do you do that?" This is your invitation to explain what you do in greater detail. However, when you are speaking in front of a group and people don't have a chance to ask how you do it, it is important that you describe what you do in a memorable way that means they do not feel they need to ask you for more information. Here are some examples:

Personal Chef: "I create delicious, healthy meals for busy executives that have no time to cook."

Computer Technician: "I rescue stressed out business owners when their computers crash."

Caterer: "We take on the worry and preparation of entertaining for busy professionals" OR "We help busy professionals have effortless dinner parties."

Yoga Instructor: "I help women feel good inside their bodies."

Change Consultant: "I help ICT companies unite and move forward quickly after a merger" OR "I help ICT companies feel less pain after a merger."

Match Making Service: "We help young professionals find the perfect life mate they have been searching for."

Professional Organizer: "You know how sometimes mothers have so much going on that they can't find anything? Well that's what I do, I help busy moms get rid of clutter and find what they need fast."

Stephanie Ward, *www.fireflycoaching.com*

It can take some time to create your own set of elevator pitches that will work well for you in every situation. Practise on your friends and get their feedback then try them out and see which work best when you are with complete strangers. And just as you may keep changing your location or what you do, remember you may need to change your elevator pitch too.

FOLLOW UP

If you find yourself networking consciously or unconsciously as much as I do, it can be hard to keep track of all the new contacts you make. You can never hope to remember everyone you meet, or to keep in touch with them all. But you can make a commitment to keep in touch with about three people you meet at an event. I usually write a few notes about each person on the back of their business card so that it will jog my memory later. Though this can be messy, particularly, if they have text on the back of the card. Maintaining a database or using a card scanner can be a good way of keeping information about key people in one place. I also make a point of emailing them all soon after the event to say how much I enjoyed meeting them. Once, I have had a few emails back and forth with someone I am more likely to really remember them and they me.

Once a year it's a good idea to remember all the people you have met over the last 12 months, with either a Christmas card or a short email. Try to keep yourself in the minds of those contacts, and at the same time to remind yourself of them too.

If you've had an informational interview, write the person a thank you note within 24 hours. In this instance, a letter expresses greater appreciation than an email.

I try to categorise the people I meet into, say, media, human resources, entrepreneurs and writers. I put their email addresses into separate groups in my email program and then when I get useful snippets of information that I think could be of interest to a group I send out an email to them all. As I mentioned earlier, I also have a database of local people for this same reason. This allows me to keep on giving them 'presents' – but it also keeps me in their minds.

Buy yourself a filing cabinet, a card index, card scanner or a business card holder. Equip yourself so that you can keep track of all these contacts, and try to keep contact details updated as people often move or change email addresses. Every now and again, flick back through these records to remind yourself just how many people you have met over the years. You never know when they could come in useful.

BUILDING RAPPORT

In business, as in social life, most decisions are made based on rapport rather than technical abilities. This is because we are more likely to buy from, agree with and support someone we can relate to than someone we can't. People like people who are like them, we have said.

Rapport is about being on the same wavelength and appreciating each other's feelings. It is the ability to enter someone's world and make him or her feel you understand him or her, and that you have a common bond. It's a means of creating trust and understanding and being able to see each other's point of view (though not necessarily agree to it). Building rapport is fundamental to being able to communicate effectively with others, to negotiate, teach or introduce change.

Neuro Linguistic Programming (NLP) demonstrates that skilled communicators and influencers are able to build rapport. The process of building rapport can be broken down into its various components.

People in rapport will often unconsciously 'match' or 'mirror' each other; they adopt similar body gestures, posture, and rhythm in speech and movement. NLP found that when we adopt the same physical posture as someone else we experience similar feelings and start to think alike. One of the core beliefs is that 'Mind and body are part of the same system. What occurs in one part will affect all the other parts,' as Sue Knight writes in her book *NLP at Work*.

NLP recommends starting with adopting the other person's physical posture, voice tone and words in order to build initial rapport. Research has shown that only seven per cent of our communication is through words, while 38 per cent comes from voice tonality and the remaining 55 per cent is physiology, or body language. That means that the words you use make up just 17 per cent.

The steps to getting into rapport are as follows:

Physiology

Adopt their posture, gestures, facial expressions and blinking patterns. Match their breathing too if you can. You can 'cross mirror', which is to do the same movement as they are doing but with another part of the body. So while one person is tapping his foot, you can tap your fingers but using the same rhythm.

Voice

Match their voice as soon as possible by mirroring the pitch, tempo and range of their voice.

Words

Listen to the key words used frequently by the other person and then use them yourself. Try to find common experiences and associations. Use the same kind of predicates that they use too. These are their preferred verbs. As we stated earlier in this chapter a visual person will say things like 'I see' a lot, while an auditory person will say 'I hear' and a kinesthetic person will say 'I feel'. Also match the size of their sentences, notice whether they are long or short.

When you are in rapport

When you have achieved rapport you should feel warm inside and both your faces will heighten in colour. Sometimes you'll find yourself suggesting that you have met before or have a third party in common. If you shift your position, the other person will unconsciously start to mirror you.

As soon as you've achieved rapport, you can 'pace and lead' them, changing position and physiology to watch them follow your lead. This is often used in situations of conflict, when someone is angry for example. In this case you would match them and then when you have established rapport you can calm them down by pacing and taking the lead.

We build rapport at the unconscious level by matching the other person's physiology. Words work at the conscious level, while physiology works on our unconscious. The brain thinks, 'OK, this person is like me, so he must be all right,' and this creates a bond. You can do this with someone across a room without conversation and they will either start talking to you or smile or feel drawn to you.

The skill is to build and maintain this rapport beyond the level of body language. To do this you need to really listen with your whole body, be curious about them and give your total attention. Don't sweep away their concerns or try and impose your solutions. Rather acknowledge them and find out how to meet their needs. You are not being a hypocrite or giving up your identity when you match someone. You are in effect being flexible and honouring them. When you are matching them you are getting the benefit of their feelings, experiences and thoughts.

NLP believes that we have responsibility for our communication – and if you try to persuade someone to do something and they don't, the fault is in your communication. The real key to establishing rapport is flexibility and not assuming that everyone has the same map of the world as we do. We need to adapt our words and behaviour until we can match their model of the world.

Learn To Present

The list of tasks required if you are to create and maintain a thriving business seems endless. And no one can deny the importance of marketing and networking. But public speaking and giving presentations, workshops and seminars can give your business the edge. To my mind it is the most productive form of networking I can do. How else can you attend a meeting of some kind and ensure that every single person in that room goes home knowing who you are?

I learned to present in an unthreatening and wholly supportive environment back in 1996. Since then I've never looked back.

Back in Stavanger, Norway, I belonged to the women's networking group, WIN, as you know. Today I admit that I owe much of what I have become to WIN. Not only were there monthly meetings with a motivational speaker, but there were a number of sub-groups for WIN members to join. There was no fee attached and members met once a month, informally in each other's homes. I joined the group that called itself 'Presenters'.

HOW I LEARNED TO PRESENT

There were usually only four or five of us at 'Presenters.' At each session we would write down a couple of topics on scraps of paper and put them into a hat. As the hat went round we each picked a random topic. We allowed ourselves 15 minutes to prepare our speech and then five minutes to give it. The topics could be as crazy as 'lost socks,' as fascinating as 'dreams' or as unusual as 'ferret farming'. One of the other members was chosen to be the heckler, another to be over-enthusiastic, another to be bored, and this audience would then listen to each talk and give constructive criticism later. The results were dramatic, humorous and immensely useful. Six months later I found myself being the guest speaker at a WIN meeting, talking about my pet subject: portable careers. Three months later I was paid to develop and present a three-hour workshop on the same subject to a group of about 20 expatriate women. A year later I presented the same workshop to more than 100 people at the 1998 *Women on the Move* Conference in Paris. Since then I have offered keynotes, seminars or workshops to networking groups, companies and conference delegates all over the world.

THE POWER OF PUBLIC SPEAKING

It was after the Paris presentation that I came to realise the power of public speaking. My workshop had lasted over two hours, but the queue of people who wanted to buy my book, ask additional questions or exchange business cards, lasted a further hour. There were several hundred delegates at the conference and it would have been impossible for me to meet them all at the various break times. Now, after a giving a presentation, I could be identified by more than a third of the attendees. Thanks to the copious handouts I had passed around they also knew my contact details.

When I returned home I made the effort to contact every single person who had given me his or her card. I just wrote a short note to thank them for attending and to suggest that they could contact me again at any time if they had further questions.

Today, as I said earlier, I have learned to ask for those who would like to receive my email newsletter, *The Inspirer*, and extra notes for my presentation, to sign up there and then at the conference. In this way I add to my contact base every single time I speak in public.

> 'I give talks but usually on a voluntary basis. I earn a good fee though when I speak to the homeopathy schools. Sometimes I teach foot zone therapy to small groups. I believe that you should always be prepared to do some things for nothing. When I give a free talk on, say, health, homeopathy or foot zone I always end up acquiring a handful of new patients from the audience.'
> **Angelika, German in Norway, *www.career-in-your-suitcase.com***

CONFERENCE SPEAKING

But before you race off to learn presentation skills and begin to count the money you will make from conferences, you need to know that conference speakers are not always paid a fee. Often though, the conference fees and a hotel room for a night or two may be underwritten by the organisers. Those speakers with a service or product to sell are often happy to fund their own travel expenses for the opportunity of showing their face and addressing a captive audience. Of course, there are many ways to be paid, and handsomely too, for speaking to audiences, but this chapter is about marketing your business and so we will concentrate on the 'pro bono' variety.

Many of the conference delegates will have arrived alone. Whilst talking to total strangers can be daunting, striking up a conversation with the speaker you have just heard is much easier. Similarly, speakers find it as easy to start chatting to someone they have seen in their session as to a fellow presenter. Networking can be much simpler and more productive at a conference. After half an hour or so on stage, you are more likely to be remembered than if you had merely chatted to someone for a few minutes during a coffee break.

Since that first presentation at WIN I have now spoken to organisations and corporations all over the world. A month doesn't pass when I don't speak to my target market. More often than not I am paid to speak too. But one thing that does not change is the networking potential of these engagements. When *Woman Abroad* magazine was first launched on the international market we decided to market it by giving away up to 20,000 copies of each issue. In order to do this many publishers would have bought numerous databases of potential customers. We bought none. Thanks to the exponential effect of contacting all the people I've met along the way and asking them to tap into their own networks, we have accessed hundreds of thousands worldwide.

You may not have a 'Presenters' group near you to kick start your own speaking career, but you can always start one. Go on a short course, buy a book or practise on your own in front of your video camera. The Toastmasters organisation offers training in a non-threatening environment in many countries worldwide. This is a great place to start. Go to *www.toastmasters.org* to find them. If you already have some experience and want to hone your skills and learn from some of the most generous and highly paid speakers in the business look no further than the US-based National Speakers Association (NSA) at *www.nsaspeaker.org* and UK-based Professional Speakers Association (PSA) at *www.professionalspeakers.org* and their sister groups. Membership will provide you with regular meetings, conferences, a newsletter and audio CDs. Never underestimate the power of public presentation.

MAKE IT MEMORABLE

In February 2007, I heard a presentation by Nick Oulton, who runs a presentation company called M62 (*www.m62.net*). He told us that people attend a presentation for one of three reasons:

- To buy something
- To learn something
- To modify their behaviour

It is worth knowing that those people who attend will only remember about five things about your presentation, so it is important that they remember the five things you want them to recall. Not the fact that you wore a low cut top, that you kept scratching your nose or could not get the beamer to work.

'If you give people information without pausing and giving them time to process it you will have a very low retention rate,' says Oulton.

Further, the memory is such that you will only remember 50% of what you heard the next day, and then 50% of that the day after that. And so on. The more they can remember the next day the better.

A stream of slides covered in text and bullet points is not easy to remember. However, if you combine pictures with text you will help the audience to have a much better chance of remembering than if you have text alone.

SEVEN STEPS FOR PREPARING POWERFUL PRESENTATIONS

After several years of presenting I decided to call in an expert to assess what I'd been doing and to see if she could improve on my work. Christine Searancke runs a consultancy called Be Clear and specialises in writing presentations for people; she also runs an affordable assessment service and has written a valuable book called *How to Write Winning Presentations*. You can find out more at *www.beclear.co.uk*.

Christine believes that, as a presenter, it is her job to 'paint pictures with words' and that it's well told anecdotes that most stay in the mind of the audience.

Step one
State the objectives and write them down:
- At the end of the presentation I want the audience to think ...
- I want them to do ... I want them to say ... I want them to feel ...

Step two
Answer the basic questions:
- Why am I making the presentation?
- What am I going to say?
- What does the audience want to hear?
- Who is the audience?
- Where will I be talking?

Step three
Use a clear and logical structure:
- Break your material into manageable chunks like the chapters in a book. Share the structure with your audience. It will help them too.

Step four
Tell the audience what they want to hear, nothing more:
- They don't want to hear everything that you know, or have done. They want to hear the parts that are relevant to them.

Step five
Think of your presentation as telling a story:
- There should be a beginning, middle and an end. Each part should flow logically from the previous part and it should be told in your natural style of speech.

Step six
Spend time on the opening words of the presentation:
- You need to grab the audience's attention while you have the chance; once you've lost their attention it is very hard to get it back.

Step seven
Rehearse with someone who doesn't know the subject:
- They can tell you whether or not it is clear, whether you've left something out and more importantly whether it will meet the objectives from step one.

6 getting a "proper job"

This chapter outlines the universal fundamentals of the job-hunting process and will help anyone looking for employment – whether full time, part time, freelance or on a contract basis with an established company. Much of this chapter, including the new extended section on Cyber Chutzpah has been compiled and researched by Galen Tinder, REA Manager.

'Work is much more fun than fun.'
Noel Coward

In this chapter:

- Job hunting
- Finding out about vacancies
- Cyber chutzpah – Your Internet Search Strategy
- The curriculum vitae
- The cover letter
- The professional portfolio
- The interview
- And don't forget to network
- Your search strategy

Job-Hunting

If you have bought this book, the chances are that you're interested in working. Not everyone reading this will want to work for himself or herself or run their own business. If you are among those who would prefer to find a 'normal' job, that pays you a salary, then this chapter is for you. If you'd rather work freelance then there will still be occasions when you need to look for contract work, submit your CV and write cover letters.

I've been freelance for more than 20 years now and I tend to think that, while I never apply for a single 'real' full-time, salaried position, instead I have to apply for many more and repeatedly. When you are freelance you are constantly job-hunting. Whether I am applying for a short-term contract, a one-day training job, part-time work over an extended period, or persuading a publisher to buy my work, many of the same principles apply. I need to make a proposal face to face and / or on paper. I need to be interviewed too, though sometimes this is by email or telephone rather than in person. Additionally, because I also offer a consultancy service, opportunities arise weekly when I find myself in a position to promote myself. Running my own business means that it is vital that I am always positive about my work, that my passion for what I do is palpable and that my enthusiasm persuades others to hire me. If you, however, want a 'real' job, whether it be full-time, part-time or peripatetic, you too need to acquire similar skills. The process, however, is more clear-cut, as you will discover below.

The fundamentals of job hunting haven't changed dramatically in the last 50 years. Job seekers still need a curriculum vitae (CV), also known as a resumé or biodata, to summarise their experience, skills, responsibilities and qualifications. Employers expect a cover letter to accompany and introduce the CV.

Few applicants will be offered a job until they've had at least one face-to-face interview with the employer. It's worth noting, however, that many people get jobs without ever speaking to a recruiter, and this will certainly be true of those reading this book. Getting through job-hunting protocol can be a daunting prospect - yet it's unavoidable.

The society in which we now look for careers and jobs is more competitive, complicated and confusing than a generation ago. Much of this has to do with the accelerated pace of change – and, of course, the impact of the Internet on our economy and society. Fortunately there's a growing range of books and websites that aim to ease the job hunting process and many recruitment agencies, both on and offline, offer valuable reading material and resources. Through libraries and the Internet we can find out about CVs, interview techniques and the companies in which we are interested.

TEMPORARY WORK ONLINE

Not all job hunters are interested in full time employment, and those looking for temporary work should consider subscribing to sites offering contract opportunities such as the well established US-based Contract Employment Weekly: *www.ceweekly.com*. Look too for *www.smarterwork.com*, *www.elance.com* and other similar sites. Like conventional job sites there are too many to list here. Look out for email bulletins such as 'Jobs for Journalists' from the European Journalist Network at *www.ejc.nl* and at *www.freelance.com* you can find information on projects around the globe.

VOLUNTARY WORK ONLINE

If you're having problems with your work permit, or want to do something different, have a look at *www.workingabroad.com* – an information portal for environmental and humanitarian voluntary projects.

CAREER COUNSELLORS

If you're fortunate enough to have a career counsellor or coach, then he or she may be able to suggest other ways in which you can find out about employment opportunities. Your counsellor may suggest particular vacancies, agencies, publications or networking groups that she personally knows about. Some career counsellors provide a service that includes finding you a job, or making enquiries directly with human resource departments – though this is not standard practice in the US.

It's worth managing your expectations here. Few companies can find jobs for you and even recruitment agencies are in the business of finding the people for the jobs rather than the jobs for the people. There is also a huge difference between the ways career counsellors work between countries. From the US perspective, there is considerable confusion about what recruiters, career counsellors and consultants, and so-called placement agencies do (see *Chapter Ten* for more information about the various types of consultant).

FINDING OUT ABOUT VACANCIES

There are many ways to find out what career opportunities may lie in wait for you. Consulting newspaper advertisements is one. Even though most people get their jobs through networking, there is a value in finding out which skills seem to be in demand, and how often certain companies appear to be hiring.

NEWSPAPERS AND MAGAZINES

Take a look at the recruitment sections (these are called classified ad sections in America) of both national and local publications. Remember, many publications are also available online and that the vacancies appear here too.

NEWSLETTERS

Often the free newsletters produced by local networks and clubs are a source of vacancies. Some may be voluntary positions, but don't disregard unpaid work as it can provide valuable experience.

JOB CLUBS

Keep an eye out for organisations that seek out locally available vacancies and then compile an email or online list of vacancies for you to view. Some of the Outpost networks available to Shell spouses create such a list and distribute it by email. Often you will find that a local organisation or website specialising in newcomer services will compile a similar list. At worst they should be able to inform where you can find them. Where there is no compilation of vacancies perhaps you will find a real-time job club where you can meet other job seekers. This can be a good source of information about vacancies.

NOTICEBOARDS

Sometimes you'll find temporary or volunteer vacancies advertised on noticeboards at libraries, in supermarkets or at information centres.

EMPLOYMENT AGENCIES

Companies pay employment agencies to fill vacancies by sending them qualified candidates. In rare cases the job seeker may be charged for this. Most employment agencies are honest and reliable – but you must bear in mind that their client is the company, not you. Be sure not to sign any contracts without taking at least 24 hours to examine and evaluate them. Read every word of small print.

Employment agencies will usually submit the names of as many qualified persons as possible for each available position. So if you use an agency, you may find yourself going through two screenings, one by the agency and the second by the company itself.

In the last decade, an increasing number of agencies have specialised in particular industries. They are also placing people in positions that require skill and training. You will enhance your chances of success with an agency if you use one specialising in the field in which you're looking for employment.

Don't overlook agencies that specialise in temporary or contract placements, even if your goal is full time employment. It's not unusual for temporary placements to be extended or to develop into permanent positions.

Even when your placements remain temporary, they offer you a good opportunity to expand your skills and experience, get acquainted with one or more companies in the new area, and add to your contact network. A full time temporary position will curtail your ability to look for a permanent job.

Before accepting an assignment, you may want to check on how flexible the company can be in allowing you time for interviews elsewhere.

EXECUTIVE MANAGEMENT FIRMS

This type of organisation offers a blend of recruiting and career management services for a price that you, in this case, will pay.

Some of these firms regularly advertise their services in the 'help wanted' sections of the country's larger newspapers. Their goal is to form long term relationships with established and upwardly mobile managers and executives who either command, or can be expected soon to command, salaries approaching and exceeding $100,000. These firms promote their ongoing relationships with major companies and may appear to function like recruiters. Beware of firms that promote their special access to the decision makers in companies, but are vague about just whose door they will usher you through. You can end up paying $10,000 for little more than basic career counselling in lush, dark wood-panelled offices. It's interesting to note that, in the US, many of these companies seem to be continually in court defending themselves against lawsuits for misrepresenting themselves.

JOB FAIRS

In the last decade, job fairs have gained legitimacy and shed their old image as the last hope of the desperate. Most job fairs combine group and employer presentations with individual booths. If you go to a job fair, plan to take in both - not just for the exposure to potential employers, but also to gather information about companies that are hiring.

When you attend a fair, be prepared with copies of your curriculum vitae, your business cards (even if they only contain your contact details) and a notepad and pen. Dress as if you were attending an interview, though it is unlikely you will be invited for interview at the event. Use the event as a networking and information gathering opportunity. Be prepared to tell people about yourself and prepare in advance a one-minute self-introduction or 'elevator speech'.

Not all professionals will profit from attending job fairs. If you're a lion tamer or a cruise ship director, there are better ways to spend your job-hunting hours. Job fairs that feature your industry however, should be part of your comprehensive campaign. When you attend them, set out to make the most of the opportunity to meet many potential employers and sources of valuable information in a short period of time.

Cyber Chutzpah -
The Internet Job Search

The Electronic Era and the Internet particularly have produced marked changes in how most of us live and work. To cite just one example, many adults in the Western world no longer rely solely on their doctor for medical guidance. Instead, they research their condition or malady on the Web and make the final decision on their preferred treatment. Is this an improvement on the kind of medicine practiced in the middle of the 20th century? Most would say it is.

Similarly, most people who have sought to change their career direction or find a job in the last several years will say that the Internet has transformed these endeavours from what they were just 10 to 15 years ago. It has increased almost beyond calculation the amount of information, advice and opportunity that lie at the fingertips of the contemporary career or job seeker.

The purpose of this section is to describe the main features of the Internet job search and how these can be used by the average person and to recommend key websites that can further introduce you to the breadth and depth of the Internet's resources. Even with a relatively well-defined topic such as ours, the Internet's resources are vast and potentially overwhelming. Successful use of the Internet requires knowing what one is looking for and developing a plan of action to find.

The Internet is relevant to all aspects of the job search from career choice to resumé distribution and salary negotiation. In its nascent, growing years the Web initially enabled us to do faster what we had already been doing. Very quickly it aided us in doing a lot more than before by giving us access to information that was not available in the pre-electronic era. Now, in the last several years, Internet technology has entered the phase of interactivity (sometimes dubbed Web II) and is restructuring the ways in which human beings interact. Today, this restructuring is the Internet's growing edge and is affecting how people look for work.

At the same time, the building blocks of the average job search are similar to what they were 50 years ago. We still need resumés and cover letters, still need to prepare for interviewing and will still engage in face-to-face networking as the most effective job search tool. Post-interview thank you notes must still be sent, though their cyber journey is almost instantaneous. That old saying is at least partially applicable here- the more things change the more they remain the same.

There are many thousands of career sites on the Web. A recent estimate put at 40,000 the number of job sites alone, and by the time you have finished this sentence that figure will be 40,005. These numbers underscore your need to tame this munificent generosity with a plan that will structure your encounter with the Web in accordance with your purposes. This section is designed to help you do this.

If you are not familiar with or adept in using the Internet, you will be glad to know that there are numerous introductions to the basics available on the very beast you hope to tame. Three excellent ones are cited by Richard Bowles on his website- Primer to Using the Internet *www.cameratim.com/computing/Internet-primer*, Your Internet Guides, *www.thirteen.org/edonline/primer*, and Basic Web Lessons *www.aarp.org/learntech/computers*.

Most of the sites we have noted in this section plus thousands of others feature articles of advice on career and job search topics. You may already have identified several sites that appeal to you. But if you are just venturing into this ocean of information, one of the best places to begin is *www.quintessential.com*. Quint has many excellent articles, a number penned by its two webmasters, Katherine and Randall Hanson. And Quint will also link you with other reliable sources of information.

Another good source to consult is *www.careerjournal.com*, a production of the Wall Street Journal. CareerJournal stays on top of the latest trends. It also carries a reserve of archived articles, so it pays to check an article's publication date, particularly if it is about the Internet. When it comes to the online job search in all its permeations Peter Weddle is one of the premier experts. Go to *www.weddles.com* for expert advice on his Tips page and his archived newsletters.

The Internet and this technological age have caused enormous changes in the way we live, work and search for employment opportunities. It has also altered the types of positions available, while creating new markets, skills and techniques to learn and develop.

By using computer technology you can add a valuable dimension to your job search. Many recruitment sites allow you to search for vacancies according to keywords, submit a CV online and start the process wholly by email. This is not a substitute for the conventional methods of job hunting, but it is a new and powerful way you can add to these techniques to improve the success of your search.

The Internet is the world's largest network and it's worth noting that 80 per cent of job openings are never advertised in newspapers. The Internet is available 24 hours a day anywhere in the world with a reliable telephone connection. Importantly, your Internet job search demonstrates your skill and familiarity with this new technology, which is vitally important these days.

To work smart online, you must clarify exactly what kind of information you're looking for – though often this clarification comes from exploring what the Internet makes available. Once you have identified your needs you can evaluate a site's strengths and weaknesses accordingly. Your goal will then be to find as many sites as possible that fit your profile.

Especially if you are new to the Internet, you'll also want to spend some time just 'playing around' – trying a number of different sites and following a series of links to see where they take you. The Internet has thousands of job, career and employment sites, and new ones are popping up every week.

JOB LISTINGS

The Internet is host to hundreds of sites that function like a huge electronic newspaper classified section. Job openings can also be found at a number of career sites on the Internet. At the better sites you will find the job title, company name, a description of the qualifications required and salary information. The site's listing can be accessed through search criteria such as geography, company name, industry, position, discipline and specialist area.

In checking into various sites, bear in mind how long the site has been in business, how many employers use the site for recruitment and how many individuals have been using the database as a resource. See which organisations endorse the site too. It's worth noting that the best sites are not necessarily the oldest or the biggest. The so-called 'niche' sites specialising in one industry, for example, are indeed small but are more effective for people in that particular industry than the huge sites like *www.monster.com*. And organisational endorsements, like the blurbs on the dust jacket of the latest techno-thriller, mean little.

'I found work on www.craigslist.org. The only recommendation I have is to follow up with a letter in the mail. If you are close to the company, hand deliver a resumé. Online companies receive hundreds of resumes. Stand out with a well-printed resumé.'
Ursula, South African in America, *www.marketingmentorexpert.com*
and *www.expatwomen.com*

ONLINE CV DATABASES

Just as you can search the Internet to find out what jobs are available, hiring employers can search the Internet themselves to find potential candidates to fill their available positions too. Online databases offer you, the job seeker, a 'billboard' on which to advertise your credentials and your interest in finding a new position. Hundreds of CV databases are online today, each offering different services. You'll need to understand the various features and then decide which arrangement will best suit your needs. A few sites charge a fee to show your CV, but most are free for the job seeker.

'I found my current job on CareerBuilder and signed up for the company job alerts directly. These email notifications let me know of openings in the company. Ultimately I got my 'in' because the recruiter was Irish.'
Lizzy, British in America, *www.expatwomen.com*

PARTNERJOB

If your company is a member of Partnerjob, you will be able to post your CV on a member site for viewing by all other member companies. In addition you will be able to search for vacancies. This site is designed to offer just the kind of short-term contract work that is perfect for mobile spouses. Find it at *www.partnerjob.com*.

COMPANY WEBSITES

The Internet is such a boon these days that it is very likely that you will be able to find a local business directory, research every featured business in detail at their own website, look to see if they have any vacancies and apply online too. Of course, this means that you have no excuse to go into an interview unprepared. With so much available information out there you can be very prepared.

HOW TO BEST USE THE INTERNET

The Internet is perhaps best known for its job postings, but it actually has five distinct uses. These are, in the order we will discuss them:

- Research
- Looking for open positions
- Resumé posting
- Networking
- Getting expert advice

Given the enormity of what is available, it might seem appropriate to shower the reader with dozens upon dozens of sites to explore. In practice, however, this can be more confusing than enlightening. Instead, it is better to work with a relatively small number of first-rate sites that can direct and point you toward other sites of potential interest.

Here is a short list of several of the best career and job search sites on the Web. They are divided into three groups: First, come those designed for a US based audience but applicable, in a number of features, to other parts of the world. Second, we list several premier international sites. Lastly, we take note of several creative and informative career blogs. As we move forward, we will refer to a number of these Internet addresses. Nearly all of them are multi-function sites that offer research, advice, job postings and networking advice and opportunities. Most of them can also direct you toward more specialised sites.

US-BASED SITES

www.weddles.com
www.quintcareers.com
www.eresumés.com
www.rileyguide.com
www.acinet.org/acinet
www.jobstar.org
www.jobhuntersbible.com
www.careers.org
www.careeronestop.org
www.job-hunt.org
www.asktheheadhunter.com
www.executive-resumés.com
www.jobstar.org/index.php

INTERNATIONAL SITES

www.overseasjobs.com
http://overseasdigest.com
www.utexas.edu
www.escapeartist.com/jobs/overseas
www.international-job-search.com
http://careers.asp.radford.edu
www.goabroad.com
www.transitionsabroad.com
http://intraspec.ca/jobsearch.php
www.globalcareers.com

BLOGS

www.jibberjobber.com/blog
www.workforce50.com
http://occupationaladventure.com
http://blog.penelopetrunk.com
http://alisondoyle.typepad.com
www.careerbuilder.typepad.com
www.blueskyresumés.com
http://blog.careergoddess.com
http://dbcs.typepad.com
http://getthatjob.blogspot.com
http://workmash.wordpress.com
www.time-blog.com

RESEARCH

There are thousands of websites where you can do career and job related research, so at the outset it is valuable to know what information you are seeking. Many people enter cyberspace unsure of what sort of work to look for. These people may be soon-to-be freshly minted graduates, people thinking about a career shift, or mature men and women who have not worked before. If you are unsure what you want to do next, you will find abundant help on the Internet.

One of the most complete and reliable sources of information about careers is the United States government, specifically the US Department of Labor and Bureau of Labor Statistics *www.bls.gov*. Under the aegis of the Occupational Outlook Handbook, also available in print in a new edition every two years, this site breaks the world of careers down into industries and occupations. Its discussion of each occupation usually features nine headings.

- Nature of the Work
- Training, Other Qualifications, and Advancement
- Employment
- Job Outlook
- Projections Data
- Earnings
- OES Data
- Related Occupations
- Sources of Additional Information

On a neighbouring site you can find even more detailed information about the economic outlook that will be affecting any specific kind of work in the years to come. While this information is obviously US-centric, the vocational and professional information has broad applicability to many other parts of the world.

If you are unsure what kind of work you next want, you may find that taking one or more career assessments (sometimes called tests or inventories) helpful. The Internet offers enough career assessments, both for free and at cost, to occupy several 40-hour weeks. This plenitude and variety are problematic; how can you determine which ones will be appropriate for you? You won't, or can't, without guidance, and for this I recommend you go to one of the best all around job and career sites, *www.quintessential.com*. Quint, as it sometimes calls itself for short, recently celebrated its 10th birthday and it has several pages of career assessment options; they are even broken down by age and stage in career appropriateness. Some are onsite at Quint, while others will take you to another Web location. You can see more information on assessments in *Chapter Two*.

You may legitimately wonder whether you would be better off taking assessments under the guidance of a live career consultant. Some people will certainly prefer this option, partly because you are not left to interpret the assessment results on your own and can pursue questions with a professional career guide. But if you are a person who does not have the time or the money to take this route, Web assessments can be a good substitute. The better ones will give you a broad understanding of your results, and some even provide for an online conversation with a professional. For more information on your options, go to the Quintessential Careers site and click on "Career Resources." If you want to explore working with a live person, enter "career consultants" or "career coaches," plus a location, in your search engine.

There are thousands of Websites in addition to Quint that feature or include career resources and lists of research destinations. Among private sites here are several good places to begin - careeronestop (*www.acinet.org*), its cousin site (*www.careeronestop.org*) and Jobweb (*www.jobweb.com*)

Once you have a pretty good idea of what kind of job you are looking for, the next subject of research may be the companies in which such jobs are found. The three sites listed above are again good places at which to begin. In addition, nearly all medium to large sized companies have websites and many smaller ones do, as well.

The purpose of company research is not just to identify promising looking organisations of potential interest. It is also critical to your success when you get to the point of sending out resumés and cover letters. It is vital that this application package be customised for the particular company. An effective resumé will be fine tuned for the particular company and the cover letter should characterise one's qualifications for the particular position you are seeking. The days of sending out scores of generic resumés in a scattershot approach are over.

Thanks to the Internet, Human Resource and hiring managers can get hundreds of resumé/cover letters a day. The sheer number makes it hard to separate the wheat from the chaff. But discarded with the rest of the chaff are usually application packets that were obviously sent in identical form to scores of other companies. Generic applications alienate the people who sort through stacks of resumés to decide whom to interview and are routinely consigned to the circular file. To avoid this fate, a resumé should be geared toward the particular requirements of the position being applied for at that particular company and the cover letter should explain or characterise one's interest in that company. This is impossible without company research.

It may be valuable for you to conduct other kinds of research. To explore other possibilities, use the recommended sites.

> 'I found the Internet an invaluable tool for job related information either directly or by finding a contact and then contacting them directly. I have had two experiences of using the Internet to find employment. I subscribe to a few expat/HR type online newsletters and within my first week of being in Mumbai came across an advertisement from an American intercultural consulting company looking for representatives in Mumbai. I got that job.'
> **Victoria, New Zealander in India,** *www.expatwomen.com*

LOOKING FOR JOB OPENINGS

As we said, job seekers face a staggering array of online options in their hunt for promising looking openings. If you don't bring some sort of order to this process you will end up wasting large amounts of time, provided you don't first lose your mind. Some people forego any plan and satisfy themselves with sending out large volumes of resumés in almost miscellaneous directions. This may give one the illusion of having accomplished something substantial, but as already indicated, this strategy is ineffective. Even with a good plan for choosing the sites you scour, you will only see a fraction of the postings online. This is one reason you don't want to put all your job search eggs in the Internet basket. More on that soon.

Websites presenting open positions can be roughly divided into four categories. First, there are the large generic sites like CareerBuilder and Monster. Second, there are the sites that specialise in particular industries or vocations. These are sometimes referred to as niche sites. While they do not offer as many postings as the large multi-speciality sites, their offerings are more specialised and they attract less traffic. You can find a representative list of niche sites on *www.about.com*, which lists 718 sites in 51 career fields. Along with the major fields like health care, computers, finance, science and insurance you will find headings for zoo, winery and funeral jobs.

The third category of sites centres on a geographic area such as a state, province, area or city. Most major sites have geographically organised job listings. In addition, *www.about.com* has a by-state listing. Other places to look for local sites are craigslist *www.craigslist.org*, and American Business Journals *www.bizjournals.com*. Most local newspapers these days have an online presence that includes classified ads. All of these locations can be Googled.

Speaking of Googling, if you are looking for a type of website but have no address, you can usually get there with a Google or two (or by using another standard search engine). If you want actuarial jobs in Montana, for example, simply enter "actuarial jobs Montana" in the search engine. Looking for elephants to care for in Brazil? "Elephants Zoos Brazil" will point you in the right direction.

The fourth category of job sites are what we used to call special interest, but are now identified as affinity sites. These are geared toward a particular segment of the job seeking public, such as teens, women, African-Americans, disabled people, professionals making over $100,000 a year, graduates of particular institutions, association members and so on. Again, your search engine will help you track these down.

Fifth, the most overlooked and under exploited job postings are to be found on company websites. Surveys have shown that the first place companies harvest resumés for consideration is their own site. This is mostly because they assume that these resumés have been submitted by persons with special interest in this company. Surprisingly, recent surveys tell us that most job seekers ignore company sites and the advantage they bring.

Lastly, there are jobs posted by various recruiting and job search agencies. Before responding to any of these, read the section on recruiters. Remember that they are paid not by the job seeker but by the company where they place new employees. In addition, recruiters prefer to work with people who are currently employed. So, don't expect recruiting firms to show avid interest in your next job. Most people report that resumés sent to recruiters are never acknowledged.

If you use a career management firm, be sure to work with a written contract that states how much you will pay for exactly what kinds of services. While there are reputable firms of this kind, others say they have special connections with choice employers but then hand you a list of companies you yourself could have gotten on the Internet.

To make the best use of Internet job postings you should decide on a list of sites that you will check regularly—at least every other day. Most people will do best with a mix of sites that includes a CareerBuilder or two, a couple of niche sites, an affinity site or two and at least one site that covers the local area. And don't forget the company sites.

The balance between the different kinds of sites will depend on your particular circumstances. For example, if you are looking for a high tech job in Frankfurt, Germany, you will probably skip the large generic sites while focusing on niche and company sites.

> 'I found a job listing, applied with my CV, was asked for an interview and secured the job. I have secured four jobs this way. Having worked in career and professional development for many years, I probably have more knowledge than most about how to create strong career marketing materials and present a compelling case in the interview. However, as a career coach, I do not recommend that my clients depend on job listings to find a job, as many jobs are never published.'
> Megan, American in Italy, *www.careerbychoice.com*

SENDING AND POSTING YOUR RESUMÉ

The third major job-search use of the Internet is the mirror image of the previous one. If you spend time looking for relevant position postings you will likely be sending out resumés and cover letters in response to those that interest you. In addition, there are resumé-posting sites that attract employers who review the resumés there for candidates of interest. Some of these sites charge a fee for candidates to post resumés or for companies to review them. Recently several new sites have been created by consortiums of companies looking for better access to viable candidates. Depending on the job you are looking for, it may be worth your while to use a fee based posting site. When a fee is involved, the site managers should be able to tell you roughly what sorts of companies use it to locate candidates. Some of these sites also offer other services such as career advice and job search tips.

This is the point at which many people begin to wonder how productive it is to use the Internet for finding a job. After all, it does take time and energy. And for all the impact of the Internet on the contemporary search, it is still not the means by which the majority of people find jobs. Most jobs are still landed the old-fashioned way – through in-person networking. Some people have adopted unrealistic expectations about what they can accomplish on-line. One inveterate resumé poster remarked that posting resumés that is about as useful as posting a dead cat outside one's front door to attract good luck to the family inside. Another job seeker who had posted dozens of resumés on a number of sites said, more prosaically, that It's like "casting your resumé into a black void." A third person said, "it is like a crapshoot with the odds stacked against you".

Nobody knows for certain how many people get their jobs through the Internet, but it is far less than half. The exact figures will depend on who is doing the counting. Some figures are as low as seven or eight percent, while other sources report percentages of 30% to 35%. This significant disparity reflects the differences in who is conducting the survey and the population of people surveyed. A survey issued by a career website that has sampled a population of web designers will tilt toward the high percentage. A newspaper that zeroed in on a middle-class cross-section of respondees would find their figures much lower.

Judicious estimates put the percentage of successful Internet searches that resulted in jobs at 15%, give or take a few points. Based on this figure, some experts recommend that job seekers put only that percentage of their time in on the Internet. But a 15% overall success rate does not mean that each Internet using job seeker has a 15% chance of Internet success. As suggested, for some it will be lower while for others considerably higher. But there is no question that in-person networking is by far the most fruitful way of finding a job.

The important point is that the Internet can be valuable for uses apart from efforts to find suitable positions or posting one's resumé. When you consider the time it takes to carry out careful and effective research on the Web, it would not be out of line to commit 40% of one's time to career and job sites. But people who spend much more time than that are nearly guaranteeing themselves a considerably longer search and a less than satisfactory outcome.

The Internet is best exploited by people who bring a measure of organisation and discipline to their efforts. Here is one way to do so:

- Decide what job you are seeking and confine your efforts to this decision.

- Determine in advance the job sites you will focus on for at least a week at a time and don't deviate from this list. If you run across other interesting sites, note the URL and incorporate it into your next weekly round.

- Have in front of you a job description that represents what you are looking for, and hew to this description. It is not true that casting a wide net affords the best prospects of success. A lack of focus dissipates energy. If you are responding to positions in both accounting and the zoo management of chimpanzees, your likelihood of success plummets.

- Once a week or so reevaluate your site selection, dropping and adding appropriately.

- Remember to get on the phone and out of the house. There is no substitute for meeting people face-to-face.

If you use the Internet for your job search, you will be asked for your resumé in different formats, the most common being the standard Word text and the so-called electronic resumé, also referred to as ASCII. You should know how to lock a Word document before you dispatch it. For a clear and concise review of how to cast your documents in different formats, see Katherine Hanson's excellent article at *www.quintcareers.com/e-resumé_format.html*.

The Curriculum Vitae & Cover Letter

TYPES OF RESUMÉ

There are basically two kinds of CV: the *chronological* and the *functional*. The *chronological* CV begins with your most recent work experiences and moves back in time. This traditional résumé format is still the one most widely used and preferred by employers. Its chronological format makes it easy for the reader to match responsibilities and achievements to the appropriate position.

The *functional* CV is a common alternative and allows you to list skills, abilities and achievements first and then, separately, a concise work history. Although this approach is often used by people with gaps in their work history, it is not really effective for this purpose. For one thing, a resumé must still always include a work history with dates and this history will give evidence of any gaps. Second, functional formats tend to raise a question in the mind of the reader: 'What is this person trying to hide?' So a functional format that also includes a sporadic work history can raise the red flag from the outset.

There are, however, two legitimate uses for the functional format. The first is when a person has held a number of similar or identical positions over a period of several years. The second, and this is the most common use, is when a person is changing careers or focus and needs to emphasise transferable skills.

Other CV formats include the *combination* CV, which combines elements of both. For example you might have responsibilities in bullet form beneath job positions but have a separate section that enumerates achievements. In academic fields a CV is taken to differ from a resumé in that it is a much longer document and includes details of all published papers, qualifications, research and presentations – though in this publication we are considering the CV and the resumé to be the same. Finally, the biographical statement or 'bio' is a short narrative statement summarising a person's professional history and achievements. A bio should rarely exceed one page in length.

GETTING IT RIGHT

Perhaps you've heard the saying, 'You only have one chance to make a good first impression'? In many cases this chance is embodied in the CV. Moreover, the expectations against which a CV is evaluated are higher than ever before.

For example, do not use the same CV for every job opening. It's important that you customise each CV you send out in order to highlight the skills required for that position. Some agencies and employers may scan your CV and for this reason you should use a simple font, such as Helvetica or Times New Roman, at about 12 points, using black ink on white paper. Fasten separate sheets with a paper clip rather than a staple and only print on one side of the paper. Put your name on each page in case they get separated.

The average CV will be two pages long, though job hunters with less than five years' professional experience can do well with a single page. At the same time, veteran employees should be cautious about exceeding two pages. Remember, the purpose of the CV is not to get the job but to obtain an interview.

If you are struggling with the two-page maximum, try the following:

- Condense your earliest employment experiences and/or eliminate those going back more than 15 years
- Reduce the size of the font to 11 points
- Narrow your margins
- Make sure you are presenting only the information that is most relevant to the job you are seeking

Triple check the resumé for typos and spelling errors and have another person do the same. Even a single minor error can propel your CV into the waste bin. If you are applying for work in a country with a native language other than English, then consider producing a second version of your CV in that language.

The recruiter or hiring manager is likely to speed read your CV. Resumé screeners rarely devote more than 15 or 20 seconds to a CV and are accustomed to making quick decisions. This is why it's so important for a resumé to be concise. If a CV has unnecessary words and information, the essentials will be harder for the reader to home in on. So try to lay out your CV in such a way that the salient points leap off the paper.

You can write numbers in figures rather than words and use abbreviations, such as '15%' rather than 'fifteen per cent'. Be consistent in your formatting and design – always keeping your job titles in bold face, for example, and the company names in capitals. And the more white space you have on the paper the easier it will be to read your CV.

THE OBJECTIVE

Resumés nearly always need objectives at the top. An objective serves the dual purpose of an organising principle for the author and a guide for its readers. None of the people who read resumés like having to guess what kind of job the person is applying for. Don't rely on your cover letter to perform this function since a good percentage of them are never read or are quickly separated from the resumé. A good objective is brief, using only a few words.

YOUR QUALIFICATIONS

Always list your educational achievements, with dates. List the degree you earned but don't detail your course of studies unless directly applicable. If your degree is recent, awarded in the last five years, and it bears directly on your objective, you may want to place the education section on page one, before professional experience.

Check out the standard terminology for your qualifications in the host country. Remarkably, only PhD (doctorate), MBA (Masters of Business Administration) and TEFL (Teaching of English as a Foreign Language) are terms recognised worldwide. Find out what terms your potential employer will understand and make sure your qualifications will be clear to them.

Any specific training you have undertaken, such as informal computer courses, languages or personal development, should also be listed as briefly as possible, with dates included.

As a general rule, you should list both your educational and your professional qualifications in reverse chronological order.

If you're going to transmit your CV electronically, try to send it as an attachment in a widely used program such as Microsoft Word or as a PDF (portable document format) file. Be aware, too, that stationery sizes differ between countries. So make sure your CV will print out in the right size for the paper at the other end.

YOUR PROFESSIONAL ACHIEVEMENTS

Start with your current or most recent job first. You may want to consider grouping similar positions together in one section. However it's not worth masking long gaps with a period of 'self employment' as this could lead to embarrassment in the interview – and even suggest that you may not be a trustworthy person. Nothing rings alarm bells more quickly than trying to disguise periods of unemployment as a bogus stint of self-employment. It's no longer considered a black mark against you to have been out of the workforce, even for a lengthy period of time – especially if you give the reason in your cover letter.

Always state the start and end date for each position you've had. State the position you held and the name of the company and its location. Then list your responsibilities and achievements. For past positions use verbs in the past tense and for your present position use them in the present tense. Make sure your bulleted phrases begin with active and engaging verbs. Avoid passive constructions like 'provided for' and 'responsible for'. Keep sentences as short as you can while also stating specifics such as percentages, dates, profit margins and so on. Remember to say whether you worked in a team (were the members multinational?) and whether you were a team leader.

144

After you've listed your responsibilities and achievements for the most recent position, state each prior position, going back ten to fifteen years. Try not to repeat yourself if you did much the same thing in another company – merely say that the responsibilities were the same.

When a company representative looks at your resumé, she has one question uppermost in mind: 'What can this person do for us?' This makes it important to list not only your responsibilities but your achievements too.

> 'When I first put my resumé out, no one at all was interested. So I had to find someone who knew a little about hiring staff, as luck would have it I found a HR director at Qwest Communications and she sat and went through my resumé with me, helping me re-word literally the whole thing. Even then it took a further 6 months for a company to hire me. If you are not fussy, commission jobs are ten a penny but in the current climate that does pay the bills.'
> **Lizzy, British in America, *www.expatwomen.com***

A selection of three example CVs are provided on the following pages.

Jane Doe

25 Johnson St. ● Orlando, FL 32800 ● 100-200-3000 ● Jane@Doe.com

ACCOUNTING / FINANCE PROFESSIONAL

Cash Reconciliation / Account Analysis / Systems / GAAP & SOX Compliance

Goal-oriented *self-starter* with 9 years of accounting and administrative experience in challenging corporate environments. History of rapid advancement based on demonstrated initiative and willingness to take on new challenges, additional responsibilities and special projects adding significant bottom-line revenue. Record of integrity, dependability and exceptional customer service.

- Highly skilled at resolving discrepancies, reconciling cash accounts, and removing accounting backlogs
- Working knowledge of GAAP and Sarbanes Oxley audit compliance requirements
- Strong systems and process orientation – PeopleSoft, MS Office, proprietary databases
- Provided leadership through training and consulting to other departments and associates.
- Consistently rated above average for "exceeding expectations" on performance reviews.
- Meticulous attention to detail; exceptional analytical, organizational, and problem solving abilities.

PROFESSIONAL EXPERIENCE

CAREER EDUCATION CORPORATION, Corporate Headquarters, Hoffman Estates, IL   2004 – Present
(Multi-billion dollar educational services company comprised of 6 divisions and 80 campuses worldwide)
Financial Analyst (3/07 - Present)
Accounting Associate (3/04 - 3/07)

Promoted 3 times in 3 years based on efficiency and initiative in improving accountability.

Financial Analyst responsible for a wide range of account analysis, account maintenance, and customer service functions supporting $13 million division with 5 entities in four states. Position requires extensive research, analysis, and problem solving.

Responsibilities:
- Manage budgeting and forecasting process for five campus locations.
- Manage month-end close process in coordination with Corporate School Accounting team.
- Manage and monitor payroll for all campuses.
- Oversee Student Accounts to ensure accurate and timely posting of payments and cash deposits.
- Track capital expenditures, in addition to marketing and advertising expenditures.

Accomplishments:
- Promoted from Accounting Associate to develop accounting and administrative/operating infrastructure for new division including all accounting processes, procedures and tracking tools to facilitate smooth day-to-day operations and monitor financial performance.
- Created templates and Excel spreadsheets for tracking monthly expenditures, capital expenditures budget, inventory, and accrual analysis, daily cash and deposit reconciliation.
- Developed and implemented monthly financial review process with management team of each campus to report, analyze and effectively monitor purchase orders, accounts payable and payroll.
- Wrote financial policies, procedures and standard practices for each campus that enhanced accountability.
- Developed a uniform mapping and naming filing system for system encompassing 75+ schools.
- Collaborated with procurement team in developing standardized procurement process.

Jane Doe

CAREER EDUCATION CORPORATION, Corporate Headquarters, Hoffman Estates, IL   2004 – Present

Accounting Associate responsible for preparation of financial statements, balance sheet reconciliation and timely month-end close process for multiple locations. Also responsible for evaluating financial trends and operating performance of individual schools and communicating performance to management teams.

Accomplishments:
- Promoted from Accounting Assistant within the first year in the position.
- Repeatedly sought out to help other divisions in doing complex cash reconciliations dealing with alternative loan funds, Title IV funding, student refunds, daily operating accounts, and Pell Grants.
- Maintained cash aging items within 45 days, well below 90 day guidelines.
- Reconciled and reversed a 4-month cash backlog amounting to $2.3 million for the Culinary Division.
- Participated in Sarbannes Oxley annual audit process.
- Created check lists for SOX compliance month-end processing that were implemented school-wide.
- Member of PeopleSoft conversion team that automated the balance sheet accounting reconciliation process.

ST. ALEXIUS MEDICAL CENTER, Hoffman Estates, IL   2001 – 2004
(331-bed community hospital –member of the Alexian Brothers not-for-profit hospital network)

Managed Care Associate
Refund Coordinator
Performed a wide range of data entry and accounting/administrative functions for 331-bed community hospital.
- Analyzed and interpreted contracts and patient claims for managed care contracts involving all major insurance providers.
- Reviewed terms and processed insurance and patient refunds to ensure contract compliance.
- Maintained spreadsheets and processed refunds, adjustments, and voids into Meditech system.
- Reconciled outstanding checks on a monthly basis.
- Communicated with managed care payers in resolving reimbursement issues, reconciliation of payment reports and collecting outstanding medical claims.

Accomplishments:
- Reduced liability from $2 million to under $300,000 and resolved claims outstanding from two years to under 45 days within the first year in the position.
- Resolved all credit balances within 45 days.

ROBERT HALF INTERNATIONAL, Hoffman Estates, IL   2000 - 2001
Contract Accountant, Accounts Receivable

BANK ONE, Mount Prospect, IL   1998 - 2000
(Bank One was acquired by Chase in 2004 – a leading financial services firm with assets of $1.4 trillion)

Bank Teller/Customer Service Representative
- Responsible for cash handling and daily balancing of cash drawer in addition to bank opening and closing.
- Performed customer transactions in a timely and efficient manner.
- Maintained standards for bank security and customer privacy disclosure.

EDUCATION

Bachelor's Degree, Accounting, *With Honors* (3.83 GPA)
Roosevelt University, Schaumburg, IL, May 2007
Worked full time while pursuing full time degree to finance education.

Jane Doe
17 Jane St.
Trenton, GA 30004
(100) 200-3000
JaneDoe@Doe.com

Senior Accounting & Finance Manager

Financial Analyst / Senior Accountant / Controller / M & A

Team-oriented professional with a career history of accuracy, integrity and bottom-line orientation. Strong analytical skills with proven expertise in cost analysis and forecasting within the financial services industry. Successfully managed inter-company mergers and acquisitions involving complex consolidation of processes, systems and policies to ensure compliance and streamline operational efficiency.

• Financial Statement Preparation	• System Conversions	• Capital Budgeting
• Inter-company Transactions	• Budgeting & Forecasting	• Incentive Calculations
• Internal Procedures & Controls	• Fixed Assets	• Cash Flow Management

Technology / Systems:
  Accounting/ERP: Hyperion, PeopleSoft, Oracle, Great Plains, Real-world, Macola, PeachTree
  Database & Office Management: MS Office (Excel, Word, MS Project, Access, PowerPoint), Crystal Reports
  Trust Accounting: TrustMark Participant Accounting, NCS Trust Accounting

---

PROFESSIONAL EXPERIENCE:

WACHOVIA CORPORATION - Wachovia Retirement Services (WRS), Charlotte, NC   Mar '03 – Dec '06
(WRS is a $400 million division of Wachovia Corporation)

Finance Manager / Team Leader
Provided leadership to team of Financial Analysts with total responsibility for month-end financials supporting $400 million Division. Multifaceted responsibilities included:

Accounting: Review and analysis of month-end financial data involving complex business transactions (revenue, expenses, accruals); preparation of accounting data to ensure accuracy and meet rigorous time and compliance standards; general ledger maintenance including journal entries (monthly accruals and revenue recognition).

Finance: Monthly and ad-hoc financial analysis and reporting; preparation of financial statements, proformas, variance analysis, revenue and expense forecasts; planning and development of annual operating and capital budgets. Provided support for annual financial audits and contract audits. Defined, analyzed and communicated key metrics and business trends for the management team via dashboard and score cards.

Achievements:
- Managed processes and facilitated transitions to ensure efficiency and consistency of reporting.
- Served as resource and collaborated with sales, marketing, operations and human resources to support corporate initiatives, new product development, and organizational restructurings.
- Managed system conversions and led integration of accounting information and processes for three acquisitions.

TRANSAMERICA REINSURANCE   Oct '02 – Mar '03
Contract Accountant - Statutory Reporting and Investment Valuations

QUEENS UNIVERSITY—attended graduate school full time (MBA attained May '06)   Aug '01 – Aug '02

Jane Doe, CPA   Page Two

PROFESSIONAL EXPERIENCE (Continued):

SCHWAB RETIREMENT TECHNOLOGIES --Charlotte, NC   Oct '96 – June '01
(Wholly-owned subsidiary of The Charles Schwab Corporation)
Senior Manager of Finance
Oversaw accounting and finance department supervising staff of three. Collected, summarized and interpreted
financial data for Senior Management Team and Corporate Finance. Developed budgets and forecasts for
operations and projects including capital budgeting. Measured actual performance against plan and standards.
Interpreted and presented monthly results to management, including preparation of monthly financial reporting
package for upper management. Responsible for organizing, directing and controlling work of staff. Oversaw
monthly close and reporting to Corporate. Prepared annual budget, revisions and estimates. Communicated
effectively with Cost Center Managers concerning budgets and variances. Prepared proposed project funding
requests. Performed profitability analysis. Created metrics.
Achievements:
- Promoted from Senior Accountant to Senior Manager after 18 months.
- Developed new pricing model for new product.

FIRST NATIONAL BANK OF COMMERCE--BANK ONE, New Orleans, LA   11/95-9/96
(Regional Bank & Holding Company)
Assistant Vice-President, Trust Officer & Employee Benefits Analyst
Prepared accrual basis periodic valuations for trust accounts including Profit Sharing plans, 401(k) plans, Money
Purchase plans, Keogh & ESOP plans. Allocated earnings, contributions, distributions and forfeitures across
sources and funds based on plan documents. Verified eligibility, vesting and participant statements. Reviewed
and verified rates of return for specific funds. Reconciled participant loans including principal and interest
payments. Prepared participants' year-end 1099R documents. Prepared IRS Form 5500 for trust accounts.
Performed IRS required testing.
Achievements:
- Organized conversion of trusts from newly acquired Central Bank.

SIGMATRON INTERNATIONAL, INC., Elk Grove Village, IL   9/94-10/95
($60M Electronics Contract Manufacturer with 350 employees - Public Corporation on NASDAQ)
Controller
Supervised staff of four including Accounts Payable, Accounts Receivable, Billing and Cost Accounting.
Coordinated monthly close and account analysis. Prepared month-end general journal entries and accruals
including interest. Prepared and analyzed monthly financial statements. Reviewed intercompany transactions for
six divisions including a Taiwanese operation and a Mexican Maquildora. Supervised quarterly physical inventory
and inventory valuation. Maintained fixed asset sub ledgers. Forecasted daily cash flow using $15M revolving line
of credit. Assisted in budgeting and projections. Complied information to assist with external audits, 10Ks and
10Qs. Served as contact to Macola software support.
Achievements:
- Controlled California-based affiliate's entire accounting operation including general ledger and financial
  statements. Established and implemented new procedures and internal controls.
- Organized and supervised accounting computer system conversion from Qantel to Macola.

ALLIBERT USA, INC., Huntersville, NC   10/92-8/94
General Accountant & Network Administrator

EDUCATION:
Masters in Business Administration (MBA), May 2006
Queens University, McColl School of Business, Charlotte, NC
Bachelor of Science in Accounting (BS), June 1992
University of North Carolina at Charlotte

PROFESSIONAL AFFILIATIONS:
American Institute of Certified Public Accountants, North Carolina Association of CPA's

149

JANE DOE

17 Jane Street
Alfredo, GA 12345

100-200-3000
Jane@Doe.com

International Trade

- Strong working knowledge of international customs regulations and trade agreements, including "prior notice," visas, quota entries, visa entries and TPLs.
- Experience with FDA and Hazmat regulations.
- Voted out of 50 employees as *Employee of the Quarter* for going "beyond the call of duty."

SUMMARY OF QUALIFICATIONS

- **Academic Qualifications:** Bachelor's Degree in International Trade,
- **Leadership Ability:** Founded and held leadership roles for two international student organizations.
- **Communication & Negotiation Skills:** Established relationships with major retail accounts; negotiated contracts and pricing for advertising campaigns.
- **Sales & Marketing:** Built internet business to profitable status while attending college full time.
- **Management:** Recruited and supervised interns.
- **Technology:** Collaborated with IT department to setup e-commerce website.
- **Computer:** Microsoft Word, Excel, PowerPoint, WordPerfect, Adobe Premiere.
- **Languages:** Proficient in French, fluent in Yoruba.

PROFESSIONAL EXPERIENCE

EXPEDITORS INTERNATIONAL OF WASHINGTON, INC., Savannah, GA   May '06 – Present
(Global Third Party Logistics Firm)

Export Brokerage Customer Service Representative, Customs Import Department
- Provided logistics support for licensed brokers dealing with major retail accounts including Walmart & GAP.
- Managed customs declaration process for imports entering the US through the port of Savannah from China, Australia, Canada, Egypt, Belgium, South America, Turkey, Jordan, Kenya and other countries.
- Processed prior notice entries, late entries, TPL visa entries, and FCA/FCC certified entries through all stages including receipt of entry, auditing, EDI input, transmission, problem resolution, and delivery.
- Developed relationships with Compliance Specialists at key accounts including Walmart, GAP, among others.
- Conducted audits of shipping documentation and bills of laden; resolved discrepancies to expedite delivery.
- Generated customized reports to track and monitor compliance with customs regulations.

INTERNATIONAL TRADE INTERNSHIP
The African Connections (http:www.theafricanconnections.com)   Jan '05 – Present

Founder / Operations Manager
- Created online web presence to promote communication among Africans in Diaspora.
- Recruited interns and collaborated with university IT department in setting up and maintaining website.
- Researched and identified online target markets; negotiated banner advertising to promote traffic.
- Managed website operations that generated 15,000 hits in the first week.

Prior experience: *Worked full time during college to finance education:*
- Public Library Customer Service, Security Officer, Maintenance Mechanic

EDUCATION AND ACTIVITIES

Bachelor of Science in International Trade, May 2006
Georgia Southern University, Statesboro, GA
Hope Scholar, President's List - Spring 2006

Leadership Activities:
Organization for African Interest, Founder, President, 2004-2006
African Student Association, Public Relations Officer, 2003-2004

COVER LETTERS

Whenever you send your CV you should always include a cover letter that is printed in the same font and on the same paper as your CV. Some countries call them 'cover letters', others call them 'letters of interest' or 'motivation letters'.

In some countries, it's standard to enclose a photograph. In others, such as the US, the employer is required to dispose of it. Some countries require original copies of transcripts and references to be attached to your application – so find out locally what may be required.

Many practised job hunters confess that they agonise over cover letters more than they do their CVs. If your cover letter is below standard then there's a chance that the recipient won't even bother to look at your CV. Be aware that the letter introduces you to your readers and sets the mental framework with which they interpret the CV.

Here are some useful tips about how to write your cover letter:

Be Concise

The acceptable length for a cover letter is one page, no longer. The cover letter must be succinct, without being abrupt or perfunctory. A good cover letter selects and presents the most important information about the author that's most relevant to the position.

Sell the CV

Cover letters don't get you the job, but neither do CVs – they get interviews. An effective cover letter wins an interested reading of your CV. It distinguishes you from other well-qualified candidates. While cover letters may seem like a peripheral extra to the basics of the job search, they require the same care and attention that you devote to the CV and interview.

Proper Style is Essential

The effective cover letter avoids both stilted formality and casual familiarity. It should be comfortable and relaxed, conveying confidence and professionalism without sounding cocky or smug.

Individualisation is a must

Like CVs, a basic cover letter can be adapted for different situations and purposes. Your cover letter will usually be in direct application for a particular open position you have seen advertised. Mass mailings of identical resumés and cover letters are a waste of time and effort. If you use a generic letter to cover all your CVs, many readers will assume that you have no special interest in the particular position they are trying to fill and will therefore have little interest in filling it with you.

An effective cover letter accomplishes three overlapping objectives:

- It introduces your CV to the reader
- It establishes the frame of mind that the reader brings to the CV and can give your reasons for the application
- It can add positive background and supplementary material that could not be incorporated into the CV. The cover letter should not merely repeat the information in the CV, but should lift up and elaborate on its most important elements in relationship to the particular position you are applying for. Sometimes a cover letter can discuss a qualification, such as volunteer experience, that doesn't easily fit the resumé format.

The Beginning

The first paragraph of your letter sets the stage for the body of the letter in which you demonstrate how you can benefit the organisation. It can do this briefly, often in a sentence or two, by confirming to the reader exactly which position you're interested in. Some companies are interested in knowing how a vacancy came to your attention.

The Middle

The middle of the letter is its heart. Employers complain that too many cover letters dwell on what the candidates are looking for in their next job. Remember, the employer wants to hire people who will perform well and contribute to the company's success.

You want to characterise the critical skills, experience, and personality traits that recommend you for the position. Be specific about what you bring to the table and concrete in your illustrations of what you can accomplish. Talk about your achievements and how they benefited your previous employers. Do enough research on the company in question to discuss how your past qualifications can translate into benefits for this particular employer.

Wherever possible, the results of your efforts should be stated in measurable terms. State by what percentage business increased, or by how much wastage was reduced. The more concrete the better.

The Conclusion

The last paragraph should be clear and quietly confident. Unfortunately, many people end their cover letters on a pleading or overly grateful note. Try not to sound desperate! Don't leave your fate in the hands of the recipient. State when you will call to follow up on the CV and then make sure you do it. You can see a sample cover letter on the next page.

Sample cover letter

This letter, in response to an advertisement, was supplied by Ricklin-Echikson Associates.

Byron Smith
128 Main Street
Sometown, Connecticut 99999
(000) 999-5555

August 26, _____

Mr Thomas Long
Vice-President for Financial Management
Marvinvest
70 Lexington Avenue
New York, NY 10005

Dear Mr Long,

With an MBA in Finance and a successful track record in both equity and high yield research/ recommendations and portfolio management, I think you will find my qualifications an ideal match for your open position of Portfolio/Equity Manager.

Requirements	My Qualifications
Proven track record in management	Assisted Portfolio Manager in managing $400 million portfolio in client account funds including institutional and variable annuity funds for past 5 years.
Manage and analyse small to medium capitalisation stocks	Extensive experience in management and analysis of these stocks as illustrated by enclosed stock performance list.
Bachelor's Degree and 5 years experience	BS in Economics and MBA in Finance from Fordham University; NASD Series 6 and 7 Brokerage Securities Licences; 5 years experience in equity management.

I am particularly interested in your position because of its focus on high yield portfolio management.

During the last several years I have increasingly specialised in managing such tricky but enormously lucrative investments. Clients who have placed resources in these niche vehicles that I have managed have realised a 17% gain over a two-year period. I would welcome the opportunity to meet with you and will call in about a week to arrange an agreeable time for us to talk. Thank you.

Sincerely,

Byron Smith

Stationery

Be aware that stationery or paper sizes are of different dimensions in different countries. The United States standard is 8 x 11 inches whereas the European A4 standard is 210 x 297 mm. When you're transmitting your resumé and cover letter via email, go to 'page setup' on your computer and reformat your documents to the recipient's standard. Otherwise, when they print it out at their end, half of your material will be missing! The same is true for sending a fax. If you transmit material typed on 'regular' size paper, half of it will be missing on the other end. If at all possible, purchase stationery that has the same dimensions as the recipient's and mail or fax your resumé and cover letter on this stationery.

THE PROFESSIONAL PORTFOLIO

Historically, artists, writers and designers have used portfolios of their work to market their talents as they maintain a constant search for freelance work. Now other kinds of professionals are beginning to use portfolios. The portfolio does not replace the CV, but is used at the interview in order to illustrate the quality of work one is capable of performing.

In the UK, The Institute of Personnel and Development (IPD) introduced the professional portfolio several years ago as part of its Continuing Professional Development (CPD) scheme and made it obligatory for members.

Your portfolio is for artifacts as well as facts. It can be made up of certificates, references, samples of work, thank you notes, employee evaluations, statistics or newspaper clippings. The most important part of the portfolio is the section that showcases actual work samples and therefore substantiates the claims of the CV. In his comprehensive book *Portfolio Power*, Martin Kimeldorf suggests that you compile your collection using clear A4 wallets inside a ring binder. He recommends that items should be categorised into sections such as Learning, Communication and Persuasion Abilities, Managerial or Leadership Skills, and Information Gathering. An alternative is to organise the portfolio around your different jobs or key accomplishments. Each item should be displayed with a title and a caption. Care should be taken to be consistent with type style and positioning throughout. You may want to arrange your portfolio in reverse chronological order.

Kimeldorf suggests you start by throwing samples and artifacts into a box, categorising them one at a time as you go. Include information answering the questions of 'what, why and when'. As you go along, bear in mind the skills that you want to portfolio, to substantiate and illustrate. Don't be tempted to include too much material, for this will obscure the information that is key for the interviewer to see.

When you take your portfolio along to an interview, ensure that you tailor it specifically for that vacancy. Keep extra items at home for other purposes.

When you visit the Bank Manager for a loan or to present a business plan, you would not need the same artifacts as when you're approaching a potential client.

Compiling a professional portfolio is a rewarding exercise. It reacquaints you with your own strengths and achievements and renews your confidence and self esteem. There's no need to wait for a job search to begin on your portfolio – jobs are no longer for life and building a portfolio is a major project.

The Interview

Job seeking is a path lined with pitfalls and surprises. So it's vital to understand the way potential employers think and what their selection criteria are, if you want to be primed effectively for the job market.

What are your interviewers looking for? Professional candidate selection comprises a three-dimensional enquiry into the knowledge base, the skills and the intrinsic human qualities of the candidate.

To be best prepared for the interview, put yourself in the shoes of the interviewer and ask yourself what areas of knowledge and experience are essential to doing the job. After establishing that there is a match with your own qualifications, focus on how you can verbalise this match in the most convincing terms possible. Assess your skills carefully and think of summing them up in a series of 'can do' statements. Think of any additional skills not specified in the job description that will strengthen your candidacy.

Last but not least, don't underestimate the importance that recruiters and hiring managers attach to a candidate's personality. They will want to know whether you'll fit into the corporate culture, how you react to stress and whether you can work constructively with others both in and outside your specialist field.

Be yourself. There's no point in pretending to be a great salesperson if you're timid by nature, because you won't be happy or successful in that job. A professional recruiter, or a human resources or hiring manager, will be capable of discerning your real skills and natural aptitudes.

Develop an awareness of cultural differences as soon as you can. Your interview panel may comprise people of different nationalities. Some may not approve of your questions about salary at this stage. Others may want to know about your family as much as about your professional qualifications. Also, be aware of local norms regarding eye contact and body language.

MAKING AN IMPRESSION

When going for interviews, remember that appearances count. Try to be open and positive, while concentrating on your objective to get this job. Smile, but don't paste a mechanical grin on your face.

Be as informed as possible about recent business developments and the news in general. Avoid gossip, particularly about previous employers, and move the conversation towards areas you know well and feel comfortable with. If you need to disagree with your interviewer, do so gently, saying: 'That's one way of looking at it, but I also wonder ...'

It's a good idea to try to surprise your interviewer at least once. When the opportunity arises, draw a graph showing the growth of the department you directed. You might also show an example of a publicity campaign you were responsible for, or an article you wrote.

Without exaggerating, remember to confirm what your interviewer says: 'You are right, I hadn't seen things that way before ... You are certainly right about that ... and that reminds me of ...' (followed by an anecdote).

Don't respond too quickly. If a question isn't clear, ask for clarification. If you don't have an answer, don't bluff. Bluffing could cost you the job. There is nothing wrong with confessing that you don't know the answer to a question or would need more information to give a well-considered response. In answering questions, restrict yourself to a minute when possible – and never exceed two minutes.

Watch your interviewer for non-verbal cues. If she begins tapping nervously, looks out the window, or interrupts you with another question, retire the topic on which you were expounding.

Respond only to questions, not to comments. Skilled interviewers will sometimes make off the cuff comments to see where you may take them. Resist responding to these remarks since it is here, in the course of informal exchanges, that people are most likely to say something inopportune. If the interviewer comments on your education or experience, take note of it without responding unless it is in your interest to offer further information.

Always return to the main topic: how you'll contribute to the development of the company and how good you will be at the job in question. Now and again try to sense what the recruiter thinks of your professional capabilities and your profile: 'How do you think I will contribute to your business, considering my experience?' Never wait till the end of the interview to ask this sort of question.

Close the interview gracefully. You can ask about the selection process but take care not to seem overanxious or needy.

BODY LANGUAGE

Non-verbal behaviours such as eye contact, posture and gestures make up our body language and are powerful signals that become especially important during the interview process. They help create the 'gut reaction' or 'chemistry' that interviewers often refer to when they are asked about why they did or didn't hire someone. Because non-verbal behaviours can elicit positive or negative responses, it's important that we become aware of our own non-verbal behaviours and how they either contribute to or detract from a professional presentation.

When body language conveys confidence and supports what we say, it can go a long way towards assuring interview success. It sends messages about important intangibles like integrity and attention to detail. Actions do speak louder than words. The interviewer is as likely to remember *how* something was said as *what* was said. Although a job candidate spends only part of the time speaking during the interview, the interviewer is getting messages about him or her throughout the interview. Here are some tips about non-verbal behaviours that are especially important in the interview process:

HANDSHAKE

A handshake should signal cooperation and friendliness; you should try to match the pressure extended by the interviewer. Be sure your hands are warm and reasonably free of perspiration. Use only one hand and always shake vertically. Extending the hand parallel to the floor with the palm up conveys submissiveness; extending the flat hand outward with the palm facing down is often seen as being too aggressive. Smile confidently and maintain good eye contact.

EYE CONTACT

Looking at people shows interest in them and is important in making a good impression. Your goal should be to maintain a calm, steady and unthreatening gaze. To avoid the appearance of staring, create a mental triangle incorporating both eyes and the mouth and allow your eyes to follow a natural continuous path along the three points. Try to maintain this approach for roughly three quarters of the time. Feel free to break your gaze to look at the interviewer's hands or to refer to your notepad as you speak.

SEATING AND POSTURE

Wait for the interviewer to offer you a seat. If he or she fails to motion you in one direction or another, ask: 'Where would you like me to sit?' If you have a choice, choose a chair that's upright with arms. Sit back in the chair with your back straight. A slight forward leaning posture as the interview progresses shows interest and friendliness toward the interviewer. Be aware of any tendency you have to slouch.

DRESS AND GROOMING

The way you dress tells people how you feel about the interviewer and the interview process itself. And, since memory is most closely connected with visual images, overall appearance may leave as lasting an impression as the words you speak. Your attitude, your confidence and your delivery are affected by the clothes you wear. Taking time to present an attractive professional image when you interview will add to your self-esteem and confidence. Generally, the standard for an interviewee is one notch more conservative than that for employees. When in doubt, make it two notches. Be aware that the interviewer will scrutinise both your overall image and the details of your appearance.

NERVOUS HABITS

Practice, awareness and asking for honest feedback on your interviewing skills will help you uncover and minimise nervous habits that could detract from your presentation. Here's a list of some of the most common nervous habits that can interfere with interview success:

- Using repetitive words or 'fillers' such as 'like', 'um', or 'you know'
- Decreasing the volume of your speaking voice
- Rapidly nodding your head while the interviewer is speaking
- Furrowing eyebrows or chewing your lip while listening
- Tapping feet, pens, fingers, and so on
- Any habitual behaviours like earlobe rubbing and chin stroking

MOST ASKED INTERVIEW QUESTIONS

Many interviewers have their favourite questions, which are often a slight variation of the most common interview questions. By being aware of these questions we can rehearse and prepare some of our potential answers. Questions often fall into the following areas:

- Abilities and competence to do the job
- Past experience and achievements
- Future aims and aspirations
- Personality and skills
- Scenarios
- Salary and benefits scale and expectations

The questions asked will probably include some of these:
- Why have you applied?
- What appeals about the role?
- What do you know about the company?
- Why do you want to work for us?
- What interview preparation have you done?
- Tell me about yourself.

- Why are you leaving your current job?
- What are your main strengths?
- How have they been demonstrated?
- What are your main weaknesses?
- How do you overcome them?
- Use three key words to describe yourself.
- How would your boss describe you?
- What experience do you have of working on your own?
- What experience do you have working in a team?
- Which do you prefer and why?
- Why should we appoint you?
- What are your main achievements?
- What is your style of leadership?
- How do you keep your knowledge up to date?
- What are your aims and ambitions – one year, three years, ten years?
- Identify a task you were involved in that didn't go well.
- What would you do differently and why?
- Describe the role you played in...
- What would you do if...?
- Describe a situation when you used... skills.
- What are your interests outside of work?
- What skills do you use in that particular sport/hobby etc?
- What is your present salary?
- What salary do you want?
- Are there any other current benefits you have?
- Does relocating to this area present you with any issues?
- Have you any questions for us?

Some questions to consider asking:
- How is the organisation structured?
- What recent developments have there been?
- What future plans do you have?
- Do you have a vision/mission statement?
- How might my career develop from this position?
- What training would I be given?
- From this interview do you think I have the abilities you are seeking?
- Why is the position vacant?
- How long has it been vacant?
- What is the next stage of the recruitment process?
- When are you looking to appoint?

Types of questions you may be asked:

The above list gives samples of questions, what follows is examples of the types of questions you should anticipate: open; closed; probing; hypothetical; continuity; playback.

Open

- Could you give me some examples of ... ?
- I'd like you to tell me about the sort of work you are doing in your present job.
- What do you know about ... ?
- How have you tackled ... ?

Closed

- Who else was involved?
- Where were you at the time?
- How did that situation arise?
- When did that happen?

Probing

- What was your precise role in this project?
- What exactly did you contribute towards the team's success?
- What knowledge and skills were you able to apply to the project?
- Could you tell me more about what you did?

Hypothetical/situational

- What would you do if ... ?
- How would you respond to rudeness from a customer?

Continuity

- What happened next?
- What did you do then?
- Can we move on now to ... ?
- Can we talk about your next job?

Playback

- As I understand it, you resigned from your last position because you disagreed with your boss on a number of fundamental issues – have I got that right?

160

INTERVIEW DOS

✓ Remember everyone you meet is already a member of the company. They could be asked their impression of you – therefore treat everyone you meet politely and try to smile
✓ Shake hands with all members of the interview panel confidently and giving eye contact
✓ Accept a drink, if you are not too nervous, to use the drink as your thinking time
✓ Look at the person asking the question
✓ When answering a question try to include other panel members with your eye contact
✓ Be enthusiastic and professional without being over the top
✓ When asked an open question, be confident and answer fully
✓ If you don't understand a question ask for it to be repeated
✓ Relate your answers to the position you are being interviewed for
✓ Listen well and indicate that you're listening through eye contact, smiling and nodding occasionally
✓ Be honest in your answers
✓ Take your time to consider an answer, remember your preparation
✓ Ask questions
✓ Take a final opportunity to sell yourself
✓ Relax!

INTERVIEW DON'TS

✗ Ignore everyone until you meet the interview panel
✗ Interrupt the interviewers
✗ Argue with the questioner
✗ Smoke, even if invited to
✗ Accept a drink if you are too nervous to drink it confidently
✗ Give one word answers to open questions which demand a full answer, even if the question has been badly asked
✗ Be dishonest in your answers. You will be found out later in the interview
✗ Be disrespectful or critical of your past or present employers
✗ Discuss salary or benefits unless invited to do so it can usually be discussed separately
✗ Ask too many questions at the end
✗ Try to crack a joke or be sarcastic if you're unfamiliar with the audience
✗ Use jargon
✗ Swear
✗ Stress negative or weak points
✗ Underestimate your skills and abilities

AND DON'T FORGET TO NETWORK

Networking Online

Since its inception, the Internet has been evolving quickly. Soon following the advent of the 21st century the Internet began to incorporate significant new elements, which come under the general heading of interactivity. Some Web experts describe this development as an evolution from Web I to Web II. The difference is simple: Web I was the era of one-way communication. Information flowed from the Web to its users. In the era of Web II, however, we use the Internet to push information in the other direction in order to communicate with other people. The era of Web II has given birth to Internet based networking. It began with Facebook, MySpace and YouTube and has now extended into many arenas of human endeavor. There are now, yes, thousands of sites devoted to business, professional and job search networking. The impetus for the development of these sites came from employers and employees looking for more effective ways to connect and promote their interests. The interactions that take place in these domains is still referred to as 'social networking', but much of it has broader business and career objectives. To learn more about these sites and how to use them read the tutorial at *www.quintcareers.com/Internet_Networking/tutorial_1.html*

Networking offline

While *Chapter Five* covers networking in depth, it's worth saying here that personal recommendations and referrals are responsible for many vacancies being filled. You can never have too many contacts.

Join professional and informal networking groups and build relationships with as many people as you can. While a person may not know of a vacancy herself, she may well know someone else, in her own circle of contacts, who does.

Many people learn of job opportunities while at informal social gatherings. Don't be afraid to speak with people you meet about the kind of job you are looking for.

YOUR SEARCH STRATEGY

Getting and staying organised

It will be impossible to conduct a focused job search without having a method of organising the information you're collecting and of recording the concrete steps, such as sending out CVs, that you have taken. Getting and staying organised has several advantages over just trying to remember what you've learned and done. Unless your search is short, or you are blessed with an extraordinary memory, you won't remember everything.

A nearly universal curse of looking for work, especially if you have just moved to a new location and are unemployed, is the sense of not being in control. Staying organised with notebooks, folders, files, forms or computerised tracking systems will help you maintain your feeling of being in command – and this, in turn, will boost your morale and the self confidence with which you present yourself.

One of the critical elements of an energetic and successful job search is following up – the exercise of charming persistence. It is impossible to maintain scheduled follow-up in a search of any complexity and depth, unless you keep track of what you have done.

Keeping orderly records helps you to internalise and track the information you have learned and actions you have taken. This helps to build your self-confidence and sense of purpose, and to maintain momentum.

Once you're convinced of the merits of an organised search, you may be interested in the best way to get organised. Here I must say that there is no single right way, which everyone must follow. But I can certainly make suggestions about what systems you may need in order to get and stay organised.

The goal of organisation is to achieve order and clarity with the least complicated arrangements possible. To organise your job search you may need the following supplies:

- A calendar that provides plenty of room to record appointments, action steps and information
- A street map to familiarise yourself with the area
- A notebook for quickly jotting down information and notes to yourself
- A notebook for recording important information you want to preserve
- Folders to separate and organise materials
- An alphabetical filing system
- Forms with which to record and monitor your goals, research, actions, results and follow-up plans

Set detailed goals and implementation plans for every week and each day. Write down these goals and plans on paper and share them with other people to help keep yourself committed and accountable.

Reward yourself along the way for successes, like getting an interview, and for achieving goals you have established for yourself.

Most job searches that last any longer than a month or two hit 'dry stretches' during which it feels as though nothing positive is being achieved. When you hit a patch like this, don't permit yourself to wallow in self-pity or negative thinking. You may have every right to be depressed, but negative thoughts will do you no good in the long run. Depression and discouragement easily evolve into self-pity. Just like disorganisation, negative thinking can spiral out of control. Fight back. Connect with people who will encourage and affirm you while keeping your distance from pessimists and naysayers. Even so, few people go through a job search without going through times of discouragement and low morale. Remind yourself that feelings are not facts and that their main source of power comes from whatever energy you give them yourself.

7 working for yourself

Working for yourself demands self-motivation, flexibility and strength of character. It also requires a business plan.

'When you work you are a flute through whose heart the whispering of the hours turns to music.'
Khalil Gibran

In this chapter:
- Starting on your own
- Time management
- The business plan
- More bureaucracy
- Market research
- What to charge
- Marketing your business
- Marketing materials
- Marketing on the internet
- Brand you
- Making it happen
- Learning the language
- Goal setting
- Teamwork

Starting On Your Own

Working for yourself is an excellent alternative to the rough and tumble of the international job market. But do you have what it takes? According to Inc. magazine, you first have to evaluate the viability of your business ideas and strategy. That's right, it's self-analysis time again.

Ask yourself, and answer honestly:

- Can you clearly articulate your idea (in 50 words or less)?
- Where did the idea come from?
- Do you really know the industry?
- Have you seen the idea used elsewhere?
- What will you do better than your competitors?
- Has your idea passed the time test? In other words, will you still love it tomorrow?
- Next month? Next year?
- Are you ready to commit yourself to the idea for the next five years or more?
- Do you know the difference between a product and a business?
- Having a good product is only one part of business ownership.
- Is this an idea for you, or would it be better for someone else?
- Do you really have the skills and desire to make it work?
- What are the potential rewards – monetary and otherwise?
- Are you plugged into the right networks to pursue your idea?

Also, people with their own businesses will tell you that the self-discipline and self-confidence required to be your own boss successfully is not for everyone. The hours are long and the rewards are few (at least initially) but there will be one undeniable, and immediate, benefit: you'll finally have a boss you can respect!

TIME MANAGEMENT

Your time will be your own and, for this very reason, you will have to structure it. In many jobs, we structure our time based on the job description, or on the organisation's priorities, which have been handed to us by our boss or those above him. When you have your own business, you need to structure your time based on your own priorities. This can become even more complicated if you're trying to take advantage of the fact that you are in control of how you spend your time and apportion less time on work than your business requires. Yes, it's great that you have the flexibility to attend a school play or take long lunches with friends. But you need to consider setting limits and boundaries too.

In your diary, Palm Pilot or other scheduler, you'll want to map out your days and weeks very carefully, with adequate time allowed to transition from the business to the personal and to get from appointment to appointment.

Time management can be a real problem for the less organised. I've found that a large format desk diary is invaluable, so that I can diary my tasks directly onto the pages in advance. I also use the calendar facility that comes with my email program, using it to note regular and individual commitments. For example, the first day of the month is always the day I try to send out my email newsletter, *The Inspirer*. I try to keep Fridays for exercise, and my online diary reminds me of this every week. I print out the monthly diary and stick it on the wall beside my desk so I can glance at it at any time. Further, I download my calendar to my Ipod nano along with my podcasts and other items on a weekly basis. They say that you have more chance of meeting your goals if you write them down so I use a number of other lists too. I have also found it useful to print up three sheets entitled Monthly Tasks, Weekly Tasks and Long Term Master Plan. First I write all my tasks for the coming year or more onto the Long Term Master Plan sheet, then I transfer a few of each onto the Monthly Task sheet. Then, at the start of each month I divide the monthly tasks up between the available weeks. You can find samples of my charts on *www.career-in-your-suitcase.com*.

'Anyone who is serious about building a sustainable and profitable business needs to be sure they are spending their time and energy on the right things. Are you are beginning to see that a long to-do list that isn't prioritised with actions that aren't connected to actual dates for completion isn't efficient?

'It can be scary to integrate your to-do list into your calendar and I promise, it is worth it. What do you have to lose? Try it and if it doesn't work you can always go back to the never-ending list of things that never get done. Stop living in denial about what you can realistically get done and choose to plan and execute profitable actions that will grow your business.'
Stephanie Ward, *www.fireflycoaching.com*

Few things sap motivation more than an impossible workload. Life throws the unexpected at us too, and we need to ensure we have enough slack in our time schedule to be able to cope with emergencies, urgent jobs or ill children. If you aim to write a manageable number of tasks into your weekly and monthly lists then you can keep your motivation and optimism alive. In addition, I find that while some plans *sound* fine it is only when I see them on paper that I realise I have bitten off more than I can chew. Hence the value in having all these lists and charts printed out.

Make sure too, that you diary in time off, a short lunch break, opportunities for fresh air and to recharge your batteries. Be aware that you may need a mixture of solitary and less solitary activities, so try to create a balance. When I worked from home and lived alone in my mid twenties, I would make a point of taking a good walk each lunchtime and plan social activities for the evening. Now that I live with my family, yet also work from home much of the time, I know myself well enough to realise that I can only handle going out two or three evenings a week, and that business trips abroad can only happen once a month. Equally, I realise that I work best alone, in silence and I dislike interruptions. However, as an extrovert I need the company of other people regularly in order to feel energised and connected. Because of this I try to plan my weeks so that I have time for being alone as well as time to be with other people. I have found that while writing provides the solitude I crave, teaching and consultancy provide the lively atmosphere I welcome too.

Email, mobile phones and other labour saving devices in fact only serve to make us busier than ever. It's increasingly difficult to switch off. It is not uncommon for people to receive more than 50 emails a day. Some entrepreneurs receive four times that, and the increase in spam, which you need to look at in order to deal with, can make things worse. So try to discipline yourself. Maybe you could try to answer emails only three times a week, or perhaps to not allow yourself to log on until you have done at least three hours' work? Switch off your mobile phone at weekends or in the evenings. If you're one of those people who always attempts to respond to every message you receive then you'll find your inbox rarely reduces in size as your recipients, in turn, reply to you – even if it's simply a 'thank you'!

> 'It's a fact that the key to successful time management is discipline.'
> Carol, American in Saudi Arabia, *http://delhi4cats.wordpress.com*
> and *www.expatwomen.com*

A DAY BOOK

Not all entrepreneurs use a day book or planner, but many do. When you go to meetings, do you take along a lined note pad? Then, do you have another pad or book by the telephone, and then have another where you jot down leads or ideas? If you're anything like me, you will either rarely get around to sorting out all these pieces of paper, or you will forget where you've put important notes. If, instead, you take to using a large format lined hard backed book, and use this same book for all those notes, ideas and messages, you will find it much easier to trace your movements, find that telephone number or remember what exactly it was that you promised to do at a meeting with a potential client.

A good planner can cover several essential functions. Between two covers it can house monthly, weekly and daily schedules, daily To Do lists, records of each day's significant events, an address book and more.

THE BUSINESS PLAN

One way to determine whether your business idea is practical and exciting for you is to prepare a business plan. Seeing the plan in black and white is often the 'litmus test.' Ask yourself (and ask friends and colleagues, who can often be more objective), 'Now that I have this business all mapped out on paper, am I still excited about it? Would this plan appeal to potential backers? Would I be excited to be a customer of this business? Are there some things I haven't looked at carefully enough? How can I rectify that to the satisfaction of myself, potential backers and customers?'

'But,' you might protest, 'I just want to start a small home based business with no employees and almost no investment. I don't have to prove my credit worthiness to any backers. Why do I need a formal business plan?'

Most people who have started a business, however small and informal, stated later that they wished they had created a formal business plan. With a business plan you ask yourself some very important questions:

- What is my business's mission?
- Who are my primary customers and what are my markets?
- How will I finance my business?
- How will I market and manage my business?
- What are the risks and how can I minimise them?
- How can I keep my business on-track financially?

If you can answer these questions upfront, you'll run into fewer surprises and less trouble later on. And if you decide to expand your business vision, you'll have a basic plan to work with, which can be modified to fit the new realities and plans.

The following are the basic elements of a business plan.

That Mission Statement, again!

You do not need to have a lengthy mission statement in your business plan – but you should, at least, incorporate a short one. In fact, some of the world's largest companies have had very simple mission statements. If Mary Kay, the founder of the successful cosmetic company, can boil her mission down to 'Make people happy', your small business can certainly have a succinct mission statement as well.

A management consultant's mission statement might be: 'To make the workplace more humane for employees at all levels'. A graphic designer might have a mission: 'To provide graphically pleasing, impactful, highly customised marketing pieces at a price below the larger design houses'. You can find out more about writing your own mission statement in *Chapter Two*.

Summary of the Business

This should indeed be a summary: no more than a few paragraphs and perhaps only a sentence. The summary should be easily comprehensible to you and to anyone reading your business plan – especially potential backers.

Legal Form

You should define the legal form that your business will take. You have a number of choices here and will want to choose the one that best fits your circumstances and with which you are the most comfortable. Keep in mind that a business that starts as a simple sole proprietorship may grow and need to 'metamorphose' into a different form. You should be familiar with all these options so you will recognise when your business is ripe for a different legal form. You can find an overview of all the different legal forms at *www.career-in-your-suitcase.com.*

Unique Selling Proposition

This is an important section whether you are marketing your business to potential backers or just firming up its marketability in your own mind. After all, if you can't enumerate why your company is superior to others, why should anyone want your services?

Here you will want to combine optimism with objectivity. Perform an objective review of the competition in your geographic area. Is there a strong need for additional providers of this service or product? Do you contribute a unique spin or variation that no one else has thought of? What are the unique selling points of your product or service?

Management Team

In this section, include the business biographies of you and every member of your management team. Of course, if you are preparing the business plan primarily for yourself and not to sell yourself to investors, this section will be positioned differently. On the other hand, it can serve as a healthy reminder to yourself of just what you have to offer in a crowded, competitive market. If you're using the plan to attract investors (either outsiders or family) be sure to include all the business experience and competencies that would inspire confidence from these investors. You'll find that this segment can also be a confidence booster and ego builder for you; you may find yourself greatly impressed by your own achievements, many of which you won't have given yourself credit for.

Marketing Plan

The plan usually begins with an overview of your industry, the competition and the opportunities for market penetration. In the case of a service like my client Robin's graphic design business, she obtained this information by talking to her employer's customers (diplomatically, of course) as well as freelancers in the industry. Robin also identified her potential customer base – small and medium sized businesses within 20 miles of her home office. She chose her customer base carefully and elected not to travel to the large city an hour away by train because she wanted to remain available to her children. A good marketing plan also addresses how you will publicise and advertise your business. Pricing is another important consideration. In Robin's case, she was able to price herself well below larger graphics houses because of her low expenses. As her business grew and she consistently demonstrated her value-added services, her clients actually encouraged her to raise her prices!

> 'Always have your 'grand to do list' that derives from your own marketing plan. Look at your list before you go to bed, so that when you get up you know you have a plan to work from. You do not have a boss of peers that can motivate you, therefore your motivation has to come from the inside and from your internal drive.'
> **Ursula, South African in America, www.marketingmentorexpert.com and www.expatwomen.com**

Management Plan

This will be very simple if you begin as a sole proprietor and remain this way. But even a partnership begins to need a management plan so that roles and responsibilities are clearly defined; that way there are fewer hard feelings between partners and all tasks are covered.

Depending on the size and structure of your business, the management plan may include employees – their qualifications, compensation, training, benefits and incentives. Regardless of size, you will usually need to identify the outside resources and vendors you will use. In the case of a very small service business, this may just be your friendly neighbourhood 'techie' to help you when something goes wrong with your computer and choosing among the post office, Fed Ex and UPS for delivering packages.

Risks

This is one of the biggest oversights in starting any business. A business plan forces you to address it. If you're using your own money, you want to know the risks of losing some or all of it. And if you are seeking outside funding, your potential investors, whether they are family or outsiders, will demand to know their risks.

Financial Plan

Every business must make money to survive unless your spouse's or family's resources are so great that not making money or even losing a moderate amount of money are plausible options. To make a profit, you've got to have a financial plan. Moreover, this plan must be realistic and you've got to monitor your finances continually to see whether you're on track.

Even the simplest sole proprietorship needs a basic financial plan. What initial expenses will you be incurring? How soon will you be able to pay them off and begin to make a profit? How far will your initial loans go before you have to start using household funds?

If your business idea and form are simple, you may be able to use simple spreadsheets to make your projections. As your business plans get more ambitious and elaborate, you'll want to make use of an accountant or other financial professional. Even in a sole proprietorship, you will probably want to enlist the help of an accountant. Enlisting a few hours of an accountant's services beforehand can save you a lot of headaches later. And in a more complex business with partners, products and/or inventory, formal financial plans become even more important.

A skilled accountant (make sure he or she has experience with small businesses, not just individual tax returns) will probably help you create the following documents:

Balance sheet
This measures your business's assets and liabilities. You will need one if you're applying for a loan at a financial institution, and your family lenders may ask for one if they are financially savvy.

Pro forma profit and loss statement
This is a projection of estimated revenue and expenses. Even if you're not seeking outside funding, this is a good 'think piece' for you and an outside lender will want to see a well prepared one.

Projected cash flow
Business people have a saying: 'cash is king'. You may have wonderful profits on paper but if you run out of cash, you usually are out of business. This is particularly true in a small business which has very little to fall back on. In fact, Ben and Jerry's almost failed in the very beginning when a lack of cash prevented them from paying a major business loan on time.

Speaking of cash, almost every business, no matter how simple, needs some cash to get started. Even if you're like my client Robin, who set up her graphics business in her home, you're still going to need some software packages (both graphics and financial), a juiced-up computer and promotional materials.

There are many sources of cash. However for the start-up business, the most common ones are you, family and friends. There are some very good reasons why outside sources like banks and venture capitalists are less likely to lend you money for your business. The bank is looking for a guarantee that you will be able to pay back the money and may view a business venture by an inexperienced entrepreneur as an unsafe risk. This can be doubly true if you are moving from another location and new to the community. And a venture capitalist is usually looking for a unique business idea that can be leveraged into many times the amount of the initial investment. Many entrepreneurs, like Robin the graphic designer, simply cannot provide this type of leverage – nor is that their goal.

OK, so your dreams of a multimillion-dollar bank loan or venture capital investment just went up in smoke. What are your alternatives?

173

YOUR OWN RESOURCES

You may have enough savings at least to begin your business. You may also have investments that can be cashed in. If their performance has been mediocre or poor, so much the better: it's time you cashed them in anyway. Why not invest in something ultimately more exciting and potentially lucrative - yourself? Cashing in a well performing investment may take a little more courage and vision. Some of this depends on your attitude toward risk and the strength of your desire to start a business.

FAMILY AND FRIENDS

The vast majority of small businesses that need outside funding receive it from this source. However you want to be sure to advise your backers of the realistic risk they are entertaining, and you also want to share with them your business plan so that there are fewer surprises if you run into financial difficulty.

HOME EQUITY

You've probably read dramatic 'success stories' in the business press of entrepreneurs who risked it all by borrowing against their stake in their home. This is usually a last resort. Consult your accountant before taking any step as drastic as this one.

CREDIT CARDS

Credit cards? Sure. If you can buy a boat or charge your groceries, why not help meet business startup expenses on a cash advance from a credit card? This is probably best done if you know your initial cash needs are low and there is little likelihood of their multiplying. There is no reason not to charge $2,000 in computer supplies to your credit cards. But you wouldn't want to charge $25,000 worth of hardware and office equipment, since you'd probably be exhausting the limits of several of your cards and the interest would be huge.

A number of outside resources exist for financing a small business including banks, the Small Business Administration and venture capital firms. Unlike friends, family and yourself, these organisations usually have no intrinsic liking for you nor trust in your ability to manage a business. They will usually put you through a large number of checks and qualifying procedures which could delay your taking advantage of a timely business opportunity or so tire you of the project that you give up. On the other hand, if you have lots of time and persistence and don't mind giving large amounts of qualifying information, these sources may be appropriate for you.

FORMS OF OWNERSHIP

It's a good idea to understand the many forms of business ownership and which one makes the most sense for your business idea. As your business grows, you may wish to switch from one form of ownership to another. The forms your business can take will vary from country to country. In some countries it is easy to be self-employed; in others you need a local sponsor; you could choose to be a sole trader, a partner or run some kind of limited company. It's impossible to list all the different types of business here, but you'll find your local Embassy, Consulate or library will be able to help. You can also find useful information in the Going Global guides. And of course you can consult a local lawyer, or often the overseas section of your bank.

'You can significantly increase the odds of success this year, if you know who you are, what you want, where you are going, how you will get there, and what you will do once you arrive.'
Nigel Risner, *www.nigelrisner.com*

'Having a business plan is essential regardless of the specific nature of the business. It allows one to identify goals and objectives, form a mission and vision statement as well as be used as a reality check to gauge progress.'
Carol, American in Saudi Arabia, *http://delhi4cats.wordpress.com*
and *www.expatwomen.com*

'I think a business plan is often the kiss of death. It's better to have an articulated vision, which outlines what you need to do and go from there. It's a lot more flexible. And, do we really have all that time to evaluate our potential customers and marketing programs? If you're looking for outside financing, well then, go ahead and make the plan.'
Lisa, British in Italy, *http://burntbythetuscansun.blogspot.com*
and *www.expatwomen.com*

MORE BUREAUCRACY

Because this is a general introduction to starting your own business, and not a detailed 'how-to' manual, we'd like to call attention to some other issues that should not be ignored by any prospective self employed person but which can't be treated in detail here.

Legal issues

Your business idea and plan may be simple enough that you don't need the services of a lawyer immediately. However you should be aware of the legal needs of a business such as establishing a legal form and securing any relevant licences and permits. You should also know when you are out of your league or when your business has grown to the point that you do need legal help.

Employees

Perhaps you're a sole proprietor who wants to keep it simple. You may have no plans whatsoever to have any employees, let alone a huge operation. That's exactly how Ben and Jerry started out; you still need to know about employee issues in case your business takes off in a way you never imagined. And if you plan to take on employees, you must consider this in your business plan, even before you establish your business. You will want to attract and retain employees who have the right skills and motivation and who also fit your personality and working style. You also have the opportunity to design a company culture and reward structure that truly motivates your employees.

You may, however, decide not to employ people on a full or part-time basis, and instead, work with freelancers or associates. If you employ freelancers you will pay them an agreed hourly rate or per task. Many small business owners employ a virtual assistant (VA) to do much of their administrative work. When you work with associates you may agree on a commission rate or other method of reward. Commission rates tend to range from 15 per cent to 60 per cent. Perhaps you could work with someone who will do all your marketing and production and decide to share the workload for a 50/50 split. There is no one size fits all approach to this, so our advice is to talk to other people in a similar business and find out what they do. Finally, you could pass work onto third parties in exchange for what is called a finder's fee. This could be a one-off fee or a percentage of the first invoice, perhaps.

Taxes

You will want to enlist the services of an accountant who has experience with the tax needs of a small business. And you'll also want to meet with him or her as you set up the business, not at the end of the tax year when it's too late to develop the proper record keeping system and tax saving measures that you should have been applying from day one.

VAT

In some countries your service may be liable to value added tax, or some other equivalent. VAT is a percentage that must be added to your invoices and it differs from country to country. Not only must you add this to your invoices, but you can claim a rebate for VAT from goods purchased for your business too. In the Netherlands it currently stands at 19 per cent for most products and 6 per cent for others, such as books. Journalists do not need to charge, however. In the UK you have a flat rate of 17.5 per cent regardless of the business. Books, as I said, and children's clothes, do not incur VAT in the UK. You are not automatically liable for VAT and in the UK it is optional until your business has a turnover of more than a certain amount per annum. Once you reach that limit, you must become registered for VAT. In the Netherlands everyone must be registered for VAT.

Market Research

Before you embark on any business it is vital that you do some market research first. You need to know who your competitors might be and how they operate. Once you know your competition you can ensure you price your service appropriately. Further, you can choose whether to offer the same service exactly, the same service, only better in some way or a slightly different service.

Take a look at the competition, or, if there is none, at similar services, and find out what makes them succeed, or fail. Is it because they have a prime location? That they offer out of hours service? That they have cool offices? That their overheads are low? They have great brochures, are cheap or that the boss is a great networker?

You could use the Internet for your research of course, but, if you are starting a small business or have a fairly new idea you may find very little on the Internet. Not everyone has a website nor much of a presence online, Just because you cannot find another 'jewellery-making class' or 'publishing consultant' online in your neighbourhood does not necessarily mean that you will have no competition.

Just because you cannot Google for your competitors this is no excuse not to seek them out. You may need to check the member lists of the networking groups, the professional groups, business groups and Chambers of Commerce. You need to ask people who have been living in your location for a while, your local expat advice service even. Look in the classified advertisements sections of the local papers, magazines, newsletters and free sheets.

If you do find someone else is doing pretty much the same thing you hope to do and, what's more, they live down the street, do not be disheartened. Meet this person. Maybe you will find that actually, you are rather different, or your outlooks, experience or personalities complement each other. Maybe you could join forces? I do not believe that there is always real competition out there and that you should be afraid of it. I believe that there is always room for more. People do business with people they like. People do business with people who are like them. People do business with people they know. Regardless of the proximity of your competition you are bound to have different sets of friends and contacts. As they say, 'keep your friends close and your enemies closer'.

'We had been running an After-School Tuition Centre in the UK for some years and due to a deep personal interest in living in Egypt decided to look at starting a similar project there, primarily aimed at ex-pat families struggling with transitioning to a foreign country with their children. Before even beginning to set up the business however it was vital to analyse what had made the UK enterprise a success, and to evaluate whether the same key aspects would deliver the same results in an entirely different environment.

'It's really important not to assume that your product or service will succeed in a different country just because it did well in your home country. Market research is crucial and it might be necessary to change your business model. Setting up an after-school tuition centre in Egypt required introducing a completely different business strategy, and not taking this into consideration would have meant a much harder struggle.'
Diane, Canadian in England, *www.expatwomen.com*

WHAT TO CHARGE

Whether you are providing a service, product or consultancy you need to employ the same basic rules if you're going to price it correctly.

Find out what other comparable services or products cost, and remember that going rates vary from country to country – and even from county to county. A public relations consultant, for example, may have to charge about two thirds of her London rate to clients in the country.

To find out about going rates or prices, you will probably want to network with business and social contacts in your new area. You can speak to someone who provides similar services or someone you know who has used services similar to yours.

Once you've established the average going rate, you'll want to position yourself within that range. If you're new in town and hungry for new business, you might be tempted to underbid on early projects. However, make sure you state up front that you are offering a discount because you are new to the area – and that rates are subject to change depending on client satisfaction, the demand for your services and other factors.

Where you're producing a product rather than a service, you might like to provide extra benefits, or add-on products, in order to induce people to give your product a try. A buy-one-get-one-free offer often attracts new customers.

If you're charging a fee for your services then you need to think about your daily, hourly, project rates or retainer fee.

Daily Rates

You need to establish in your head a minimum and a maximum daily rate. You'll actually propose a daily rate based on the marketplace in your new area, the size and budget of the client, visibility of the project and other factors. Of course, you may accept a beginning project at slightly below your minimum to help get you started, but try not to make this a habit. And if you're charging by the day, be sure to keep an accurate record of your time so you can document it for the client.

Hourly Rates

An hourly rate can be computed as simply as dividing your daily rate by eight. You'll want to charge an hourly rate if you find that you are putting in 12-hour days every time you visit the client to provide services. Hourly rates can also be used in the initial stages of a project before it becomes a long-term assignment. Generally speaking, an hourly rate connotes less status, so you may want to avoid it for that reason. It also puts too much attention on time spent and not enough on results achieved.

Project Billing

When you need to tailor a proposal to a client's budget, you can bill by the project. You then have the leeway to decide how much time you will spend on each aspect of the project. If the client doesn't demand itemised timekeeping, there's no need for her to know. The higher level the project, the less the client wants to monitor your time and the more appropriate project billing is.

Retainers

You know you've arrived when your client puts you on a retainer. A retainer guarantees you a certain level of billable hours, such as two or three days of work a month. The client is so dependent on your services that she knows she needs to lock in a portion of your billable time on a regular basis. Any retainer arrangement should be clearly spelled out in writing and cover the exact fee, the time commitment and the type of work to be performed. In addition, you should establish a fee for the time that extends beyond the retainer.

> 'I really enjoy teaching people new things and there are always plenty of people on the expatriate circuit desperate to learn from an English speaker in a relaxed environment. I worked out of my home and had two computers so I could teach up to four people at a time. I taught beginners and intermediates about computers, operating systems, word processing, spreadsheets and graphics. I charged a rate that was satisfactory to my users. It took some while to pitch the price correctly I admit. Then the conversion rate kept fluctuating!'
> **Kitty, American in Norway,** *www.career-in-your-suitcase.com*

Marketing Your Business

You may have had the best, most brilliant idea in the world. There is a market for it. Everyone wants one, and it's cheap to make and cheaper to supply. But if you do not tell people about it you may as well not bother.

> 'Everyone has a Terrific Idea, but if you can't get out there and sell it, you might as well stay home and make cookies.'
> **Lisa, British in Italy,** *http://burntbythetuscansun.blogspot.com* and *www.expatwomen.com*

If you are lucky enough to have your target market on your doorstep then you could do very well indeed – providing you get out there and tell people.

When Sue and I published our cookbook, *Dates*, we were living in Muscat, in Oman in the Middle East. Dates were the local, indigenous fruit. They were everywhere, fresh in season, dried when not. On market stalls, in supermarkets and on the trees. They were plentiful and they were cheap. They were nutritious and delicious too. Dates were everywhere but few people knew how versatile they could be in your cookery. We had a target market on our doorstep. The first edition of the book was in Arabic and English, so our market extended from the English speaking expats there to the locals.

The market was easy to target back then too. With only two newspapers and one English radio station, we only needed to make three phone calls in order to ensure the local media interviewed us and ran our story.

Next, we had tee-shirts printed with the words 'Make a Date with the Middle East' and wore them around the city. We asked the local shopping malls (there were only three) if we could stand in their lobbies, handing out bite-sized samples of our food, selling the book and packs of dates and jars of date syrup too. They agreed. We also stood in the school playgrounds, again wearing our tee-shirts, handing out samples and selling books. And we supplied the local bookshops of course.

Finally, we took a stall at the Christmas bazaars and had a big, sponsored launch event at the prestigious Al Bustan Palace Hotel.

With our market on our doorstep it is no surprise that we sold thousands of copies in a short space of time.

Internationally, things were not so straightforward. This was before the Internet so, instead, we wrote articles for international magazines about dates or about our publishing experience and widened our net that way. Nothing, however, could beat the effect of having that market on our doorstep.

Today, ten years later, a second version of *Dates* is being published by Zodiac Publishing and will be available worldwide, including in Harrods in London, where there is a special section devoted to dates.

How well do you know your market? And how easily can you target it?

Every business needs customers and every business needs a marketing plan. It can be simple or complex, largely written or largely intuitive – but you do need one to succeed, even if it's all in your head. (Bill Gates didn't start out with an elaborate marketing plan, but he probably has exceptional brainpower with an ability to store data. And today, even he has a mammoth marketing department.) Here are some ways you can market your business without (yet) developing that mammoth marketing department.

'Never miss a marketing opportunity and use all available avenues. Don't lock yourself inside a box. Use both printed and electronic media. Join groups and organisations that are like-minded, compatible and complementary to your business. Know your competition. Take advantage of any and all networking opportunities. Remember to provide some services *gratis* and consider volunteering for charitable organisations as well. People remember those who take the extra initiatives.'
Carol, American, *http://delhi4cats.wordpress.com* and *www.expatwomen.com*

ATTEND BUSINESS AND PROFESSIONAL MEETINGS

If you are a brochure designer, you will not just want to attend meetings of your own trade association. You'll mostly meet competitors there who, while helpful, are not potential customers. However if you attend advertising or direct marketing association conventions, you'll be a lot more likely to meet potential customers. You might also want to give a talk at one of these conventions, such as 'How to design a truly effective direct mail brochure'. If you don't have enough experience or credentials to speak at a large national meeting, begin your speaking for smaller community and business groups such as Rotary or Lions. They may be small business people like yourself, so they may see you as a colleague. They may also refer you to people they know in large businesses.

ASK FOR REFERRALS

As soon as you have your first successful engagement or product delivery, ask your customer if they will refer and recommend you to others. Ask if you can use their testimonials in your marketing literature.

WRITE ARTICLES OR COLUMNS

Write articles or a regular column for a publication that your potential customers read regularly. An example might be a regional newspaper or a professional journal or newsletter. The articles should show your knowledge of your field and your business savvy. Many small businesses get their first clients in this manner. Don't forget that you can write for websites and free publications too.

ISSUE A PRESS RELEASE

Send a press release announcing the opening of your business to the local paper. A press release is free advertising and lets potential clients know of your existence and the variety of services you offer. Find any excuse to send out a press release to the publications, radio or TV stations that your target market are known to use. If you can find a link between your product, service or recent success and say, Christmas, Valentine's Day, summer holidays, the cold and flu season or whatever do so.

ADVERTISE

You don't need to spend thousands on advertising when you haven't made a penny yet. Put a display advertisement in your local paper. Get your business listed in the Yellow Pages, their website *www.yell.com* or your local equivalent. You can also buy a display advertisement in Yellow Pages type publications as your business grows or as an initial investment in its growth. If your target market is local expat women, then you may be better off advertising in the local school or women's club magazines. Go where you feel you have the best chance of finding potential clients.

NETWORK

Informal networking can be one of the biggest sources of business development. Don't keep your new business venture a secret. As you meet people in your new community (at professional meetings, a synagogue or church, social gatherings) introduce yourself and your new business. The person you're speaking to may not have the need for your services, but could have a colleague or a relative who does. *Chapter Five* is devoted to this subject.

Marketing Materials

Your well-designed brochure and business card can be produced inexpensively (perhaps even on your own computer if you have some talent in this area as well as the right software). They communicate a professional image even if at present you are sharing your home office with your son's gerbil. Business cards can be designed and printed for free at *www.vistaprint.com* providing you leave the back free for the Vistaprint logo.

You will want a logo and business card that fits the character of your business. If you provide accounting services, your card will have a more staid image than if you produce brochures and so on. And, speaking of brochures, you may want to design one of these too. Don't despair if you're not highly artistic. There are a number of easy software programs that can help you create a tri-fold brochure on a piece of A4 or equivalent paper. Special paper can be purchased at a stationery supplier. If you possess absolutely no artistic talent, take your design ideas and copy to your local High Street printing and photocopying shop, where they should be able to help you design the brochure. I usually create a trifold brochure (that's a sheet of A4 folded into three) in Word, and then pay a freelance designer to make it look better. My latest brochures were produced by Vistaprint too, while I had bookmarks made a local copy shop.

You may also want to compose a marketing letter to be mailed with your brochure. In order to really attract attention you could consider finding out more about NLP (neuro-linguistic programming) techniques that draw the reader in. Ian Halsall's book, *NLP 4U* is particularly good for this. And

Gary Courtenay's *How to Write Sales Letters with* Clout is also packed with good tips.

The letter should consist of:

- **Introduction** – who you are and what you are offering in your new community.
- **Attention grabber** – in dramatic fashion, state the problem that your services can solve for the potential client and address the consequences of not solving this problem.
- **Benefits** – describe how your unique expertise can benefit the client and help her solve her problems.
- **Action close** – tell the potential client you will be calling in a few days to follow up. Then do it. Even if the client has no immediate need for your services, she may refer you to a colleague in another department or company. It rarely hurts to mention that you are new to the area and especially eager for a chance to perform your services in this new environment.

Take a look at the home page of many websites and you will see that they too read a bit like a sales letter and draw you in, ending in a call to action, usually, signing up for something. Look at my *www.expatentrepreneurs.com* and Alexandria Brown's *www.ezinequeen.com* for more inspiration and examples.

Marketing On The Internet

Selling your product or services via the Internet can be very effective. Of course, you will need to have a website or a section on someone else's website. But it is no good simply putting up a website or webpage and leaving things to chance. You need to ensure that the search engines can find you, that your site is placed high on the ratings, preferably on the first page.

Today, one of the first things you should do when you are setting up your business is to start a website. After all, what do you do when you want to find out who, say, teaches German in your city, or where you can buy size 9 shoes? You look on the Internet. You too need an Internet presence. At the very least you should have one single page of information and your contact details. But do consider the advantages of having a newsletter sign up form, a blog, lots of articles, links, a shop, your testimonials and free gifts.

First you need to buy a domain name that will be easy for people to remember. You could play safe and simply buy your name. I own *www.joparfitt.com* in addition to my other websites. You can search to see which sites are available at *www.yahoo.com* and also from many other sites including *www.godaddy.com*, which I use. Key in the name you would like and see if it is available. If it is, then great, buy it and then ask a webmaster to help you to move forward with its creation and hosting. Often the domain name will cost just a few dollars. Sometimes, someone else has already had your idea and has bought the domain you want but rather than using it themselves they simply offer it for sale at a higher price. Now it is time to be clever and inventive and devise another domain name you like. Maybe, if .com is not available you could still buy .biz or .co.uk, but generally it is best to buy a .com as this is the suffix most people will guess first.

Unless you have a very popular website, that sees heavy traffic, you are unlikely to be able to sell expensive advertising on your site. However there is much scope for setting up reciprocal links with important sites, and getting publicity for your business on other people's sites. Offering free content on appropriate websites is a good way to get yourself some publicity and a hyperlink that takes people directly to your own site. Google's AdWords service allows you to place adverts on related sites. Search engine optimisation services will help you to appear first on the list after a search by Google, for example.

Paul Herbert of Where On Earth (*www.whereonearthgroup.com*) helps people with search engine optimisation and says that websites act like either 'corks' or 'stones'. The more links you have to sites that have many links of their own, the more like a 'cork' you will be and the further to the top of the ratings you will appear. Additionally, the more pages you have containing the more keywords (the ones that search engines look for), the more 'corklike' you will be. There is plenty of information on this available so study this carefully. Tim Ferris' book The Four Hour Workweek is particularly helpful here, as he explains how to earn lots of money working just four hours a week running an Internet-based business that sells product. Other Internet gurus I have had dealings with are Graham Jones of Infoselling (*www.infoselling.com*) and Tom Antion *www.antion.com*. Graham states on his home page that he learned everything from Tom, by the way.

Depending on what you want your website to achieve you need not spend too much money on your site. However if you don't update content regularly you will find the number of visitors may decrease. This incurs ongoing maintenance costs, unless you choose to learn how to do it yourself. There are plenty of programs that allow you to update your own websites these days, many of which are Open Source (free). If you decide to run a blog (web log, which is a kind of online diary and available from many places including WordPress *www.wordpress.com* and Blogger www.blogger.com amongst others) and keep it active this will ensure you have new content on a regular basis. Incorporate your blog into your website for the best results.

Maybe you simply want your website to be a brochure online. And indeed, no self-respecting business should omit the value of having a website of some kind, however small. But if you want to sell goods and need a shopping cart and payment facility, search options, hundreds of pages of content and a sophisticated site it can cost considerably more.

Consider inviting visitors to register their name with you so you can send them a regular electronic newsletter or ezine, as is done on www.expatrollercoaster.com, www.thebookcooks.com and www.career-in-your-suitcase.com as well as many other websites.

If you find it hard to encourage people to advertise on your site, think about setting up affiliations with other sites and receive commission on sales resulting from all business that reached the affiliate's site from yours. www.amazon.com offers such a programme.

A website is very versatile and much can be sold or promoted through it. Artists can sell their creative work, publicise their exhibitions or advertise seminars. You can buy just about anything on the Internet these days. You can also find freelance staff to work for you. You can advertise your services, source clients, information or staff. The channels for selling are multiplying almost as fast as the Internet itself.

Brand You

The business world is very competitive and to be successful you need to be able to market and sell yourself. One way to do this is to think of yourself as a brand – Brand You – and do all the things successful brands do.

So how do you go about establishing yourself as a brand? The first step is to establish what type of person you want to be and hence what type of person you want others to know that you are and/or that you are capable of being.

Mary Spillane, in her book *Branding Yourself*, suggests that Brand You is a combination of three factors – your assets, your values and your image. We will look at each area in detail so that you can create your own brand statement identifying who you are, the essence of your achievements and what you have to offer. Before that however, let's examine the characteristics and activities of successful brands so you can learn and use these to your benefit when creating Brand You.

CHARACTERISTICS OF A SUCCESSFUL BRAND

Listed below are some of the characteristics of successful brands and how you can apply these to building your own brand:

- **Be congruent and have integrity** – how you look, act and talk must be in line with your values; people are quick to sense when you are not being congruent. You may dress better, talk better and fool people in the short term – but ultimately if you are not true to yourself it will show.
- **Show yourself in the best light and appeal to all the senses** – you have 30 seconds to make an impression – research has shown that only seven per cent of our impact comes from words, 38 per cent is judged on how we sound and 55 per cent on our appearance and how we behave.

- **Adapt to the times without sacrificing your identity** – you must keep reassessing your skills to make sure they are relevant to the market place – but not at the cost of sacrificing your values.
- **Be easy to find** – don't expect a job or business to come looking for you. Make sure you get your CV or your product/service details out to as many potential customers as possible. Have a business name that does not confuse people.
- **Be easy to understand** – be clear about who you are, what you do, what you stand for and what you offer. Simplify your message and focus/highlight your core strengths/features so as to be able to drive it into the minds of potential customers.
- **Stand out from the crowd** – distinguish yourself from the rest, sell your uniqueness, what you do best, and capitalise on the differences.
- **Meet market demands** – there's no point having a great product, service or skill if people don't need it. That is not to say you can't identify or even create a need.
- **Reduce perceived risk** – the simpler it is for people to understand what it is that you offer, the easier it becomes for them to decide whether they want it or not. If you're a known quantity with a good or trustworthy reputation then people will find it easier to buy you.
- **Provide value and satisfy needs** – unless you provide a real benefit for the employer/purchaser there will be no need to buy 'you'. Make sure you add value.
- **Think global** – think global but act local; bear in mind cultural differences. This is sometimes called 'glocalisation'.
- **Remember psychological rewards** – try and define what psychological benefit people will get as a result of hiring/buying you, and play on that.

Some sample activities of some great brands

Brands spend a lot of time and money undertaking a number of activities in order to launch, establish and sustain themselves, such as:

- **Vision** – begin with the end in mind – determine what business you are in, what your offering is and what you are working towards in the long term.
- **Market analysis** – unless you know what the market needs/wants and what the competition is doing, you are, in effect, shooting in the dark. Start out by looking at the political situation, the economic climate, finding out what advances or changes there are in technology and any social trends. This may give you an insight into possible gaps and opportunities. Consider the 'barriers to entry' in your market, the threats, potential new entrants, what buyers require, the nature of your competition and what it offers, and other possible substitute products/services.

- **Constantly reassess your values and identity to make sure they are still relevant to the market** – Do a SWOT analysis- (see *Chapter Four*) – make a list of your Strengths and Weaknesses and market Opportunities and Threats. From this, determine whether what you are offering is still relevant and if any changes are required. Check that this is in line with your values and your vision.
- **Invest in research and development, reinvent yourself and introduce improvements** – companies no longer manage our careers for us, so it is up to you to develop yourself and add new skills. Make yourself a lifelong learner.
- **Market yourself** – even if you are employed keep your ears to the ground and promote, advertise and sell yourself and **your** services. This is even more applicable when you are in a new market.
- **Take advantage of opportunities** – network, be proactive, take opportunities as they arise, make things happen.

ASSETS

You need to establish what makes you special. Value your background, your achievements and your capabilities. To determine your assets make a list of your skills, your education and your experience. Highlight your achievements, focusing on things that differentiate you and in particular in three keys areas – where you have saved money, made money and saved time.

Chapter Three concentrates on analysing your assets, but it's worth noting again that we easily discount our own key strengths simply because they come naturally.

VALUES

Again, values are covered in earlier chapters – but it's worth reiterating that only by knowing, understanding and living your values can you create your life's direction and ultimate destination. It is vital that you define your values, for they are your foundation.

IMAGE

As I said previously, you have 30 seconds to make an impression and 93 per cent of what you will be judged on has nothing to do with what you say. You need to be analytical and establish how you are going to live your brand. What image do you want to project? What should your voice sound like, what kind of appearance is suitable? How are you going to manage yourself, and how will you conduct yourself?

Remember that whatever you are feeling you will project. If you are feeling negative or lacking in confidence people will sense this. Try to visualise how you would like to act. Think of a time when you were successful. What were you wearing? How did you present yourself? What made you different that day? Get yourself into a positive frame of mind, think about what your body posture would be like and then adopt that pose. Your physical state has a great influence on your mind. It's more difficult to feel down if you get your body into a 'positive' posture. How would you be if you were feeling happy and successful? Your head would be held up high, you would have a smile on your face, your eyes would be bright and shiny, your body erect and so on.

Try completing the exercise below and take action on those areas that need more work.

LOOK

Values I want to project	Already convey	Need work on looking more

SOUND

Values I want to project	Already sound	Need work on sounding more

BEHAVE

Values I want to project	Already behave	Need work on behaving more

FEEL

Values I want to project	Already feel	Need work on feeling more

Another exercise to do is the Johari Window, an example of which is below, which is featured in Spillane's *Branding Yourself*. This is useful for coming to terms with yourself and discovering inconsistencies in your personality, behaviour and perception. It allows you to recognise yourself more honestly and discover if you are sending out conflicting messages.

When you are communicating one on one with someone else, consider that there are in effect six 'people' present. You are simultaneously the person you think you are, the person you are giving the impression of being, and the real you. And the same applies to the person with whom you are communicating. Ask a friend to help you with this so that she can help you identify any blind spots you may have about yourself. Use this exercise to identify any gaps and find out what may be holding you back.

Public self	Blind spots
What am I happy to share with people?	What things don't I see?
Private self	Unknown self
Dreams & aspirations – what I know about myself but only share with nearest and dearest. What do I want to be?	What you don't know about yourself – your potential

FOCUS ON SOLUTIONS

Now that you have examined who you are and what you're capable of being, you are able to create your own brand statement that identifies who you are, the essence of your achievements and what you have to offer. Once that's completed you should set some strategies on how you are going to get to where you want to be. Be aware of which elements need to stay and which must be jettisoned from your life. Be honest about what you really want rather than simply doing what you or others think you should be doing.

Ask yourself:

- What can I do to improve?
- What do I need to know?
- What can you learn from what has already happened?
- What will get me what I want?
- What actions can I take right now to move me in the right direction?

Later in this chapter you will find out how you can set goals in the light of these five questions.

Making It Happen

So, you have found your passion, analysed your skills and assets, devised the perfect portable career that will work in your current location, decided to run your own business, set it up as a legal entity, organised your work space, put together your business plan and marketing plan and formulated a winning brand. Well done! Now what?

In the rest of this chapter we cover just a few more things that can help you to make your dreams a reality.

WORK FOR FREE

What? Work for free? You have put in all this hard work and now I'm suggesting you do it for nothing? Well, yes. Something like that.

Just as a new journalist finds it hard to find paid work until he or she has been published already – but finds the only way to build that vital portfolio of clippings is to write that first few articles for publications that do not pay – you too may find that you need to follow similar principles.

The best way to persuade strangers to buy your services or products is to show them testimonials from past, satisfied customers. But, until you have some customers how can you get hold of those testimonials?

Offer to work for the first few clients either free of charge, or at a substantial discount on the understanding that they will provide you with a testimonial. Easy.

I have employed this method many times. When I am trying out a new course, I will usually offer it at half price to students the first time. I explain that they get a special price but that I would like their honest feedback on the course and a testimonial in exchange.

Sometimes I give students free places on my courses even though they are established and successful. I do this for several reasons. One is that I like to mentor new writers and allowing those who cannot afford to pay to attend my classes free of charge is one way that I can help them. Often I ask them to provide or help serve the refreshments in exchange. Sometimes I ask them to help me in my other work, doing some proof reading or research for example.

A benefit of giving away one free place to each workshop is that my classes are always full, the interaction among students is better and, after the course, I have an extra testimonial and one more person who will refer me to other clients, who, hopefully, will be able to pay.

'In the beginning it was very difficult to find paid work when I first arrived to Saudi Arabia. I am fortunate to have had diverse experiences and skills, which are in demand so receiving calls and being asked for interviews was not a problem. However it is fairly typical in Saudi Arabia to request a prospective employee to first work on a trial basis to better allow the employer to gauge the skills, expertise and "fit" of the candidate into the organisation. This seems to be especially true when the candidate is a woman and looking for work, which is outside the traditional occupations woman generally hold in the Kingdom such as teachers, women's banks or at a hospital. Initially I "went with the flow" and performed services such as marketing analysis, risk assessments and custom curriculum design that I would have typically charged several thousands of dollars for my work. After two specific instances where, after performing work I was told I would be contacted if needed for future opportunities, I began to realise that I did not have to "go with the flow" and learned the hard way to never feel I needed to undersell myself or my qualifications.'
Carol, American, *http://delhi4cats.wordpress.com* and *www.expatwomen.com*

'I believe strongly that you should do things for free. I also treat some people for free if I know they can't afford it. An open hand both gives and receives therapy.'
Angelika, German in Norway, *www.career-in-your-suitcase.com*

LEARN THE LANGUAGE

One thing that you can do to really set you ahead of the game is to learn the local language.

Culture and language are inseparable. The key to understanding most cultures, in fact, lies in the languages spoken there. The standard greeting in most Asian countries is 'have you eaten rice yet?' What does this tell you about the importance of food in these cultures? Yet, strangely, many expatriates will decide learning the local language is unnecessary, too much work, impossible, or all three and not attempt it.

Career Your Suitcase contributor Mary van der Boon has lived and worked in six different countries, and speaks the languages of all of them.

'I do not consider myself gifted linguistically,' she says, 'but I am both motivated and stubborn. And as a media addict, I could not conceive of living happily in a place where I couldn't even read the local newspaper. I'm also convinced that forcing everyone in your vicinity to speak your language raises an insurmountable barrier between you and your new neighbours, colleagues and so on, and that you will never truly feel at home. And a final motivator: cultural experts have proven that being surrounded by an unfamiliar language for a long period of time almost always leads to alienation, paranoia and culture shock. Yes, perhaps you are the topic of conversation in the market when everyone suddenly bursts into riotous laughter – but wouldn't you rather know for certain? And wouldn't you rather be able to laugh along with them?'

Learning Styles

Not everyone learns the same way, so perhaps the first step in learning a language (or anything else, for that matter) is determining which type of learner you are. This can also be a very valuable tool in helping to decide which career path to follow. Harvard professor Dr Howard Gardner (*www.howardgardner.com*) has identified eight distinct learning styles (which he recommends should replace standard IQ testing, since they have such impact on how we gather and retain knowledge. Author and child development specialist Diane Schilling too matches your preferred style of learning with studying a foreign language.

An online test to find out what type of learner you are is available on *www.agelesslearner.com*, learning expert Marcia L Conner's excellent website which also offers free online assessments for motivation and engagement.

Learning styles could be:

- If you like words you may work best from books and audiotapes.
- If you are logical and like numbers, you may enjoy learning rules, grammar and linguistics best.
- If you are visual then you might be best learning from a course that is highly illustrated or from videos.
- Intuitive, 'feeling' types, may work best from total immersion courses or from living in the home of a native speaker for a while.
- Extroverts may like the interactive atmosphere of a classroom.
- Introverts may prefer self-study.
- Music lovers may like to learn through the music of a language, listening to songs, perhaps.
- And many may like to explore superlearning techniques, sometimes called accelerated learning or effective learning, for which you listen to music of 60 beats per minute while absorbing the language, aurally.

Whichever course of study suits your style, don't be dissuaded by the inevitable naysayers around you. Imagine how you would feel if you had been living in a foreign country for five years and were still unable to speak the language, only to see Jane-Just-Come (that's you) blithely master the tongue in months?

'When I moved to Beijing with my husband and my two kids, I thought that finding a job in China - land of opportunities - should be no problem. After all, I had 7 years work experience as a UK chartered accountant and had worked in Paris, London and Zurich in prestigious companies. But I soon realised after our move that Beijing was already flooded with local, BILINGUAL number crunchers. When I was telling recruitment companies that I could speak French, German and English but not Mandarin, they used to tell me "Poor you, we are really sorry, but you have really NO chance. Learn Mandarin for 1 year and then come back to us".'
Jasmine, French in China, www.inspiredbeijing.com and www.expatwomen.com

'Naturally without having fluency in the Arabic language results in communication gaps and loss of revenue. In my capacity as a founding partner of Global Watchers Arabia the focus at present is predominantly on the expat community within Saudi Arabia and clients from the rest of the English-speaking world [...] any business with a Saudi company requires discussions and written communication in Arabic, especially in regards to legal documents and contracts. Therefore to pursue and interact with Saudi clients results in GWA having to engage fee-for-task consultants who are native Arabic speakers to represent GWA with non-English speaking clients.'
Carol, American, http://delhi4cats.wordpress.com and www.expatwomen.com

'I was not as expressive in English as in Afrikaans. I couldn't make fast progress in my career, because I couldn't express myself well. Business language in South Africa is different than in the United States.'
Ursula, South African in America, www.marketingmentorexpert.com and www.expatwomen.com

'I spoke the language, but, if you don't want to end up as a secretary for some export office, it's best to learn the language. Take an intensive course. This is your greatest tool in getting the job you want. Not knowing the language means you will always have a problem inserting yourself in a local company.'
Lisa, British in Italy, http://burntbythetuscansun.blogspot.com and www.expatwomen.com

GOAL SETTING

Anthony Robbins, author of *Unlimited Power*, says, 'The greatest achievers in the world all started by setting a goal.'

Goals are what motivate us and give purpose to our life.

Would you build a jigsaw without seeing the picture or drive off somewhere unknown without first looking at a map? So why do many of us live life without having a plan?

Numerous research studies have found that people who have achieved success in many walks of life have precisely written goals. One piece of research was carried out on Yale University graduates in the United States. The graduates were surveyed prior to graduation and then again 20 years later. It was found that three per cent were worth more in terms of wealth than the other 97 per cent put together. This three per cent also had better health and enjoyed better relationships with others. The difference was not due to parental wealth, subjects studied, ethnic or gender base but it was found to be that this small minority had written goals when they graduated – unlike the huge majority who did not.

The reason that most people do not set goals or follow through with achieving them is because they think they will fail. They don't realise that progress towards a goal can only be made one step at a time. Each little success will provide a boost of confidence and a sense of accomplishment that will help to keep you motivated.

For example, if you wanted to write a 300-page book but had never written anything of significant length before, the task would be daunting. However, if you were to write two pages a day for 150 days the goal would seem much more realistic and achievable.

First, find your mission

It's not enough simply to know that you have goals; they need to be written down and clearly thought out. Stephen Covey is another one who recommends identifying your mission statement as a starting point. Covey is perhaps best known for his book, *The Seven Habits of Highly Effective People*, in which he suggests that we 'begin with the end in mind'. He recommends developing a personal mission statement as it focuses you on what you want to be and do, based on your values. He compares the process to the construction of a house: no one would start building without first having a design and construction plans. Use the carpenter's rule: 'measure twice and cut once'. Begin with the end in mind – clearly define what you want beforehand.

A mission statement isn't something that you write overnight. It takes careful analysis and deep introspection and could take several weeks or months to get it to be a complete concise expression of your innermost values and directions. You may continue needing to review it regularly and make changes as required, depending on your experiences and circumstances. There are ideas about writing your mission statement in *Chapter Two*.

Once you have that vision and have established your values, you have the basis upon which to set long and short-term goals. Having a vision/mission allows you to judge every major decision you make and prioritise your activities according to what is important – hence making more effective use of your time and energies.

Second, determine what you want

To decide what it is that you want, set aside some time and start to dream. Focus on what you want, not what you think you should/ought to/must want. Ask yourself: if you knew you couldn't fail what would you do? Make a list of all the things you want without limitations.

Determine the reasons why you want what you want. If they are big and compelling enough you will always figure out how to achieve them. As Daniel Burnham said: 'Make no little plans – they have no magic to stir your blood to action. Make big plans, aim high in work and hope.'

Goals need to happen in our minds before they happen in reality. The unconscious mind does not differentiate between what is imagined and what is real. The brain always strives to help us achieve what we focus on, so make sure you focus on what you want and not on what you do not want.

All things are created twice; first there is the mental vision and then the physical creation. If you think about what you want to achieve and visualise it, and then you write it down, you will have created the goal twice. When the goal is achieved, you will have created it three times.

Third, set your goals

Start by planning three-year goals and then work backwards for one year, six months and three months. Your goals need to be SMART, which stands for Specific, Measurable, Achievable, Relevant and Timed:

- Specific – What exactly is it that you want to achieve? State this in the positive, present tense.
- Measurable – How will you measure the achievement of the goal? How will you feel? What will have to happen for you to know that you have achieved it?
- Achievable – Ensure the goal is realistic. Make sure that you are not reliant on others in order to achieve it.
- Relevant – Is the goal worthwhile? Is it initiated and maintained by you?
- Timed – Decide on a time frame. Specify the date/time when you intend achieving your goal

Start by making a step-by-step plan. NLP suggests that you establish your goal into a well-formed outcome, as explained below:

Define precisely what it is that you want

If you want to make more money, state exactly how much money you wish to earn. What will achieving your goal do for you? Is the goal in keeping with your values? Consider whether it meets your higher purpose. Ask yourself what is important in achieving this goal. Supposing your goal was to make a certain amount of money, you may want to quantify exactly what that would do for you? Keep 'chunking up' (moving up a level) until you get to the meaning of the outcome. For example, your first answer might be that it would allow you to buy your own home, so what would that do for you? It might mean being able to get married. And what would that do for you? It might bring you happiness.

How you are going to achieve it?

Break it down into smaller sub goals. So, for example, if you want to produce a brochure, your sub goals could be to research other brochures, to find a designer, to write the text, ask someone to edit the text, get printers' quotes, find the capital to pay for it and so on. Remember to celebrate every win.

Can you start and maintain this outcome?

Does your outcome depend on others responding or being there? Charles Handy in his book Waiting for the Mountain to Move describes a traveller who, having travelled around the world, comes to a road and sees a mountain blocking the way ahead. The traveller sits down and waits for the mountain to move. Likewise, if your goals are not self-maintained you may find yourself waiting for the mountain to move.

How will you know when you have got it?

What will it feel like? Describe the emotions you expect to feel. What will you hear? Will you hear people congratulating you and if so what will they be saying? What will your success look like? What will be happening when you achieve your goals, where will you be, who else will be there? The more vivid you are in making the picture and including all the senses, the more realistic and achievable the goal becomes. Remember what I said earlier: your unconscious mind does not know the difference between imaginary and real. Visualisation is something we all do, but we don't do it regularly enough. The more vividly you can imagine the outcome the more your unconscious mind believes it has already happened. You need to ensure you include the sound and feeling too. Then you will begin to feel as if you have achieved your goal and you will start to act as if you have - resulting in the likelihood that you will achieve it. Successful people and athletes spend a lot of time imagining themselves winning.

When do you expect to achieve the outcome?

Set a date/time by when you intend to achieve your outcome. Don't just say 'in June', say 'June 25th'.

Is your goal challenging and stretching?

Your goal needs to be challenging and compelling in order to motivate you to take action. If it is not challenging you may not feel inclined to accomplish it.

Is it worth what it will take?

Is your goal desirable enough? Does it motivate and compel you to action? Is it worth the cost and the time?

What does your current state do for you?

We all get some kind of benefit from our current state otherwise we would not bother to maintain it. Imagine you were a smoker. By smoking at work you would probably get a few minutes' break and the opportunity to chat with colleagues. It's important to consider these needs and imagine, if you decided to become a non-smoker, whether you would want to maintain or challenge the need for a break and social contact in another way.

And finally, take action

Break your goals into smaller sub goals and set a date by which you will have achieved each one of the steps.

So what action needs to be taken? If you don't know, then find someone who does and either ask them or use them as a role model. Work backwards until you find something that you could do right now to help you achieve your goal. You don't need to know each of the steps to take but at least set the first few. The outcome is that you will be started on your path to achieving your goal. Anthony Robbins suggests that once you have decided on your goal you need to take immediate action. As they say, 'Strike while the iron is hot'.

You should regularly review your goals, at least once a week, if not daily. Try to think and to visualise your goal at least once a day and it will be come more real and compelling to you. It will feel as if you are on the road to achievement rather than a dream for the future. The goal that you set yourself may change as you go. That's fine. It's like flying a plane; you adjust course according to the wind and weather conditions to keep yourself on track.

I have found that keeping a diary or log sheet and spending a few minutes at the end of each day to review my progress really helps to keep me on track. Not only does it highlight what work still remains to be done – more importantly, it highlights what I have not done. So often we are not aware of the progress we have made and as a result we discount our accomplishments. Remember to celebrate each of your wins! The difference between success and failure is perseverance. Just keep at it, be flexible, see what you are doing, and modify your actions as needed. Keep taking action. Good luck!

'It's easy to get overwhelmed by the big picture. The way that works best for me is breaking a large goal down to smaller more manageable chunks. Like if you need to lose 10lb and you say instead that you'll lose 1lb a week for ten weeks – it's much more do-able. Translated into business goals, I start with a sheet of paper and brainstorm all the elements of the particular project. Then I prioritise them into a timeline to visually show what has to be done by when. Then each step is broken down into mini-brainstorms and lists of tasks. This was the way we worked when we were setting up the business. Nowadays it is less necessary as the pressure has reduced somewhat.'
Diane, Canadian in England, *www.expatwomen.com*

'[I believe in] making plans, which set goals and objectives to be achieved within specified time periods. As an example, I may decide that within one month I will initiate 8 new contacts or attend 5 networking events with the goal to expand my network of contacts at a factor of "x" per function. I do the same in business by setting a realistic goal although one that will also stretch me.'
Carol, American in Saudi Arabia, *http://delhi4cats.wordpress.com*

'I work with a team that is scattered at the four corners of the world and there are moments where losing the plot is too easy. A way to gather momentum and spring forward is achieved by setting short term targets, where everyone has to pitch in, in order to complete a goal. The breaking down of any objective in digestible pieces is for us all the key to overcome the discouragement that might set in when you look how distant in the future is the achieving of your goal. A concept based on the old Chinese saying "even the hardest journey begins with a small step".'
Patrizia, Italian in France, *www.paguro.net*

'What we get in life is a result of the choices we make and the actions that we take on a day-to-day basis. Hence, I achieve goals by identifying, prioritizing, scheduling and doing my best to stick to that schedule. I adjust my schedule as needed and incorporate as many things as I need to keep me on track and motivated. I keep enough flexibility in my schedule to allow for "life to happen" (I do live in Italy and so the idea of time can be relative!)'
Megan, American in Italy, *www.careerbychoice.com*

'The first week of each year, I look back at the last year and think of situations both good and bad and decide how to handle future dilemmas. Then I set my goals, personal, work and spiritual.'
Lizzy, British in America, *www.expatwomen.com*

'I really struggled giving up my work, identity and financial independence in Shanghai to move to Russia with my boyfriend. I suddenly became a 'nobody' in a very small expat community and a very undynamic city, which was a very big blow to my self-esteem and my motivation. I decided I needed to feel like I achieved something at the end of each day, no matter how small and so started writing a list of things I would do tomorrow – things as simple as do the washing, buy dinner (a challenge in Russia!!), read another chapter of my book, go for a walk and file the credit card statements, but at the end of the day I could tick those off which made me feel in control of something and that I too achieved something today. Three years later and I feel much more confident and in control of who I am (an extremely steep learning curve that a job does not define who I am), but I still plan what I'm going to achieve tomorrow, the night before.'
Victoria, New Zealander, now in India, *www.expatwomen.com*

TEAMWORK

If you move frequently, as I do, then one of the hardest things about running your own business will be the fact that you have to keep starting again in a new place, and that you have to do so alone. We have already talked about motivation, and indeed, it can be really tough finding the motivation to keep going and to make things happen when you are uprooted for the umpteenth time.

Maybe finding someone else to work with would make things easier for you? In Oman, I wrote and published *Dates* with a friend, Sue Valentine. She is a food scientist with a love of photography, as well as a great cook, and so she was the perfect teammate. Working with Sue meant that I was answerable to someone with whom I had shared goals and deadlines. Not only did I have someone with whom I could discuss the project, and who shared my passion for it, but I had someone with whom I could share the workload. This was invaluable. I have co-authored since then too. In 2002 I wrote *Grow Your Own Networks* with Jacqui Tillyard. We came up with the ideas together. I wrote it but she proof-read it and her husband designed the cover. What I have learned from co-authoring is that sharing a byline does not reduce my reputation as a writer at all. Instead, it gave both Jacqui and myself a high profile as networkers and a boost to our careers.

In Dubai, when I worked at the recruitment agency, running a computer training department, having an alliance with the agency was mutually beneficial. Just as their clients became my clients, mine became theirs.

During the last 20 years I have often partnered with others on a project-by-project basis. I have run workshops jointly with others. This has many benefits. Not only does it mean that I share the work and the preparation time but it means that while I market to my network my co-trainer markets to hers, and in this way we double our potential client base. Of course, it means we share the income too, but in my opinion the benefits outweigh the disadvantages.

8 working from home

Many people who choose to create a portable career decide to run their own business, and ultimately to work from home. This chapter explains.

'*May your dreams defy the laws of gravity.* '

H Jackson Brown Jnr

In this chapter:
- Working from home
- The work life balance
- Stress busting
- Staying motivated

Working From Home

With the home-based business, you have the perfect opportunity to set up the exact environment with all the right business tools at your disposal. With today's technology, a highly technical home office operation can be set up at relatively low cost. And if you are a transferee, you have the added advantage of starting from scratch. These things are all possible, but they don't just fall into place automatically. To start any successful business, you need to plan. And you need to think particularly about how you will balance the priorities of home and family without each one intruding on the other or suffering in some way.

One advantage of commuting to an office is that there's a natural separation between the 'working' you and the 'family' you, with some transition time in the car or train to change roles. In the home-based business, you have to work harder to delineate and differentiate these roles – but it can be done and the work/family balance can be significantly enhanced. So it's important to create a working environment for yourself that will make you feel professional and that will help you switch roles easily.

You can start thinking about what you want in your home office before you even arrive at a new location. What follows are just a few helpful hints.

SPACE PLANNING

Because you're relocating, you have a golden opportunity to select your new home and plan the space in it to best accommodate your new business. You don't necessarily need a separate, private, room, but this is usually a good idea. If such a room is impractical logistically or financially, you can make double duty use of an existing room or space – or use alcoves, garages or even a shed. Of course, the space must meet the needs of your business and be a reasonably pleasant environment for working in. Many people turn a built in wardrobe in a bedroom into a hidden workstation.

A spare bedroom or family room is often a good place to start your home business. Keep in mind, though, that you may want to put up overnight guests in these spaces, so the business should be reasonably self-contained and its boundaries explained and delineated to any overnight guest. You may also be planning to have more children; consider where you would put your business if this took place.

If you plan to use your living room as office space, you may want to use a screen or other barrier to separate the living space from the working space. And you'll probably have to clean the house more frequently if you will be entertaining business visitors.

The family room might be a good place for your business, especially if it isn't used for too many things already. But some family rooms lack privacy (such as doors) and if they also contain the TV, computer and toys, you may be constantly interrupted and your home office may not be taken seriously.

The bedroom is often the least appropriate place to set up a home business. Bedrooms are traditionally for other activities, such as sleeping and personal intimacy. Setting up your business in this space can easily have a harmful effect on your relationship with your partner. If you absolutely must set up shop here, establish some kind of physical barrier between the work and living space. Arrange times when you absolutely are off duty and the business cannot intrude on your personal life.

Basements, garages, lofts and other such places can lend themselves well to starting your own business. Because these spaces weren't set up originally for this purpose, you may have to do a little creative remodelling, but it does not necessarily have to be extensive.

A key in planning your space is to ask yourself: 'Will I feel comfortable here?' 'Will I feel professional here?' And perhaps most importantly, 'Is this space set up so that my work and family environments are appropriately contiguous and separate?' You need to be able to keep your eye on pets and children if necessary, but you also need to have privacy to devote full attention to the business.

FURNITURE AND EQUIPMENT

As I mentioned earlier, this is your opportunity to furnish the workspace exactly to your requirements and taste. If you like, and your budget allows, you can set up a streamlined and beautiful home office. But if you're like most of us, you will want to set up a comfortable, functional (not necessarily elegant) space that supports the needs of your business and supplies a pleasant working environment that you enjoy entering every day.

Perhaps most important are a desk and chair. With all the technical advances in office technology, most of us still spend most of our time at a desk sitting in a chair. You don't need to spend $1,000 on your chair (and you may already possess an appropriate one) but it should be comfortable and well matched to your desk and the configuration and height of your computer equipment.

Make sure your work area is well lit. If the overhead lighting is poor, invest in some recessed, fluorescent or track lighting or buy a good quality desk lamp. Make sure that your office space looks inviting and professional. After all, you will be spending a lot of time in it.

Look at your existing furniture to see how it can be used for the storage and organisational needs of your business. Will it serve the purpose? And will it make you look and feel professional? A 30 year-old filing cabinet with a rusted-out bottom may not fit the bill. You may want to invest in a new cabinet that meets the needs of your particular business and shelving that is pleasant in appearance and gives you organised, easy access to your records and materials.

A tremendous benefit of the home office is your ability to control factors such as noise, temperature and humidity. For instance, you may want to relocate your stereo to be near your home office space. You can decide if you want a screen, sliding door or regular hinged door to define your space and provide the right amount of privacy. You can have bare floors for the clean look, wall-to-wall carpeting for subdued sound and the elegant look or area rugs for a more casual atmosphere.

YOUR COMPUTER

The computer and other office equipment must also be customised to your space and business requirements. Not every office needs every piece of equipment (for instance, a graphics studio needs a state-of-the-art printer to produce camera ready work, whereas an accounting service does not need a highly artistic presentation of ledgers and bills). Because every home office is different and office equipment is so highly technical, we'll give you a broad overview here rather than a detailed technical explanation of every piece of equipment.

An answering machine may be enough when you start your home business. However, as your business grows, you may want to consider voice mail. Many home business owners find it more professional and it allows them the ability to leave instructions for how to order products or describe services or products.

An answering service may also be helpful, particularly if you receive calls of an urgent or emergency nature during non business hours.

To separate the business and the personal, it's a good idea to have a separate line for your business. It makes a difference if the message on your business answerphone is a professional one.

These days fewer businesses have a fax machine, though it is undoubtedly still useful. Many PCs can operate with a multifunction printer to scan and fax items, and of course, thanks to the Portable Document Format (PDF) and broadband many documents can be emailed. Large documents may need to be 'zipped' (try Aladdin Stuffit) in order to be sent, but even the largest of all can be transmitted using intermediary sites such as *www.sendthisfile.com*.

No home-based business can exist today without a computer. You'll want to buy one that has enough storage, speed and other capabilities to meet the needs of your business. You may already own such a machine – but if the rest of the family already uses it, you should consider purchasing another one. If your family likes to use the Internet during the evening, and you need to work late, then you may also need to consider broadband or a second phone line for that reason.

When purchasing a computer, keep in mind both the present and future uses to which it will be put. When you buy a three year old his first bed, you can't plan on him staying the same size for the next 15 years – and you can't assume your business will stay the same size either. A computer should be able to accommodate the projected needs of your business, not just the current ones.

Technical support will be particularly important to you as you set up your new business. If you worked for a corporation, technical support was right down the hall in the IT department. Now you need to find your own reliable resources or your business can go on hold until the problem is fixed. When purchasing equipment, make sure the company has a reputation for skilled, local, round the clock technical support.

You will also need software to support your business. Consult others who have set up small and home-based businesses (as well as your retail outlet) to find out about user friendly packages. If you are a speciality business, such as graphic design, you will need to network with specialists in your area regarding the latest technical developments. For basic business programs, speak to people in both large and small business environments.

All small businesses need a word processing program such as Microsoft Word. You may also need a presentation program such as PowerPoint and a spreadsheet program such as Excel. These are conveniently packaged together into a package of programs called Microsoft Office. You may also want financial software to write your cheques, keep basic financial records and perform basic accounting. You may even link a tax preparation program to your financial software. A contact database can be very handy in managing current clients and keeping track of potential clients. It is always advisable to use standard, popular software, so that any files you transmit can be read easily by their recipients. Today, there will be very few problems communicating between PCs and Apples. I use both.

If you choose to buy a laptop rather than a desktop computer be aware that the keyboard may be smaller than standard and the mouse may be incorporated into it. I find these hard to operate and, as I have Repetitive Strain Injury (RSI) in my right arm from too much typing I have attached an external ergonomic keyboard to my Apple laptop for many years. More recently I purchased a pen mouse and ergonomic keyboard, which are less painful for RSI sufferers. My laptop is a godsend for when I travel, and as it has a wireless card I can pick up emails from hotel rooms and when abroad. However, back home, I hook up to all my external equipment as well as a much larger flat screen, which is better for my eyes.

Printer, scanner, beamer (LCD projector) with screen, video camera, digital cameras and maybe video or DVD player with television round out the list of equipment that may be useful to your home-based business. Every business needs a printer, but the quality and resolution will vary depending on the nature of the business. Three-in-one or multifunction printers are commonplace and can be printer, scanner, fax and photocopier in one. Inkjet printers are cheaper to run and the ink (you may need to buy up to six separate ink cartridges for this) can be bought cheaply if you shop around. Refilling is widely available. Inkjet printers produce copy that will smudge when wet. Laser printers are better quality and do not smudge, but are much more expensive to buy and their ink is pricey too. Digital cameras can be very useful if you want to display your products or keep an attractive up to date website. I recommend ensuring your computer has a DVD burner. You may need speakers (they are not always standard) too. A large capacity memory stick (flash) is useful for transferring large document between local computers. And you should also have an external hard drive for regular back ups, though some broadband providers offer this service.

FAMILY MATTERS

Because your family is in such close proximity to your business, you will have to manage them as well. You need to let them know when you are at work and when you are free to attend to family matters. Not to do so can interrupt your concentration on your business and result in dissatisfaction and grumbling among family members. Don't make them feel that they never know when they can ask you a simple favour. Have a chat with your partner or significant other before you start your business. Discuss how your respective roles will change once your business gets rolling. How will household responsibilities be adjusted? How will child care arrangements change? Will you need your partner to be available during evening hours for some childcare if your business schedule demands some evening time? This is not as simple an arrangement as a family with one wage earner and a stay-at-home partner, nor is it even as simple as the typical two-career couple (and no one ever said *that* was really simple). This is a brand new working arrangement and it can bring your marital relationship much happiness or dissension depending on how you communicate to structure it.

You also need to take time out from the business. Remember, one of the advantages of the home-based business is the time flexibility it offers. But if you let the business run *you*, you'll soon find it affecting your partner relationship. No one is going to give you a specified holiday period. You have to allot this to yourself and plan it to coincide with your partner's holiday schedule. And just like a standard two career couple, you have to make time in the week to spend quality time with each other and coordinate with each other to ensure that all the home and family responsibilities are covered.

Kids are another matter. They may be the most important reason why you elected to work from home. But you cannot expect work and life just to fall into balance because you are home. However, you will be more in control and be in closer proximity to family in times of need or crisis.

If you work at home, your children can see what you do all day. They get to know the whole person you are, the working self and the family self. And children can even give you ideas or contribute effort to your business. It helps to be realistic about the effect a home based business will have on children of different ages and the effect the children will have on the business.

The home-based business can be a true blessing to the parent responsible for a baby, toddler or pre-schooler. These are the years when a child is most dependent, and the most emotionally difficult for parents who must work. During this stage, though, you must be flexible to the needs of the child. For younger children, crying and feeding usually can't wait long for a response. You may not need all day childcare, but you might want some help during peak activity periods (your business's or your child's).

The child in the middle years (five or six to twelve) is in school most of the day. Your flexible at-home schedule can make for a more relaxed morning routine. You don't have to rush around like a crazy person, trying to get yourself ready for work and your children ready for school by 7:30am. And if they miss the bus, you can even take them to school without being late for work yourself.

But the older school child needs to be taught the boundaries of the business. You may be at home, but you're also at work. The child needs to know when one begins and the other ends. Let him know your office schedule – and that when you are in your office, you can only be interrupted for emergencies. Set some ground rules. Maybe you could suggest that they may interrupt you only in the case of 'blood or fire' as one stay at home novelist mother would stipulate when her children were small.

The high school child can understand these boundaries better and is more self-sufficient. One was even heard to comment: 'I like it when Mum is holed up in her home office. It keeps her out of my hair.' On the other hand, you can enlist the child of this age to help with the business. The caveat here is that the help should be mostly voluntary (a little prodding is allowed for all parents) and that it should represent a true contribution to the business that matches the child's skills and age level. A seven year-old can stamp envelopes, an 11 year old can sort index cards alphabetically and a 16 year old can probably give you some pointers on setting up your computer system and using the software.

'I have had a home office twice, first after my first pregnancy leave and now.

'After having my first child, I had negotiated with my employer that I would work 1 day 1/2 from home. I managed to convince them by acting very professional and putting together a "case": a Word document of 50 pages with the benefits of working from home and many success stories. BUT reality seemed a bit more difficult. It worked pretty well till my baby was 6 months old but became impossible afterwards. My baby wanted of course to be with me and was making very sweet noises that sounded quite inappropriate during my conference calls. Also, I had many interruptions to feed her, change her nappy. At the end, I was feeling like I had to work 10 hours to accomplish work requiring 5 hours. In the end the benefit of being with my child was becoming a huge stress. I think that a home office does not really work with small children at home unless you have a nanny to help you.

'I also work now exclusively from home. My two kids go to school so the house is very quiet. Now the problem is the opposite: it is too quiet and I sometimes feel rather isolated. I managed to sort this problem by working a bit at the nearby Starbucks. Working from home is a big plus: I work when I want to work. Perfect for a mum with small kids.

'I tend to work a lot at night, which could be a problem but I am working for my own business so I am happy to do that!'
Jasmine, French in China, *www.inspiredbeijing.com* and *www.expatwomen.com*

'We run our business from home and from an office located a few miles away, but we need to be in constant communication with several other countries as well so having Internet connections is vital. We are in the process of starting an Internet-based business as well, and the beauty of this is that it can literally be run from a beach in the Bahamas or your front room. I can't imagine being without a computer within a few yards of me at all times. It's great to be able to have a meal bubbling on the stove while I work in the office and yet can keep an eye on what's going on in the kitchen.'
Diane, Canadian in England, *www.expatwomen.com*

'I appreciated the convenience (and the commute) of having the office in the home but at the same time, because it was within the corporate residence, the company corporate headquarters always expected me to be readily available in spite of the 11 hour time difference.'
Carol, American in Saudi Arabia, *http://delhi4cats.wordpress.com*

'I have a designated work-space, which is off-limits of the rest of the family, so to convey the sense of "I-am-at-work" to the others. But the reality is that working from home, no matter how virtually connected you are still in many ways lacks the human enriching experience of the "coffee-machine gathering", where you learn and stay on top of everything by being exposed to other people's problems views and interests.

'The hardest part is to combine social availability with work schedule. In my network few people work and they have got the time and the desire to pop-in, therefore finding the right balance is essential to avoid being removed from the social scene for lack of response and yet prevent to be overwhelmed by it. After all who would not trade a menial web-research for a nice chat with a friend while strolling along the Seine?

'Also, recognise the importance of the work-mode: think of it as funny, but when I have important meeting online, I dress up as if I were to show up in a conference room. It helps me focus and gear up for the conversation to come.'
Patrizia, Italian in France, *www.paguro.net*

'Use your office space only for your work. Don't take your laptop to the other parts of your home. Separate your work from your personal life.'
Ursula, South African in America, *www.marketingmentorexpert.com* and *www.expatwomen.com*

'I love the 15 second commute from my bedroom to my "office", in the morning, as well as the casual dress code. Pajamas or jeans are acceptable forms of attire many days of the week.

'Currently I have clients in 14 countries. Because of this, I work with 80% of them on the phone or through video chat (I am set up with VoIP and a wireless internet connection). This means I can work wherever I can take my laptop – even out on my terrace when the weather is nice. Technically, I am completely portable, so my office is more of a virtual office than a home office.'
Megan, American in Italy, www.careerbychoice.com

'You do need to be a very motivated, dedicated and determined person otherwise you would never get anything done. I planned my day the night before - listing what I wanted to achieve and then would make sure I would get those items completed (my plan also included the household chores and so the daily plan was very realistic and included things that were important to my 'well being' and work life balance such as friends and exercise.'
Victoria, New Zealander in India, www.expatwomen.com

'For about a year I worked from home helping Brits obtain financing for homes in the States. The down side was that I felt isolated and not part of a team. Something I particularly like. I would also find myself doing housework in between working.'
Lizzy, British in America, www.expatwomen.com

The Work-Life Balance

Work-life balance does not mean having it all. And even when we do manage to 'have it all' we're usually too tired to enjoy it! A working woman can indeed have a nanny, and a cleaner, and live off ready meals – but business dinners still mean missing out on bedtime stories. And then there's the guilt. In her book *Foetal Attraction*, Australian novelist Kathy Lette suggests that when we give birth, a 'guilt gland' suddenly appears from nowhere.

For women, the issue of work-life balance rears its head daily, as we race from packing lunchboxes, to school runs, cram in some work, scrabble together supper, then start ferrying children to Rainbows, swimming lessons or karate. Action is everything. And it is not until the house is silent that we can flop in front of the television and sigh.

Even if women abroad are not working, balance is no more achievable. And, in many ways, the rollercoaster life of the 'multimover' is even tougher. In order to stay sane, we need to maintain social contact, and fill our time with work, voluntary work or study. Add to the usual list of daily tasks, the need to prepare for and recover from regular moves, and each day can feel like a crisis. Whether we work in the traditional sense, or provide support services to our employed partner and family, what we do outside of 'me-time' must still be regarded, and valued, as 'work'. Keeping soul and home together is a lot like spinning plates. Try to stop *juggling* and start *balancing*.

SOLUTIONS

I'm the first to admit that it is far easier to talk about taking time off than actually asking for permission to go, particularly if the person who needs to give that permission is yourself. Years of conditioning have made women, particularly mothers, willing to accept a martyr's role.

'Without setting work hours and a designated workspace it can be more difficult to "leave the office" and "call it a day". Being strict about setting those limits and spaces is important for balancing work and life. In my opinion it is essential to create structure and schedule for your days. Although it is in my nature to plan and schedule (I am a coach after all) for those to whom this does not come easy, too much unstructured time can lead to procrastination, inefficiency and hence longer working hours. And for extroverts who are energised by working with others, creating opportunities to connect with people if you are at home most of the day by yourself is also important to do. In the end, no matter what your strategy, it really comes down to identifying your priorities, allotting time for them by creating a reasonable schedule, and then keeping to your schedule. You can adjust your schedule as you go along and discover what works in practice. The real challenge is keeping to the schedule. I have found that different people have different blocks – and different strategies for getting around those blocks – to sticking to a plan of action. For me, the benefits of having balance – such as health, peace, opportunity to spend time with friends and my husband – are things that keep me in check. Since I work with expats, I often work with them to identify what drew them to their new home country and find ways to get them to use that interest to engage with their home/community. I find that helps many people find more work/life balance.'
Megan, American in Italy, *www.careerbychoice.com*

'One thing we have begun to insist on is regular holidays. It's so easy to go through a whole year without stopping. Now we book breaks ahead and make sure we work to deadlines to ensure we can get away. The other thing I find important is to have a hobby or interest that is completely different from work. For me it is cooking and reading, as well as walking in the countryside when I can. That offsets the brain-strain a bit.'
Diane, Canadian in England, *www.expatwomen.com*

'If you are considering working from home I suggest you take on board commitment outside of the house that forces you to interact with people. In my case I volunteer for a women's network and organise breakfast events for entrepreneurs, where I work with another lady and seek speakers, decide topics advertise the venue etc. There is a double gain there, I get to meet other entrepreneur and to be exposed to topics I have a keen interest in.'
Patrizia, Italian in France, *www.paguro.net*

Stress Busting

It can be hard to stay positive when it's slow going, or when external events get in the way. When things appear not to be going our way it is easy to feel stressed, negative or demotivated.

The first step to eliminating stress is to determine what triggers it for you. Start to notice where the ongoing stress is – is it at the office or at home, with particular people, before certain events, doing a particular task, or when something specific is said to you? Getting problems down on paper sometimes helps to give you a more objective perspective and stops the negative thoughts going round and round in your head.

Once you've identified the source of your stress, you can make a plan to neutralise it. For example if a client is repeatedly finding fault with your work, do not simply allow yourself to get repeatedly stressed about it. Why not ask him what you could do to improve your service? If it is simply a case of him picking on you, try humouring him or ignoring it.

'The cause of almost all relationship difficulties is rooted in conflicting and ambiguous expectations around roles and goals,' suggests Stephen Covey, author of *The Seven Habits of Highly Effective People*. Try to clarify expectations in advance. When expectations are not clear and shared, personalities can clash and communications will break down.

James Scala, author of *25 Natural Ways to Manage Stress and Avoid Burnout*, recommends keeping a stress diary. In this way you can identify your stressors, think up solutions and then look back to see how far you have come in eliminating it.

Start by summarising the stressor in general terms using one or two sentences. Then write beneath this how your stress manifests itself. Perhaps you have headaches, stomach aches, feel depressed, tired or angry? Or perhaps you procrastinate? Write down how the stressor is making life difficult for you. Next you need to write down the actual problem, or cause of your stress. Finally, you need to write down a possible solution.

An example could be:

- **Stressor**: Having to make cold sales calls.
- **Manifestation**: Not making the calls and so end up feeling guilty; or making the call, not coming across well and feeling bad.
- **Problem**: Fear of rejection and of not being good enough.
- **Solution**: Determine why your services or products are good and how they can be of benefit or add value to your clients. Make a list of all the possible reasons why people might not buy your services. Write down all the objections they might have. Now write down the ways in which you can deflect these objections or handle them. Remember that you would not be trying to sell them anything on the telephone at this stage but that – you are trying to get an appointment would allow allowing you to identify their needs, and then determine whether they may have a use for your services.

COPING STRATEGIES

Having identified your stressors, spend some time building coping resources and avoidance strategies. This will serve to increase your self-esteem and energise you. Take a look at the following coping strategies and consider which ones may help you.

WELL-BEING

Take up aerobic exercise (it burns up stress hormones) and get enough rest (sleep is needed for physiological recuperation and is close second to exercise for preventing stress).

CONTROL YOUR THINKING

Our thinking creates much of our stress. Feelings are not caused by events themselves, but by beliefs we have regarding the event. Our self-talk and beliefs are based on our past experiences, some of which are self-defeating. Some negative beliefs are so deeply ingrained we don't even realise we have them. One example of a negative belief that most of us have at some stage or another is 'I'm not good enough'. Challenge the reality of these beliefs. Ask yourself how true your belief really is. If you believe it's so, then who says so and is this always the case? You will often find that this belief isn't real.

TIME OUT

Every day make a point of relaxing, even if for only a few minutes. Try meditation, walking, stretching, yoga or taking up a hobby. We need to give our brains some quiet time when it is not nervously reacting to everything around it.

SPIRITUALITY

Try to find time to be a human *being* rather than a human *doing*. It is easy to neglect being as we rush around busy doing and having.

PRE-PLANNING

Once you become aware of the stressor, attempt to prepare to handle it. Control your thinking, try to avoid exaggerating the situation and don't underestimate your ability for coping.

PATTERN BREAKING

Thinking about the past and the future can be stressful. Try to bring your thoughts back to the present by centring your attention on your breathing, an object or another topic that interests you. Doing something different like laughing out loud or pinching yourself can also help as it breaks the pattern of our thoughts.

GET CLEAR

Do not ignore the stressor, bring it into focus and get clear about it. You won't be able to deal with it until you have understood it. Ask help from friends if you're stuck.

COPING RESOURCES

With our attention dominated by a stressful situation we often forget or don't realise that we have coping resources. Matheny and McCarthy suggest making a list of possible coping strategies that you have used in the past or intend to use. Then you just have to remember to put them into practice. You possess many skills and resources. Recall past successes and visualise yourself coping. Build your confidence by spending time making an inventory of your resources and thinking about past successes.

BE PROACTIVE

If the situation is controllable, take action to control the stressor. Any action you take will reduce the stress since when you shift into action, the body lowers its production of the stress hormone, epinephrine. Remember that you won't know if the decision is the right one until you have made it. Give yourself a pat on the back for taking action; proactivity will energise you.

Be open to negative feedback; you may have to step back and adopt a new course of action.

If the stressor is uncontrollable, you will need to focus on controlling your emotions. Reframe the situation to look for positive elements. Ask yourself what you might learn from the situation.

Robert Kohls, author of *Survival Kit for Overseas Living*, found that the most important skill for living successfully abroad was the ability to fail. So keep looking for the positive in any situation and realise that there is no failure, only feedback.

ASK BETTER QUESTIONS

To change how you feel about anything, including stressors, you need to change what you are focusing on. Ask questions that give you useful answers. If you ask yourself negative questions you will get negative answers. Instead of asking why life is so unfair or why something always happens to you, seek out the positive aspects of your situation. Ask yourself what can you learn from this experience. Or what can you do differently to make you feel better or move towards your goal. This will get your brain thinking of solutions for you.

DEVISE YOUR OWN ANTI-STRESS REGIME

Jutta König is a clinical psychologist and movement psychotherapist who offers workshops in a range of meditative arts. She suggests that we should develop our own anti-stress regime. This should include learning a meditative art, such as Qi Gong, the Five Tibetans, Tai Chi, Yoga or Watsu and practise daily to stay sane.

Jutta also believes that it is vital to eat plenty of fruit and vegetables and to take exercise. She recommends consciously spoiling yourself with little attentions – flowers in your home, listening to your music you love, buying your favourite perfume.

OUTSIDE INTERESTS

In addition to the above methods, I have found that having an interest or hobby separate from work does wonders for taking the mind off your problems.

LAUGHTER

Spend a few minutes every day having a good laugh. Research has shown that laughter relieves stress and makes us feel better – so watch a movie or comedy show, listen to a tape. Look for the funny side of life and learn to laugh at yourself. Lighten up, stop taking yourself so seriously.

Ten Tips to a Stressfree Business Life

1. Take a five-minute break every hour and a half that you work. Use the time to get up from your desk and stretch your legs, relax, breathe deeply, meditate or walk around.
2. Do not rush or leave things until the last minute. Try to arrive early for every appointment.
3. Recognise your boundaries. Learn to say no.
4. Organise yourself and your day and stick to it.
5. Notice the things you are grateful for. Say thank you.
6. Aim for a clutterfree desk and office.
7. Set aside a few minutes a day for worrying and refuse to focus on your worries randomly throughout the day.
8. Reward your achievements; it will encourage you to keep moving forward.
9. Admit you are responsible for your actions and move on.
10. Go easy on yourself. If you think a task will take one hour, allocate an hour and a quarter. If you think you will complete an assignment by Monday, say you will deliver it on Tuesday.

'For me, probably reading works best. I am an avid reader. When I feel really fed up with the world I read a light historical novel, set in a world without the pressures of consumerism, commercialisation, globalisation, politics and global warming. Pure escapism. As well, I do Tai Chi, meditate, use Bach Flower Remedies and aromatherapy, and enjoy listening to music. If I have a block of time I like to paint. I also find stupid TV shows help on occasions when my brain just feels lazy! Oh, and I mustn't forget the pets. We have cats, fish and a rabbit who demand love and attention. That is remarkably relaxing, even cleaning out the litter tray can be done meditatively!'
Diane, Canadian in England, *www.expatwomen.com*

'For each person this can be so different. I find exercise, meditation, watching films, reading, writing and connecting with friends by phone or email are helpful ways to reduce stress.'
Megan, American in Italy, *www.careerbychoice.com*

'I sometimes write a thank you letter to a customer, ex-colleague, boss, etc. When I give I de-stress myself.'
Ursula, South African in America, *www.marketingmentorexpert.com*
and *www.expatwomen.com*

'A beer always helps and having joined an expat group in Denver, it's a great release.'
Lizzy, British in America, *www.expatwomen.com*

Staying Motivated

Job hunting, starting to run your own business and advancing your career all take hard work. Of course you will have down times, and times when you feel like giving up and joining a commune. Self-motivation is one of the key attributes required by all freelancers and anyone who repeatedly has to reinvent themselves or pick up a temporarily shelved career. Margaret Chapman recommends four essential actions that you can take to stay self-motivated. She suggests we employ positive self-talk, build our own support network or hire a coach, think about our inspirational mentors or role models and create an environment that lifts our spirits.

POSITIVE THINKING

Most people repeat negative statements to themselves such as 'I hate myself', 'I am stupid' or 'I can't do …' They spend so much of their time focusing on the negative that they see faults in everyone as well as themselves. This creates a process called 'self-fulfilling prophecy' and they set themselves up for failure as they get caught in a vicious circle.

Your subconscious doesn't know the difference between a real and an imagined experience. If you keep telling yourself that you are going to fail then you will – because the next time that you attempt the same thing you will find yourself remembering the previous failure. As soon as you expect to fail, you do. One way out of this self destructive loop is to condition your mind with positive thoughts, self-talk and affirmations.

An affirmation is a statement that you read and repeat throughout your day. If you like you can write yourself notes and post them all over the house, so that they are never far from your thoughts.

The requirements for effective and powerful affirmations are that they must:

- Start with the pronoun 'I'
- Be stated positively
- Be in the present tense
- Relate to your goals
- Be visual

For example: 'I, (insert your name) am confident and a competent public speaker'.

For extra emphasis you can try repeating the same basic affirmation but in the second and the third person.

For example: 'You (your name) are confident and a competent public speaker. She (your name) is confident and a competent public speaker.'

The reason for this is that our current views of ourselves tend to be formed by a mixture of what others say about us, what we say to ourselves and what others tell us.

Read your affirmations at least once a day. Alternatively record them and listen to them in the car, before going to bed or first thing in the morning. When you are reading or listening to your affirmations, make sure you visualise them in vivid detail. The more clearly and deeply you can visualise, the more you will programme the mind to believe it and make it be true. If you think you can, you can. So always think and tell yourself that you can. A lot of people see themselves in the past or in the present when they read their affirmations and visualise. Try to visualise yourself the way you want to be and make sure you are looking into the future. Don't dwell on the past, unless it is positive and helps build the way you want to be.

If someone instructs you not to think of monkeys, it is impossible not to picture one. Your unconscious mind doesn't recognise negatives. If you ask it not to worry or make a mistake, you are actually setting yourself up to do just that. Successful people, in particular sports people, know that they are more likely to achieve positive results if they focus on positive outcomes. Our thoughts strongly influence our performance. So concentrate on what you really want, and your mind will propel you forward to achieving it.

Like negative self-talk, optimism will also create self-fulfilling prophecies. Studies have shown that people with a positive sense of self will work harder and longer and in turn their perseverance will allow them to do better.

'Have the courage to take a risk. Practise believing the *impossible* until it becomes *possible* and then *actual*. Remember achievers achieve the unachievable,' writes Norman Vincent Peale, author of *The Power of Positive Thinking*.

'For me motivation can only come from knowing that what I am doing is making a difference to other people's lives. Our business is after-school tuition in English and Maths, and we know for sure that many of our kids have gone on to have better lives than they would have done if we hadn't been able to help them. On a more mercenary level I am also motivated by the knowledge I am saving for my retirement, and helping my daughter have a better standard of living, and that helps to get me out of bed in the morning too!'
Diane, Canadian in England, *www.expatwomen.com*

'Setting goals and achieving them; trying projects that involve new research, techniques and information; sometimes having to give myself an occasional pep talk [keep me motivated].'
Carol, American in Saudi Arabia, *http://delhi4cats.wordpress.com*

'[To stay motivated I] read positive affirmations or poems when I feel lonely. Call peers and have a 5 minute marketing discussion with them. I have to pay my own medical insurance and bills - that motivates me. A big motivation is to have a goal and a vision board - write your goals and plans on this board, and when you get demotivated look at it. Make the vision board colorful, put pictures of things you would like to achieve, purchase on this board. In less good times, your vision board will be a good source of strength.'
Ursula, South African in America, *www.marketingmentorexpert.com* and *www.expatwomen.com*

'I look at the Rocky Mountains on a daily basis and think how lucky I am. It's truly inspiring.'
Lizzy, British in America, *www.expatwomen.com*

'I stay motivated by sharing my ups and downs with my friends and with the women in a small Mumentrepreneurs group that we created a few months ago. Having a support group made of people in the same boat than you is in my opinion the best way of staying motivated. I guess the success of this group is also that all women onboard are dynamic, fun and positive.'
Jasmine, French in China, *www.inspiredbeijing.com* and *www.expatwomen.com*

9 coping with change

A portable career is perfect for today's mobile dual career family. But if you are mobile then you are inevitably going to have to be able to handle change. Galen Tinder investigates.

'Change alone is unchanging.'

Heraclitus

In this chapter:

- Relocation and change
- Change and transition
- Expatriate partners – their special situation
- The challenge of change

A well-known rating system measures the amount of stress a person has experienced over the course of a year by assigning a certain number of points to several dozen common life events. The more points accumulated, the more likely you are to suffer from physical illness and emotional deterioration. Some of the events on the lengthy list are 'positive', such as marriage and having a child, while others would widely be considered 'negative' – losing a job or landing in jail, for example. Relocation, which can have both positive and negative features, ranks third in the number of stress points earned, following hard on the heels of the death of a close relative and divorce.

Whether stress-inducing events on the list are considered positive or negative, they all share a common feature – all involve change, a change in personal circumstances. It's not just that negative events are stressful, but that change itself makes heavy demands on our coping resources.

The concept of 'managing' change may be a misnomer. It's not as though we can manage change to the point of eliminating its sometimes painful and undesired effects on our life. Managing change is rather like herding cats – even the best of intentions and maximum effort do not guarantee pleasing, much less perfect, results.

So, by managing change we don't mean conquering or nullifying it, but facing it with courage and openness and thus using it to further our own growth and betterment. The external events that affect our lives may sometimes be desirable and sometimes not. The feelings these events elicit may be pleasurable or painful. But whether our management of change has a positive or negative affect on our lives depends on whether or not we integrate it into our lives in a way that enhances our personal, emotional and spiritual advancement.

Relocation and Change

Relocation is one of the most common and also disruptive sources of change in contemporary life. We have so accepted moving as a routine feature of our global society that we often forget how emotionally exhausting and challenging it can be. But to appreciate the stress caused by relocating we don't have to mine any source of knowledge more sophisticated than our own common sense and experience:

- It's **hard work** - the selling or renting of a house, securing housing in the new location, packing and transporting family goods and the endless but necessary tasks of 'settling in'. This is to name just a fraction of the nerve wracking logistical details that accompany relocation.
- If there are **children**, they need extra attention of various kinds, depending on their age and the nature of the move.

- It is a time of **saying goodbye** to friends and to familiar and beloved places – a time, in other words, of loss.
- The **entire family** needs to adjust to everything being different in the new location.
- Nearly every aspect of **common family life** changes: daily routines, schools, community associations, friendships, even the physical landscape.

For the majority of people, this multi-faceted upheaval is tackled while moving within the borders of a single country. But for some, it's an international experience. People who have made both kinds of moves agree that foreign relocations make the heaviest demands on a person's emotional resources. Here are just a few of the challenges facing expatriates:

- Communicating with people who speak another language.
- Adjusting to the myriad differences in every day life.
- Learning native customs and manners.
- Discovering how public entities and organisations work, from the library to the police force, from the food store to the traffic authority.
- For the expatriate partner: finding fulfilling vocational and non vocational pursuits.

In an expatriate family the accompanying partner may shoulder more stress than the employee. She (only about 15 per cent of international accompanying partners are male) is in the more exposed and vulnerable position. Although the employee too must negotiate much that is new, he has the advantage of being grounded in his profession and the familiar disciplines of his work, and of spending most of his waking hours with people who speak the same language he does, both literally and figuratively.

The partner, on the other hand, is initially both more isolated and more exposed. She has no band of colleagues with whom to huddle – but as the captain of family logistics, she interacts daily with a world dismayingly unlike the one she came from. She may not have her work, so there may be no refuge there. On the contrary, she may have resigned from a fulfilling position back home and feel partly the victim of the corporate advancement practices of her husband's company. For these reasons, the challenges posed by international relocation changes are often unusually stressful.

Change and stress go together. How many people have we heard say, 'I just love change; it's so relaxing'? External events don't themselves produce stress. But they do trigger a cluster of feelings that constitute stress. Stress consists of an unruly combination of strong and unprocessed feelings, usually including anger, fear and anxiety. When these feelings run around in our systems untamed they consume nearly all our energy, to the point of interfering with our daily life and perhaps to the point of overwhelming us.

But we don't need to be a hapless victim of change and its emotional byproducts. Our key question, then, is this: How do we manage all the changes of relocation, especially international relocation, in a way that enriches, rather than diminishes, our lives? You can find many tips on handling stress in *Chapter Eight*.

'In a country like Egypt you need to have unlimited reserves of patience, as things simply don't happen overnight or in the way you expect. Whatever your time-line is, it'll be best to double it! It's also crucial to have someone who has the ability to speak the language, preferably a local, as misunderstandings are inevitable if you do business in English only.'
Diane, Canadian in England, *www.expatwomen.com*

CHANGE AND TRANSITION

William Bridges, an organisation psychologist who has studied and written on how people react to change, differentiates between change and transition. Change consists of external events, while transition is the set of internal processes we go through in adjusting to change.

Just as Elizabeth Kubler-Ross delineated five stages in a person's coming to terms with his or her approaching death, Bridges observes that most people react to change by making an inner transition that consists of three distinct stages – *Endings, a Neutral Zone* and *New Beginnings*. People achieve successful transitions when they adjust to change through the healthy navigation of each of these three transition stages. When we fail to accomplish the essential tasks of each stage, we can get stuck in an incomplete and unsatisfying transition characterised by prolonged stress and maladjustment. This failure cripples our ability to live a satisfying life in our new area.

Broadly speaking, *Endings* consist of saying goodbye and leaving. The *Neutral Zone* is a way station between departing from one place and arriving at another. This is where we pause to gather our energy and inner resources for stage three. *New Beginnings* signal the stage of investing energy in the new features of our world. When we fully engage these three stages we'll still experience stress, but a stress that ultimately energises rather than disables.

Bridges did not conceive these stages with relocation particularly in mind, but his tripartite distinction is especially apt in its application to the dynamic of physically moving from one place to another. Let's take a look at several of the most common 'sticking' points in the process.

ENDINGS

Change always begins with an ending, sometimes one that we don't recognise at the time. But when we move from one location to another it's hard for the ending to slip by us unnoticed. For most people, the ending stage of relocation begins when the final decision has been made. At this point, whether we realise it or not, we begin to disengage psychologically from the place we're leaving. This disengagement begins subtly, becoming more conscious and intentional as we grow closer to the move.

When we prepare to move we're confronted with a combination of logistical and emotional challenges. We tackle a seemingly endless list of tasks that come with uprooting ourselves from one place and settling into a new 'world' in which we are a stranger. At the same time, we typically feel a sense of loss about all that we are leaving behind, not just the concrete places but also a whole way of life. This sense of loss can feel like grief and takes many shapes.

- **Mild shock** – 'I can't believe it. We've only been here a couple of years. And what is the sub-continent? Can you drink the water?'
- **Anger** – 'What ivory towered manager thought this would bolster my husband's career?'
- **Anxiety** – 'I can't imagine how I am going to get everything ready. I don't even know what to get ready for.'
- **Sadness** – 'I am going to miss … (people, places, activities, events).'
- **Fear** – 'I was just getting to love the people in Spain; what are the Belgians going to be like?'
- And finally, there is what we might call **groundlessness**, which some people describe as the feeling of being rootless, of not belonging anyplace and therefore being vulnerable in an unaccustomed way.

These feelings are natural and normal. They're part of ending our relationship with all the tangibles of a given place. We may fear that if we give such feelings the recognition they deserve, they will exhaust us and leave us no energy for the future. True, strong emotions like sadness and fear can tire us out over the short term. But this cleansing clears the way for healing, a newfound energy and a creative engagement in our new location. Over the longer haul, it is always the feelings we don't acknowledge that wear us down.

In some parts of the modern world we've got into the unfortunate habit of slapping the label 'negative' onto any experience or feeling that is uncomfortable. This reflex action is partly a product of our times. The mammoth engine of global commerce and mass media celebrates our entitlement to perpetual bliss. If we feel sad or unsettled, there is always a pill to take, a product to purchase, a new experience to distract us. The cure comes from outside us. So when we don't feel good for any period of time longer than a few minutes, we conclude that there must be something wrong with us. It's impossible to overestimate the destructive impact this belief has on the human spirit and on how we experience our lives.

The truth is that life involves discomfort and it includes painful feelings, especially at points of ending. A healthy reaction to such feelings is to move through them, not around them, talking about them with other people who understand us. This will help prevent us from getting emotionally stuck in the old location while our bodies and our lives have moved to the new one.

> 'I felt unfulfilled while working I felt that I made a difference, I contributed to the success of companies, and all of a sudden I had this empty feeling. I missed my colleagues, peers and my clients. I felt I didn't belong.'
> Ursula, South African in America, *www.marketingmentorexpert.com* and *www.expatwomen.com*

What can help us say goodbye? Every year thousands of domestically and internationally relocating families have found that parting rituals don't have to be fancy to be helpful. A last visit to a favorite pizza parlour, a romp at the local playground, visits to important sites like schools, and special goodbye times with friends are examples of simple, but effective, leave-taking rituals. Some children host a goodbye party for their friends a week or two before the move.

In the case of moving, what's good for children is also healthy for adults. Here are several tips for 'closure' at the *Endings* stage of your transition:

- Before the move, take the time to say goodbye to people and places. It gives us a sense of rounding off, of completion, and allows time to acknowledge what we will miss. Keep a journal of your experiences while living abroad.
- Encourage open communication among family members. Inform children about the move as soon as possible. When feasible, include children in some aspects of the decision making process about how the move will be organised. Encourage everybody to speak honestly about their reactions and explore your new surroundings.
- Take time to relax and have fun. Inaugurate life in your new home or apartment with a special 'Welcome to Us' dinner. Try to learn the new language.
- Pre-relocation visits to the new area help both adults and children to make the transition. Instead of wondering about the unknown, we can begin preparing ourselves while still in our old location.
- Relocation is physically, mentally and emotionally demanding. This is not the best time to abandon your normal routines of self care in the areas of sleep, nutrition and exercise.
- Have reasonable expectations of yourself and others. Recognise that relocation is inherently stressful and do not be hard on yourself for not handling everything perfectly.

225

- These suggestions apply as much to expatriating and repatriating relocaters as they do to those who move domestically, though international pre-relocation visits are difficult to arrange for obvious reasons.
- Don't hesitate to ask for help. Well, you can hesitate, but do it anyway. Don't confuse asking for help with self-pity or weakness. Admitting your limitations takes strength, and it bestows a kindness on others because most people like to help another person. Expatriates report that it is valuable to arrive equipped with the contact information for other expatriates from their own country. Network, network and network some more!
- Keep your sense of humour. If you've never had one, try to develop it.

THE NEUTRAL ZONE

This period occupies the middle stage of transition; it begins with the departure from the old home and extends into the initial period of resettlement. Its duration varies anywhere from one to several months.

The *Neutral Zone* is often marked by a sense of dislocation and anxiety. Change means heading into unfamiliar territory, and during this passage it's common to confront a feeling of emptiness. People often feel in limbo; they miss their familiar surroundings but haven't yet planted firm roots in the new area. During this period family members are especially vulnerable to disappointment as they find that their new location doesn't offer the same features, attractions and apparent advantages they had appreciated 'back home'.

Despite its unsettling aspects, the *Neutral Zone* also provides time for rejuvenation, self-examination and redirected focus. In the *Neutral Zone* people discover new talents and passions, and a capacity for closer, more rewarding relationships.

People who are relocating may feel that this *Neutral Zone* gets gobbled up by the endings at one end and the beginnings at the other. We may need to make time for the *Neutral Zone*, settling into the new location at a reasonable pace without feeling as though we must master the entirety of our new environment in the first week. We give ourselves a gift by not pressing hard towards premature new beginnings. No, our goal is not to dawdle. It's to break away from our incessant doing and to create space in our minds and our lives for self-discovery and creativity.

One expert on change has remarked that it's an interlude that deserves to be 'savoured'. Here are several suggestions for making your *Neutral Zone* a 'tasty' one:

- Accept what is. Waging a war against circumstances that are fixed is self-destructive and wastes enormous energy. You may not like where you have moved to, but by bemoaning your fate for months on end you'll only intensify your unhappiness. Accept your feelings for what they are without passing judgment on whether they are good or bad. Emotions like anger and sadness are not inherently negative. They can be either positive or negative, depending on how we treat them. But they can have a negative effect on us if we ignore them or pretend we don't experience them.
- Relocations disrupt customary patterns that give our lives structure, so it may help to quickly re-establish basic routines that provide a sense of order and structure. At the same time, try to resist the natural impulse to fill all your time with activity and busyness.
- We can remind ourselves, and not just when we are moving, that our unceasing drive towards activity plays havoc with our emotional and physical health.

The main danger of the *Neutral Zone* is getting stuck there. The two most common signs of an unsuccessful transition are emotions that are unusually intense and prolonged, and a feeling of numbness that doesn't ease with time. If you get trapped in either place, consider seeking short-term professional help.

BEGINNINGS

Veteran movers learn that the unpacking of their belongings scarcely concludes their relocation. Experience teaches them that it takes six to nine months to acclimatise fully to their new world.

So it can be difficult to pinpoint where the *Neutral Zone* merges into *New Beginnings*. But at some point people look back and realise they've made the shift. Families who have successfully relocated report that the key to making a healthy transition is to form connections in the new community as quickly as they can. Perhaps:

- They make an effort to meet their new neighbours.
- If they are religious, they seek a spiritual home within a month of moving.
- They join one or two community groups or voluntary associations – the American Women's Club, International Club, library guild, rescue squad, municipal health commission, hospital volunteer corps, town recreation programme, planning board and Rotary are but a few of the possibilities. People who are in a new country have a special challenge. At the beginning, especially,

everything can feel intimidating. Veterans of foreign moves advise that new arrivals need to get plentiful and accurate information about their host culture and immediate surroundings so that they are not hobbled by ignorance.

- They explore their new surroundings with a sense of adventure, locating important places like banks and government offices while soaking in the new culture.

> '[Not having work made me feel] devastated and insecure. I have worked all my life by choice and I did not know how to easily adapt to finding myself at home and without a job when I first arrived in the Kingdom. After allowing a "reasonable period" for self-pity I then gave myself a harsh pep talk and put together my action plan in marketing myself, my qualifications and making contacts.'
> Carol, American, *http://delhi4cats.wordpress.com* and *www.expatwomen.com*

Expatriate Partners – Their Special Situation

We often can't control events, but we can plan for what we want to do when we encounter them. Our focus in this book, of course, is on career, employment and vocation. Many expatriate spouses make tentative plans for how to continue their career in another country and then adapt this goal to the environment and circumstances they encounter. When it is impossible to obtain paid employment, these partners find and create opportunities for developing their professional capabilities through volunteering and community activities.

Planning is aided by research, and happily it's now far easier to prepare for the exigencies of expatriate vocational adventuring than it was even ten years ago. Reliable information about nearly every country in the world is now easily available. A recent check of a popular online bookshop immediately turned up almost 50 current titles on working in foreign countries. Whether or not a partner has worked in her country of origin or not, there is no reason for her not to have some idea what to expect in the way of another country's opportunities for vocational enrichment.

Many accompanying partners, depending on the country they are in, are unable to obtain remunerative employment. If you can know before you move that your country of destination restricts expatriate employment options, you can spare yourself the frustration of developing unrealistic predeparture expectations. This will also give you the time to gather information about the alternatives to paid work – alternatives that will engage and advance you vocationally, if not financially.

'Not having any work in the first 8 months after moving to Beijing with my family was extremely hard for me. Not only had I lost my professional identity but also a sense of where I was going. I started losing my self-confidence and would only speak to women at the evening social gatherings my husband and I were attending. I suddenly thought that if I was not working, I had nothing very interesting to share with the gentlemen. Obviously I was wrong.

'It was actually after one of those evenings that I realised how bad I was feeling about myself. I then took the decision to start my own business and by then save myself from depression.'
Jasmine, French in China, *www.inspiredbeijing.com* and *www.expatwomen.com*

THE CHALLENGE OF CHANGE

To paraphrase the international bestselling psychiatrist, M Scott Peck, change is difficult. Whether it is changing ourselves or adjusting to changes in external circumstances, our relationship with change engages our vital energies. The people who are most successful in 'managing' change, to cite our imperfectly stated theme, are those who have successfully initiated change in their own lives. The people who can manage change are those who possess the capacity to change themselves. The more you can push yourself to change in your present circumstances, the better you'll thrive in them.

We all encounter the challenge of change on two fronts. Firstly we need to think about how to respond to changes that originate outside ourselves. This chapter has been focusing on this area. Secondly, we need to be able to initiate and sustain desirable changes in our own patterns of thought and behaviour.

Personal change is difficult and our efforts are often met with formidable inner resistance. The fundamental source of this resistance is fear, the emotion that underlies anger and anxiety. People who are brave and venturesome push against this fear to make their desired personal changes. People who bring this capacity for self-change to meet the challenges of external change are rewarded with a rich and dynamic life.

People who have made successful relocations tend to share a number of common traits:

- They're intentional about setting goals and organising their actions around these goals. They are clear with themselves and with others about their important values.
- They neither deny nor wallow in their emotions, but accept them for what they are and work from there. Meanwhile, they keep their sense of humour.
- They communicate their feelings openly and listen sympathetically to the feelings of others.

- They focus on their own behaviour instead of trying to control the behaviour of others.
- They take responsibility for themselves and are open to personal change. They know the futility of procrastination and self-pity.
- They practise flexibility and tolerance of others.

People who manage change well are those who can make and accept changes in themselves. When a major change such as relocation appears on the horizon, they're not immune from normal feelings like fear, sadness and anger. But by facing and expressing these feelings, they move towards the future with hope and a sense of adventure.

10 talking to a professional

Galen Tinder, REA Manager, explains how to understand and use a career consultant, coach, mentor, recruiter or career management firm in order to realise your career dreams.

'But where shall wisdom be found? And where is the place of understanding?'
Job

In this chapter:

- Who can help you with your career goals?
- Our case studies
- Career consulting for expatriates
- Remote consultants
- Making the most of it

In this chapter you will learn that careers consultants come in a variety of forms, and with a number of different titles. Consultant, counsellor, advisor, coach and mentor. It does not always follow that one 'careers advisor' will do exactly the same work as another. It is not what they call themselves but what they do that matters. In this chapter we are using the title consultant as a general term.

AUSTIN

Austin is a 33 year-old computer network administrator who has decided, after 12 years in the field, to change careers. He wants to spend less time with machines and more with people, but beyond this he does not know what direction he wants to head in. Does he want to stay in the computer field but orient himself toward management? Or should he bid farewell to computers altogether? He has often thought about teaching high school students, but this would require the major commitment of returning to school.

SIMON

Simon is 42 and has just moved to Spain with his family. He wants to start his own property development business, buying, restoring and renting out interesting old houses. He has experience in the building trade and can turn his hand to most aspects of this area. He does not know the Spanish market, speaks little Spanish and knows nothing about the tourist industry and rental market.

JANICE

Since graduating from college 16 years ago Janice has worked for the marketing department of a regional supermarket chain, the last five years as Senior Vice President. By nearly all standards she is in the middle of a successful career. The only fly in the ointment is that Janice does not enjoy her work. She has decided that while she is still in her thirties it is time to move in a new direction. She has even identified her goal: Janice wants to direct the marketing efforts of a not-for-profit artistic organisation. She is not aiming for the New York Metropolitan Museum of Art; she would be happy with a county art centre with a budget of $200,000. But Janice, who was recruited by her present company straight from college, has never had to conduct a job search and doesn't even have a resumé.

SUZANNE

Suzanne is 49 years old and after raising her children into their mid teens is ready for the work world. She has never held a paying job but has been active in responsible positions for volunteer organisations. She is interested in working as an administrative assistant, but is unsure about the best way to obtain such a position.

These people represent just four of the many situations in which professional careers advisors (also called career counselors or careers advisors) can provide valuable help and guidance.

In order to understand what career consultants do, it's helpful to compare them with other professionals. Let's take attorneys and financial advisors. All three kinds of professionals possess a body of knowledge and a set of skills in applying that knowledge to individual situations. As with attorneys and financial advisors, much of what career consultants provide for their clients is intangible, consisting of counsel and advice. This is the major reason why it's not easy to be sure that you've selected the right person and are getting the services you need.

In this chapter I want to give you an idea of what career consultants do, help you decide if you can benefit from working with one and suggest guidelines to help you select a person who is qualified and well suited to help you.

Who Can Help You With Your Career Goals?

COACHES

There seem to be so many people who say they offer coaching these days. They may call themselves a Life Coach, Business Coach, Executive Coach, a Transformational Coach or a Career Coach. Some offer a combination of business and life coaching; others combine general life direction coaching with career advice. However, all coaches share one thing in common – their goal is to facilitate positive change in their clients. In discussion with a coach about adopting a new direction, a coach might ask: 'so where do you want to go?' or 'how do you propose to get there?' and 'who can you speak to in order to make that happen?' In other words a coach helps the client to elicit the answers from deep inside him or herself. They then provide tools and strategies to make your dream a reality and help you to find the motivation you need. A coach does not tell you what to do, but helps you uncover your authentic desires and map out a plan for achieving them.

Outside of sports, professional coaching is an even newer profession than career consulting. Although there are different kinds of coaches, boasting a variety of educational and training preparation, most of them assist people with overall life direction. They help people establish and pursue their significant goals in life. You'll find a coach here and there who is also experienced in career consulting – but don't assume this to be the case. Some people engage the services of both a coach and a consultant – the former for the big picture and the latter for vocational and job search issues.

234

When to Use a Coach

If you are still at the 'searching' stage and unsure what you want to do and where your passion lies, you will need the answers to these questions before you can turn your aspirations into concrete reality, then a coach may be your first port of call.

How to Choose a Coach

Sadly, there are many thousands of people out there who advertise themselves as coaches, but who have received no formal training of any kind. It is important that a coach understands how to achieve the best for the clients, the value of confidentiality and appropriate questioning and listening techniques. So, first check your coach has received at least some training. Second, ask to see testimonials from satisfied past clients. Many people come to being coaches themselves because they so enjoyed it when they too were coached. A number of these start practising a little too early. In order to choose the perfect coach, it is fundamental that you believe your coach is happy with their choice of career, that they are walking their talk, motivating themselves and setting and achieving their goals. A good coach should be a living example of what she promises to create for her clients.

'I worked with a coach who successfully helped me to make the transition from working for corporate companies to starting my own business. His talents and expertise were just what I needed to transform my skills. His coaching and programs helped me to gain confidence to go out to start networking, presenting myself in a successful way and get more visibility. I am reaping the benefits of my hard work, perseverance and selecting the right coach!'
Ursula, South African in America, *www.marketingmentorexpert.com*

'I worked with Dori Weinstein (*lifematters@mac.com*). She was amazing and it was something I had never encountered before, she made me think about things prior to reacting. Now I tend to think before jumping into a situation.'
Lizzy, British in America, *www.expatwomen.com*

MENTORS

Mentors also come in different sizes and shapes. A mentor is generally a person who is in a similar field or position as yourself, but has a greater depth of experience. Mentors typically don't help you get a job but instead share of their own professional experience in a way that may illuminate your own direction and provide you with general life and vocational guidance. Today, some companies have formalised systems of mentoring that they hope will contribute to the development of their younger employees.

When to Use a Mentor

If you know what you want to do, for example to write and publish a book, or to create a portable career, then you may need a mentor in addition to, or instead of, a coach. The ideal mentor would be someone you admire and want to emulate, someone who has 'been there and done that' and, more importantly, has lots of contacts and information he or she is happy to share with you. Plainly put, a mentor is a person who has what you want and can inspire you to do the same.

How to Choose a Mentor

Mentoring is less widespread than careers counseling or coaching and can be provided on an informal basis, often within a company, by someone higher up in the hierarchy to you. Outside a corporate environment, it can be hard to find someone who can mentor you on a formal basis. Some coaches or counselors will be able to mentor too, so ask. Choose a mentor who is a role model to you, who has shown success in the area to which you aspire and who is generous of spirit. Find someone who will share contacts, connect you with her colleagues, give you the names of websites and membership organisations maybe. Most importantly, you should consider your potential mentor to show enthusiasm and passion for what she does and to inspire you.

RECRUITERS

This is a point of confusion for many people who expect career counselors or consultants to find them jobs, and recruiters to help them with self-marketing. There is a distinct difference between them – in that career consultants work for individual clients while recruiters work for client companies. In a nutshell, career consultants help people to find jobs, while recruiters help companies to fill positions. Recruiters are in a position to recommend qualified candidates to companies, and sometimes conduct preliminary screening interviews. Career consultants work with people on career goals, resumés and cover letters, networking, interviewing and other aspects of the job search to help them market and present themselves as effectively as possible.

Recruiters are sometimes referred to as 'head-hunters' and their services are rarely suitable for people who have been out of work for a period of time, for career changers or for people who are not committed to a particular vocational field.

Recruiters are most interested in managerial and professional types who can command a salary of at least $50,000. In general, the higher your salary, the greater the chance of attracting recruiter interest. In addition, recruiters are often more interested in people who are already employed than in those looking for work.

Nonetheless, a job seeker is always free to make an initial contact with a recruitment agency. Bear in mind, though, that recruiters are flooded with resumés and enquiries from job hunters. You will need to take the initiative to follow up with them. Don't be offended when they don't return your call – remember their paycheck comes from the employers, not the employees. Some people can use recruiters for their job search, but few should rely on them as the linchpin of their campaign.

When to Use a Recruiter

Many job hunters have an unrealistic expectation that recruiters will be enthralled with their resumé and promote their interests to the companies they work for. The fact is that recruiters are rarely interested in looking at the qualifications of a person looking for a job. Imagine a recruiter with an expansive desk covered with pieces of paper from one end to the other. Those papers represent open positions that she is trying to find matches for by contacting, for the most part, potential candidates who are presently working and are not even actively looking to move.

The one circumstance in which you may be able to break through into a recruiter's field of vision is when you represent a closely-defined specialty in which that recruiter works. And that, of course, is when you should consider including, but not relying on, recruiters in your search.

How to Choose a Recruiter

First, we need to remember that there is not a line of recruiters waiting to sign us up. Recruiters do not work for individual job seekers, but for companies who want them to find candidates to fill specific open positions. Thus, a job seeker who expects to attract recruiter interest is working against the flow. Here is another count against the average job seeker: in looking for round peg employees to fill round peg positions, recruiters much prefer casting their nets among the currently employed.

But if you want to give recruiters a whirl, here are several guidelines for selecting the right ones:

- First, there is geography. Although there are numerous national recruiting firms, most are strongest in their home base city or state. Even stronger in their city and state are local recruiters who specialise in a well-defined area. Try a couple of both.

- Second, there are recruiting firms that span several industries and those that specialise in one or two. You will usually do better with the smaller speciality (boutique) firms.

- Third, recruiters are either retained or contingency. The differences are not important here, but the former work with higher paid personnel, usually people who make over $75,000 a year.

- Fourth, if you have a solid business associate who has worked with a firm before and is willing to introduce you to a particular person, pursue this opportunity first. This kind of reference is invaluable.

- Finally, even small firms sub-specialise. If you are going to contact a firm, it is worth finding the name of the person whose responsibilities most closely match your niche in the market. You can get this information in the reference section of your library. Try *Kennedy's Directory of Executive Recruiters.*

CAREER MANAGEMENT FIRMS

A career management firm offers services like those provided by career consultants. In fact, if you contract with a firm, you are likely to work with a particular consultant. Be aware, however, that some of these firms promise more than they deliver and can cost a hefty sum, as much as 20 per cent of a first year's salary. Some of these firms promise to connect you with important corporate 'decision makers', while in fact just supplying you with a list of names obtainable from one of any number of data bases. Some such firms have been accused of grossly misrepresenting themselves and found themselves dragged into court by irate clients. One large firm has even found itself a frequent target of government investigation. This does not mean that you should never use such a firm, only that you need to research them thoroughly and make sure you have in clear and understandable writing the services you will be provided and payments owed them.

When to Use a Career Management Firm

Unless you have close ties with somebody at the firm, there is no reason to use one. You are better off engaging the services of a sole practitioner consultant. This gives you better quality control and is more economical.

How to Choose a Career Management Firm

Career Management firms vary greatly in quality. Since they charge you up to 30% of your first year's salary, it is critical to choose wisely. First and foremost, you want to get in writing the services they will offer you. Don't be satisfied with vague phrases like, "Help you with interview preparation." That could mean nothing more than giving you a list of ten questions often asked in interviews. Insist on having the services spelled out. Second, you want to be comfortable with the firm's ambiance. If you feel patronised or condescended to, leave. Third, be sure you know who will be your primary counselor and direct any questions you have toward her. Fourth, find out what you can from third parties. This includes checking in with the local business organisation on the firm's reputation. Finally, ask for the names of two or three former clients who you can call. If they refuse to give you any names, keep looking.

CAREER CONSULTANTS

Career consultants can be generalists or specialists. The generalists handle everything from career development to the nitty-gritty of salary negotiation. Specialists tend to focus on either helping you decide what kind of work you want to do or helping you to get a job in your chosen field.

The generalist will administer and interpret career assessments, write resumés and cover letters, counsel clients on the productive use of the Internet, teach networking skills and train clients for interviewing.

When to Use a Career Consultant

A career consultant can be useful especially for those who have little idea about how to conduct a job search or who need an objective party who can hold them accountable for executing the several stages of the search, especially the networking. Or perhaps you feel well-qualified in general to conduct your search with the exception of one crucial step, such as the resumé. Career consultants should be willing to work with you just on this or some other component of your search. If they insist that you buy a whole package, move on and find somebody more flexible and user friendly.

How to Choose Someone to Help You Achieve Your Career Goals

A first rate career consultant is master of a formidable list of professional functions. So when we are thinking of using the services of a career consultant, how can we evaluate the quality of this mastery and its application to our particular situation? This issue is complicated by the fact that career consultants come with such a variety of backgrounds and educational training.

In contrast to law, nursing and other service-oriented professions, formal career consulting is a recent creation. It is the child of the 20th century notion that work should be not only remunerative, but personally fulfilling. As this understanding of the relationship between work and our larger life has developed over the last 50 years it has spawned a flourishing industry of people whose work is to help others work.

When you consult a lawyer you know she has a law degree. Your doctor has a Doctor of Medicine degree. Your financial planner will have the right credentials and your children's teachers will have recognised professional qualifications. But when it comes to career consultants, the picture is murky.

As a distinct profession, career consulting is so new that its practitioners share no common background, preparation nor uniform standards. College students cannot major in career consulting and there are no graduate schools that, like the nation's law schools, specialise solely in training people for this field. So where do we come from? Historically there have

239

been, and still are, three separate streams flowing into the profession – the social work/mental health stream, the educational guidance stream, and a third stream that flows out of a spiritual and religious orientation. Now we can add a fourth stream – those who come to career consulting out of a more general coaching background.

The grandfather of modern career consulting, Richard Bolles, fell into career work after writing a brief guide for people like himself – Episcopal priests who were looking for a vocation outside of the parish and perhaps outside of the church structure entirely.

Bolles' brief, informal collection of tips about how to get a job outside the ministry touched a nerve and addressed a need, not only amongst his brethren in the cloth (there were no 'sistren' at the time) but, to the author's surprise, among many people in other professions too. The pamphlet became a book that is now published in a new edition every year. *What Color is Your Parachute?* recently celebrated its 30th year, with no challengers in sight to its status as the best-selling career book of all time. Today Bolles, in his 80s, maintains a sophisticated website (*www.jobhuntersbible.com*) and travels extensively giving presentations and workshops.

During the past 30 years, hundreds of clergy have followed Bolles into the career field. You can often recognise them by the letters after their name – M.Div. (for Master of Divinity), and perhaps the advanced D.Min. (for Doctor of Ministry).

This was my (Galen's) own route into the profession, though in my case it involved an escape from the Lutheran, rather than Episcopal, ministry. Between my ten years as a parish pastor and settling into my present career I experimented with such disparate pursuits as car sales, work with the disabled and organisational development. Eventually I realised that the career field made good use of some of the skills I'd developed in the ministry (listening, counselling, helping people find direction) while also offering the ever-changing variety I thrive on.

One of the most visible educational trends of the last decade has been the shift towards preparing young people for careers at increasingly early ages. When she was newly in high school, my daughter came home one day in tears. She was in despair, it turned out, because she was one of only two people in her history class who didn't already know what they wanted to do for the rest of their lives.

But ironically, in the 21st century, the notion of people spending their whole lives in one career is antiquated. On average, people now have several careers in a lifetime, and many more jobs. It's risky to pronounce a trend irrevocable, but it is unlikely that we will ever return to the mid-20th century one-life/one-career/one-company model of employment. Generation Y will be the first full generation to embrace the new, mobile approach to work and career.

Whether this new world of work will make for happier future employees is hard to predict. Generation Y may eventually find that the lack of longer term professional relationships has its own disadvantages and that changing jobs every several years takes its toll over time. But for the time being this trend sees no signs of ebbing and one of its effects has been to produce a plethora of experts and practitioners devoted to career development and job search strategies.

A number of these people have the professional background in education that gives them the ability to teach their clients how to identify their authentic calling (or callings) and secure a suitable position.

Another source of career consultants is psychologists, social workers and other mental health practitioners who have for some time appreciated how vocational fulfillment is closely tied to a person's overall contentedness in life. So, it's not surprising to find that therapists and other mental health personnel have incorporated career consulting into their portfolio of services. Many of them are doctors of psychology or education, while others have a Master of Social Work (MSW) degrees or a Masters degree in counselling.

The diverse backgrounds of career professionalshelps explain why it is difficult for the average person to evaluate and compare them on paper. This doesn't mean that we must resort to flipping coins or drawing straws. But it does put more responsibility on consumers to do their research and then make an informed, careful selection of the consultant they will use.

Consultant Credentials

There is no magic formula for choosing a consultant, but there are a number of criteria that may carry a greater or lesser weight, depending on your situation. In looking for a consultant, remember that you're the purchaser of a service. Too many of us are still inclined to approach professionals of all kinds with cap in hand, as though they are doing us a favor by accepting our business.

If formal educational credentials are important to you, it's easy enough to ask about them. Be aware that in addition to educational degrees, consultants can boast an impressive and unpronounceable mixture of credentials and certifications. If you have no idea what a person's credentials mean, even when spelled out, don't be shy about asking. Focus on the nature of the expertise that an acronym signifies and the standards by which the expertise is measured.

As we have indicated, there are no uniform certification standards or requirements for career consultants. Graduate degrees in theology, psychology and education are common. Some consultants will have an alphabet soup of letters after their name. Again, make sure to ask what the letters stand for and the requirements the consultant needed to meet in order to earn them.

Here is a sample of other considerations for you to take into account:

Experience

First, verify that your consultant has experience working in the field and that she has worked with people like you. You may be:

- a recent or soon to be college graduate.
- a PhD research scientist.
- a person returning to the workforce after a 20 year absence.
- an accompanying partner looking for a portable career.
- a woman who was sexually harassed at work seven years ago, resigned, and has not worked since.
- a recent retiree looking for a part-time job with which to occupy his time.
- a person with disabilities or special needs.
- somebody who has put 25 years into a career and now wants to do something totally different.

And the list goes on. If your consultant has not had experience that fits your background, make sure that you feel comfortable that she can make the stretch.

In addition, if you are looking for a mentor, then you may want to pick someone who has experience, and success in exactly the area you want to work in yourself - someone who inspires you and is passionate about what he or she does for a living.

Specialisation

It's a good idea to figure out what kind of help you need before your first visit. If you want help figuring out what to do, see a career development professional. If you know where you want to go, but need help getting there, meet with a job search specialist. There are some generalists, adept at both the 'helping to figure out where' and the 'helping to get there'. Generalists offer the advantage of being available to accompany their clients through the entire process.

In working on your job search, you may not need the whole laundry list of services. If it's just a revised resumé that you need, look for somebody who writes lots of them. Ask to see samples of her work. If interviewing gives you the jitters, find a person who is expert in interview preparation. Ask the consultant how she prepares people for interviewing. Request to see examples of interview preparations sheets.

Local Reputation

The best way to find a competent professional is on the basis of recommendations from satisfied clients. If you know people who have seen a career consultant, ask them their opinion. Would they recommend the person? What are her strengths and weaknesses? What is her style and how much does she charge. If you do not know such people, ask the consultant you are considering for two or three former clients you can call. If she balks at this request, be sure to interview others.

The Fit

As the client of a consultant, you are a consumer of services. Make your purchase with the same care you would give to a decision about what new television set to buy. When you walk into a store's electronics section, do you settle on the first set that meets your dimension requirements? Probably not. Like most other consumers, you turn the set on, look at the picture, research and try the features, and determine if the set you are looking at has enough of the bells and whistles you want without expensive features you are unlikely to use. You are even likely to compare its picture with those of other models in the same price range.

Bring this same approach into selecting a career consultant. Interview several (you should not be charged for the initial 'do we have a fit' session) with a special eye towards identifying somebody with whom you feel comfortable. When purchasing a new car, most buyers research potential makes and models and then decide what to focus on when they go shopping. After narrowing down their choices, they take one or two of them for a test drive. If the feel is right, 90 per cent of new car buyers are flexible about the features. That personal fit, the 'it feels just right' sensation, is no less valuable in choosing counselors than cars.

You may talk to three distinguished consultants with graduate degrees but select an educationally undistinguished person because you sense that she's the one with whom you will be comfortable being entirely honest. As we indicated, you should never engage the services of a career consultant before interviewing the person to assess her expertise, style and your own level of comfort with the person. If any of your candidates resents this, you can cross her name off your list.

Work Samples

If you wanted to have a family portrait painted, it is unthinkable that you would commission the services of an artist whose portraiture you had never laid eyes on. Why should a consultant be any different? Ask to see samples of resumés, cover letters and materials used to prepare people for interviews. Are they well put together, the product of purposeful and careful work? Perhaps the consultant's materials are excellent, but of a style that is incongruent with the portrait you want to present of yourself.

Again, if you pick up 'consultant reluctance' at this stage of your decision making process, keep looking.

Flexibility and a Collaborative Style

Quality consultants are good listeners and do not operate with a predetermined agenda and process into which they squeeze every client. You want to work with a consultant who understands your particular situation, lays out the options available along with their advantages and disadvantages, and helps you to arrive at decisions with which you feel comfortable. Career consultants should not hesitate to give their opinions about how you should conduct your search, but they should also respect your autonomy and leave all the final decisions in your hands.

Costs and Fees

Before you begin working with a consultant, make sure you know how much her services will cost. Your consultant should be able to explain clearly how much she charges, how you will be billed, when payment is due and in what form she expects it. It's very important to have these details ironed out at the beginning. If they are left vague or unaddressed, this will undermine the consultant-client relationship.

Most consultants bill by the hour, charging for both the time spent with clients one-on-one and for the preparatory work done in between sessions. Hourly fees vary greatly according to country and region, the qualifications of the consultant and her years of experience. Generally, the more education a person has, the higher her hourly rate. In metropolitan areas fees will be higher than those in rural areas. Make sure you understand all the financial terms and can calculate your payments as you go along. Steer clear of consultants who require weekly meetings no matter what. Some consultants are willing to work on a sliding scale. Remember, don't settle on the first consultant with a friendly smile; shop around. Don't sign any contracts yet.

Some consultants charge by the month or by the 'unit' of service given – a set fee for the resumé, another for the cover letter, and so on. Resumé fees often vary, depending on the length and complexity of the document. A few consultants charge per month, though with some stipulations about the number of meetings or conversations. Some offer free, between-session email and telephone support, or membership in an online forum, support or chat group.

Some consultants will charge a one off fee for the entire process, regardless of the length of time it takes; the fee is payable only when you, the customer, are satisfied.

Before you sign anything, make sure you understand and are comfortable with all the financial particulars. If you're unclear about the costs of the services or about how payments are to be made, your uncertainty will undermine the trust necessary to a successful partnership. If you sense that the consultant is being deliberately vague, don't hesitate to go elsewhere.

Some consultants will prefer payment at the time of services. Others will send a bill or will want to be paid monthly. You need to be clear how much you are paying, when you will pay, and what, if any, services are extra. Your consultant should be able to explain all this in a straightforward manner and, ideally, have the essential information in a printed format. There is never any reason to sign a contract with a consultant stipulating the number of sessions or the overall duration of your work together. These variables cannot be determined in advance.

BACK TO OUR CASE STUDIES

Generally, there are two kinds of overlapping help that people seek from careers professional. The first, typified by the example of Austin, is career guidance, sometimes called career/life development. People like Austin know what they don't want to do, but now need help in identifying a career path that will give them fulfillment and a sense of meaning. Right now, Austin needs the services of a person who specialises in the 'what' question – what career will make good use of his talents and abilities in an environment that is conducive to personal and professional growth? To gain insight into these questions Austin can employ either a career consultant or coach.

Austin

The person Austin works with may call himself or herself a career specialist, or a career development professional. In some cases, she may even be a business or career coach – but not all coaches are trained to provide career specific advice, so do check. This person will probably ask Austin to complete one or more standard vocational or career questionnaires and lead Austin through interpreting their results. In doing so, the consultant will focus on what the results reveal concerning Austin's vocational strengths and preferences. Clients shouldn't assume that assessments will yield simple answers to their uncertainties. But they are likely to generate interesting and meaningful raw data. It's the consultant's responsibility to organise and present the data and use it as a springboard for further conversation and reflection. She will also be able to focus the client's attention on possibilities that would benefit from follow up research. Armed with this new knowledge, Austin and his consultant can customise their ongoing research to focus on a select number of vocational possibilities.

Simon

Simon knows what he wants and where he wants to go but does not have the inside knowledge he needs to get there without help. He needs to talk to other people in his industry, find out about the legal implications of setting up a business. Moreover, he needs help from someone who speaks Spanish. Simon would benefit from the goal setting and motivation services of a coach and the mentorship of someone who knows the Spanish tourism industry.

Janice

Janice presents us with a different picture. She's fairly clear about where she wants to go, but doesn't know how to get there. By way of contrast with Austin, Janice already knows the answer to the 'what' question: she knows what she wants to do. But she doesn't know how to get from where she is to where she wants to be. Janice needs help with the 'how' questions. She needs to work with a consultant who is expert not only at the nuts and bolts of finding a job, but also at transitioning into a second career.

Suzanne

Suzanne presents yet a fourth kind of situation. Although in her late forties, she has never worked before. She questions whether she has any marketable skills. She is nervous about the job search process and about entering the work force at what she refers to as her 'grand longevity point'.

Janice and Suzanne both need help in the following areas:

RESUMÉS

Many people do write their own resumés, perhaps with a bit of help from a friend or family member. The results are often adequate, but less effective than they could be. Resumés are notoriously difficult to write for oneself. In fact, most career consultants get help in writing their own resumé. A career consultant can help clients to identify their most valuable skills, abilities and achievements and to articulate them in a way that will be maximally persuasive to a potential employer. A consultant can also help her client with the formatting of the resumé, laying out the information on the one or two pages in a manner that is aesthetically pleasing and easily accessible to the reader. Recruiters and hiring managers have little patience with resumés that are awkwardly formatted and written and make them work hard to mine the nuggets of relevant information.

This is especially the case with career changers. A key challenge in building Janice's resumé will be to show how her experience with supermarkets can be transferred to the world of local, not-for-profit art organisations.

'I used a professional resumé writer. He knew exactly how to take my experiences, achievements and strengths and put it into one document that presented who I am. I have a resumé that is authentic and true to my career experiences and personality. They know what type of words to use to attract immediate attention.'
Ursula, South African in America, *www.marketingmentorexpert.com*

COVER LETTERS

A resumé usually needs a cover letter, a document that many people find more challenging to write than the resumé itself. The cover letter is by no means a meaningless formality, especially for people who are shifting their career focus. Like the resumé, the cover letter should be a collaborative effort between the job seeker and the consultant.

Some job hunters want their consultant to do all the work. 'Find me a job,' the client will say. Consultants know that nobody can find another person a job. Consultants can provide guidance, direction, advice and assistance. But they are no more in the business of finding people jobs than financial planners are in the business of giving clients money out of their own pocket. In order for a job search to bear fruit, the client must be actively involved every step of the way.

NETWORKING

Despite all the hoopla surrounding the Internet, and despite its undeniable usefulness as a research tool, most people still get their jobs through networking the old-fashioned way. Many people new to job hunting find networking confusing and intimidating and have little idea where to start or how to build a continually expanding web of contacts. A career consultant can correct misperceptions about networking and give clients practical advice on how to go about doing it.

INTERVIEWING

Some people are such consummate networkers that their formal documents – the resumé and cover letter – are of secondary importance. But even skilled and experienced networkers can lose their confidence when faced with a formal job interview. It's possible to get a job without a resumé or a cover letter, but very rarely without an interview. Career consultants are expert at rigorously preparing their clients for interviewing by:

- Generating a list of questions a client is likely to be asked.
- Teaching the interviewee to identify the primary concerns behind the interviewer's questions.
- Helping the client to formulate his own questions for the interviewer.
- Crafting answers to between 10 and 20 representative interview questions.
- Developing brief 30-to-60 second achievement statements.
- Conducting mock interviews.
- Conducting videotaped pre-interviews, for review.
- Holding a post-interview debriefing.
- Giving tips on salary negotiation.

USE OF THE INTERNET

The Internet, as we noted, has transformed the ways in which we conduct research. But for the novice the enormous volume of information available can be daunting, if not overwhelming. It's difficult to know where to start and, once underway, how to collect relevant information most efficiently. Career consultants provide expertise on how to make this tool an ally, without overly depending on it.

STAYING ORGANISED AND FOCUSED

People who are impressively organised in their personal and professional lives sometimes conduct their job search in a surprisingly haphazard manner. They can benefit from having somebody to whom they are accountable, a person who can function for their job search in a role that is analogous to that of an effective manager at work. In addition, the career counsellor can recommend, and often supply, forms and other tools with which the client can stay organised.

TROUBLESHOOTING AND ADVICE

No two job searches are the same, and each one yields its share of puzzling or unusual circumstances. Often the right course of action can depend on the subtleties and nuances of the situation. Career consultants, by virtue of their experience, can help clients assess such situations and respond to them appropriately.

SUPPORT AND AFFIRMATION

No matter how qualified and resilient the job seeker, job hunting is often distressing and demoralising. Ideally, everyone has a supportive cheering section of friends and family members – but the ongoing encouragement of a professional person outside one's usual network of support is usually valuable.

It is often remarked that there is abundant information about the job search both on the Internet and in bookstores. Indeed, scarcity of resources is not a problem facing the contemporary job hunter. Quite the contrary, there is so much information available that it can bewilder even the most sophisticated job seekers. One valuable role the career consultant plays is to connect the job seeker with the right amount of the right information. A good career consultant is an expert at marshalling and organising the right amount of the right information. She has a general knowledge of what it available and can match the client up with the resources that will be most helpful to the particulars of his search.

Career Consulting For Expatriates

As this book amply demonstrates with its numerous personal stories, pursuing vocational goals can be both more complicated and more adventurous as an expat than on your own turf. Your eligibility to work at all may be curtailed by government regulations. Some countries prohibit non-nationals from holding regular full time jobs. Obviously the best time to find this out is before the move. But don't unquestioningly assume that an official policy against the employment of foreign spouses will condemn you to several years of idleness. There are some countries that prohibit expats from working, but define 'working' as a regular full-time job with a native company or organisation. Less formal work arrangements, like those involving entrepreneurial and home based businesses, may be quite feasible.

'In Malaysia work permits are impossible to get for spouses (because there is a protectionist policy) unless you are a teacher. However, I am able to continue environmental work on a short-term contract basis/freelance for organisations such as WWF, although it is only paid on a local volunteer 'pocket-money' basis.' **Environmentalist, 2005 Trailing Spouse Survey**

Simply put, it's important to research the prospects in the area you will be moving to. A career consultant can be very helpful in gathering and interpreting this information, both before and after your move. Although native-born consultants may have a close acquaintance with the pertinent rules and regulations governing the work options of foreign nationals, you may find it easier to work with somebody who is part of the expatriate community and well connected with other expats.

Whether you can officially work or not, it's naturally important that your career consultant be familiar with all of the formalities of the classic job search as well as the informalities and idiosyncrasies of the national and local culture. She should also be able to network you into relationships with both nationals and other expatriates who can help you from the 'been-there and done-that' vantage point.

One of the themes of this book is that even in the absence of formal employment, expatriates have a wealth of opportunities with which to enrich themselves personally, socially and vocationally. Even if the vocational enrichment doesn't include monetary recompense, it can add to what you will offer your next employer upon repatriation. Experienced expatriates, including those who have spent many years abroad in different countries, emphasise the importance of being open to new and novel pursuits. Bring to your time in another country a spirit of adventure that might seem, at home, wistfully impractical. You may become one of the many expats who discover a new passion and vocation to take home with you. A good number of foreign spouses have kindled a new passion by volunteering in the host country.

A consultant can help you to identify these opportunities and to assemble a portfolio of activities that will be stimulating and career enhancing. Keep an abundant record of everything you get involved with so that upon your return home, or your arrival in another foreign location, you can assemble a portfolio to document and demonstrate your activities to potential employers. A career consultant can help you to select items for your portfolio and to organise it in a way that will attract a person's attention.

Your access to consultants who share your nationality or first language will depend on the country and on language compatibilities. Even in countries where the profession of career consulting is formally unknown, you may be able to find local citizens who can fulfill many of the functions we have identified in this chapter. If not, the expatriate population may boast several people whose experience, insight and counsel can help you to determine your direction.

REMOTE CONSULTANTS

Career consulting can be successfully conducted via the telephone or webcam, using a program such as Skype (*www.skype.com*) which is free. This is especially effective when supplemented by the use of the Internet. Technologically based consulting has several advantages. Firstly, it enables consultants to work with clients who live at a geographic distance – in another state or province, or even in another country or continent. Secondly, clients can reap the convenience of accessing services without having to leave their home. And for clients who have special transportation problems, teleconsulting, as it is known, is more than a convenience. Thirdly, there are clients who feel more comfortable working with somebody over the telephone. Some clients don't want the closer relationship that is more likely to form when people sit across from each other, while for others the telephone brings the measure of distance they need in order to feel safe in discussing painful career and vocational issues.

Most consultants today are willing to work with clients both in person and over the telephone. The two might meet in person once a month while transacting much of their work via telephone and email.

Many consultants will provide frequent, scheduled telephone consultations and then agree to communicate by email on an ad hoc basis as well.

MAKING THE MOST OF IT

The nature of your expatriate experience depends partly on whether your new home shares your native country's cultural history. For example, Americans who move to France or Italy normally have a smoother transition than their counterparts who spend several years in Zimbabwe. No matter where you are, you will probably have opportunities that will never again come your way. This is a time to explore, experiment, to push beyond those borders of conventionality that may have restricted you back home. In doing this, you are likely to discover that there is more within yourself than you had known.

For case studies and the opportunity for you to add your own please go to *www.career-in-your-suitcase.com*

11 the male accompanying partner

When in 1995 his wife's career took him first to Turkey and then to France, Huw Francis put down his briefcase and took over the role of househusband. During this time he has created a portable career for himself and a brand new identity. His story will resonate with and inspire accompanying partners, both male and female.

'And the oak tree and the cypress grow not in each other's shadow.'
Kahlil Gibran, The Prophet

In this chapter:

- The rise of a new breed of expat spouse
- What's so different about the new breed?
- Men and coffee mornings
- A shift in role
- 'And what do you do?'
- The true story of a male accompanying partner
- Benefits of having a successful portable career
- Hindsight is 20/20
- Options for the male accompanying partner

The Rise of a New Breed
of Expat Spouse

Despite the advent of female emancipation, women's rights, laws against sexual discrimination and the growth of political correctness – men still usually earn more than women, rise more quickly and higher up the corporate ladder, are thought to be more career minded and have a much greater likelihood of being sent abroad as an expatriate employee. Women, on the other hand, may be thought more family- than career-oriented and more willing to let their husband's career take precedence over theirs.

However, there are growing numbers of women who earn more and are more employable than their partners, who are more career focused, who have a more secure career, or who enjoy their job more than their partner does.

There are also men who want to stay at home with the kids while their wife goes out to work, who take a career break while the children are of pre-school age, or who accept that their partner's career will take precedence over their own.

Increasingly, these couples too decide to move abroad, or are offered the chance to do so. The advantages of such a move can be varied and include improved lifestyle, career benefits, or an escape from unemployment, redundancy, and other unpleasant situations – much the same reasons as men take an international job and their partner follows them.

Slowly but surely the number of female expatriate employees is increasing, and some surveys have indicated that almost 23 per cent of expatriate employees are now women. Consequently, as more women do become expatriate employees, as opposed to expatriate spouses, more men are becoming accompanying spouses – though a larger percentage of female expatriate employees, compared to male expatriate employees, is not married. As shown in the introduction to this book, as many as 17 per cent of accompanying partners are now male.

HUW FRANCIS – A NEW EXPAT SPOUSE!

Having worked as an engineer in the UK, I travelled to Hong Kong in 1992 and quickly found a job with an import/export company. A couple of job changes later and whilst studying for a postgraduate qualification in International Business I joined a management consultancy where I worked as a business manager and an associate consultant. I also met and married my Scottish wife Seonaid in Hong Kong and after three years our first son, Ieuan, was born there too.

With increasing economic uncertainty as the Handover to China approached, we decided to leave, and both of us began looking for new jobs – Seonaid was then teaching at the Chinese International School. We worked on the principle that whoever got a good job offer first would accept it, and the other would stay at home, look after our son and write a book!

As it turned out my wife was offered a job at a school in Ankara, Turkey, and a few months later we arrived in our new home. Having arrived in Hong Kong separately, this was our first move as a couple and it took us a while to settle into our new roles of 'breadwinner' and 'househusband/male accompanying partner'.

'Of course, one might question whether it is the growth of female assignees with male spouses that has prompted this action. In the past, dual career policies have been developed with a predominantly female audience in mind. Limited financial compensation but positive support measures have made some headway in encouraging spouse mobility but, by their very nature, they could not address the heart of the problem – namely the ability to work in the host country in the first place. One wonders whether a stronger spousal (male) voice in pursuing work opportunities is driving organisational lobbying for change or whether the requirement for greater gender equality in expatriation, reflecting the need to exploit all available talent, provides a sufficient driver by itself. Either way, the employer voice is strengthening and, judging by some of the successes achieved so far, governments are listening. Whatever the driver, improved work-permit regulations will provide a kick-start, but the organisations should not feel that this is a reason to step back. Legislative interventions need to be backed by career development initiatives so that those who want to, can pursue career opportunities alike, regardless of whether they are the primary assignee of the second career holder.'
ORC Worldwide, Dual Careers and International Assignments Survey 2005

WHAT'S SO DIFFERENT ABOUT THE NEW BREED?

As the employee, leading expatriate women face different issues than when they are an accompanying spouse – and their accompanying partners face different issues from those that male expatriate employees have traditionally faced.

For many of these couples this scenario – the woman being the prime/sole wage earner – will be a new experience and place new pressures on their relationship as each partner learns to adapt to the new role and responsibilities. These pressures can be both professional and domestic and the stresses of professional life can impinge on domestic life, and vice versa.

One woman who had worked abroad for many years as an aid worker and ESL teacher, both before and after she got married, found that when she became the sole wage earner and had a family relying on her solitary income, it suddenly became clear to her why men work long hours to keep their job and climb the corporate ladder. This realisation, that everything the family had depended on her, caused an unexpected amount of additional stress that she had not experienced before, and which also affected the relationship with her husband. It took many months for them to become used to the new balance of responsibilities in their marriage and accept that both their roles were equally important.

From the man's point of view, having been brought up expecting to be the breadwinner in a family, suddenly having to rely on his partner for money can be a severe blow to his ego and self-esteem – and this can cause resentment of his partner.

Unfortunately, the scenario is often new not for just the couple concerned, but also for colleagues, friends, relatives and employers – and they can't always be relied on to be supportive in their reactions.

For example, a female expatriate employee whose husband stayed at home to look after their children faced constant criticism from her mother, who thought that it was wrong for her to work while her husband 'lived off her'. Women employees can also find themselves commonly assumed to be the bilingual secretary in the office, rather than a career professional able to deal with clients as well as her male colleagues.

The woman can also have to listen to criticism of her partner, which can be upsetting. One woman overheard her colleagues saying about her husband, 'What type of fool must he be to quit his job for her? What was he doing before – selling hamburgers at McDonalds?' In this case it did not seem to matter that the husband in question was a trial attorney – nor that the wife of the man who made the comments was a medical doctor who had previously given up her own career to follow him.

The men can face problems too and when not employed they can find that other people consider them a failure, or even an unqualified waster.

One businessman, who had worked with international corporate banking firms, took time out to change his career path when his wife got a new job abroad. He found it took years before most of his wife's new colleagues took him seriously in any capacity, just because he was not employed when they first met him. On one occasion a fellow expat carefully explained about an investment opportunity he was looking into and condescendingly explained about stock sales, IPOs and the investment bank that was handling the deal, and then asked if the male accompanying partner had heard of Goldman Sachs. When he replied, 'Yeah, they used to be one of my clients and I worked on a number of IPOs myself,' the other expat looked stunned and quickly ended the conversation. The male accompanying partner went on to develop a successful independent consulting business and the other expat never raised the subject of Goldman Sachs again.

MEN AND COFFEE MORNINGS

For female expatriate spouses there is a plethora of women's support groups to assist, encourage and, yes, support relocated women. Dedicated support groups for *men* are rare, however. STUDS (Spouse Trailing Under Duress Successfully), in Brussels, has been active for many years, but the London branch has faded from view.

Although the women's support groups will often offer their support to male accompanying partners, both the men and the women can find it somewhat uncomfortable. Despite political correctness, men like to talk about different things than women during their coffee mornings – and women certainly don't talk about everything in front of the men.

The men can also find that activities organised by the women's group may be aimed specifically at women, and so be of little interest to them. There is therefore the problem that though the group may accept the men, the men do not always want to be accepted, as they would prefer to do 'men's stuff'.

This subtle, though natural, divide can lead the accompanying man to feelings of isolation, and that loneliness is probably one of the biggest problems faced by male accompanying partners. It can lead the man to resent his partner and position in life.

As one Human Resources manager commented, 'In most assignments, women will meet other wives who have followed their husbands, and have a built-in social circle. The male accompanying partner does not necessarily have anyone else in his position, so even if he were au fait with the idea (before departure), the reality (after arrival) may hit him in the face like a ton of bricks and he has no one to turn to (or against), but his wife.'

A SHIFT IN ROLE

As with female accompanying partners, most men will have a career before the move, and the impact on their career of leaving the country is often a major determining factor in whether or not their partner accepts the international appointment in the first place.

For many couples, the careers of both partners are important elements in creating the sense of personal worth, happiness and satisfaction that make the relationship a successful one.

No matter which partner in a couple is offered an expatriate position, and which one would be expected to accompany him or her as the supporting spouse, the change in status of either individual will affect the balance of the relationship. The change in status does not have to be negative to adversely affect the relationship. A promotion may seem to be a good thing – but the increased responsibility can mean additional time away from home, either at the office or traveling on business. That additional time away can cause tension in a relationship. It's not uncommon for spouses with children to look after to feel like little more than a domestic servant, when their working spouse returns from extended overseas travel and spoils the children to relieve their guilt about being away – while the spouse has to enforce the rules on doing homework, tidying bedrooms, bedtimes, etc.

Although women have long been expected to let their careers take second place to their partners', for men this is a relatively new experience. It is even rarer for a man to be expected to give up work altogether to allow his partner to further a career – as is likely to be the case when a married woman accepts an international posting.

Carrie Shearer, an international HR consultant, believes that, 'Men, feeling societal pressure no doubt, identify themselves by what they do. When they trail and do not have a career, they lose their identity and often their sense of self. Women, perhaps because they're more accustomed to seeing themselves in various roles, seem to have an easier time adjusting to not working, or to working part time, or freelancing.'

For the parents of the expatriate couple, though, it can be anathema for the woman to work and the man to stay at home. Any resulting loudly voiced negative reactions from family and friends can cause additional and unwanted stress during what is already a difficult transition. Of course in-laws can be notorious sources of strife in any marriage and the fact that they are half way round the world does not necessarily diminish the strength of their criticism, even when they try to pretend they are not really criticising. The forcefulness of a single 'Oh!' when you tell your parents your latest plans can take the wind out of the sails of even the most optimistic person.

Becoming an expatriate involves many changes, all of which are stressful. There will be a new home, new country, new culture, new job, new social circle and often a new language and climate to adjust to. But when a couple relocates abroad and there is also a significant change in role and status of one partner, additional stress can be added as the relationship needs to re-establish its equilibrium and the partners learn to become comfortable with their new roles. Re-establishing the structure of a relationship in a foreign country is going to be much more difficult than doing it in the home country – since many of the traditional support groups of long term friends, family and colleagues will not be so easily available.

The host culture may also be less familiar than the home culture with the concept of a woman taking the lead career role in a relationship. This can cause difficulties both personally and professionally in some countries, though in many parts of the world expatriates are expected to be different anyway, so it may cause less comment than at 'home'.

In the Middle East it is uncommon for men to look after the children, and one male accompanying partner looking after his six week old son soon after his wife went back to work was continually asked by concerned local matriarchs where the baby's mother was. One day, as he tried to explain that the mother was at work, his command of the local language let him down and he mistakenly said, 'The baby has no mother.' The matriarch's attitude changed from concern to sympathy and praise for taking on such a hard role – thereafter the man always repeated this explanation and his life became much less frustrating. In much of East Asia, however, expatriates look and behave so differently from their hosts that a male accompanying partner would not often attract much additional attention.

Expatriates often sense their differences from the local community, but a couple consisting of a working woman and an accompanying male partner is likely to be different not only from the local community, but from the rest of the expatriate community too. This complete sense of difference can be an isolating experience and can become problematic, especially for the male accompanying partner who doesn't even have his job to base their joint identity on. Problems are most likely to arise when the male accompanying partner feels undervalued by his partner and friends, or when he suffers from a loss of self-esteem and subsequent depression due to his change in situation.

An expatriate couple embracing the 'trailing male role, having carefully thought through the implications of doing so, is going to have a better chance of successfully setting themselves up in their new lifestyle than one who takes it on with little forethought. Approaching the experience with a positive attitude will go a long way towards smoothing the transition – but it will not necessarily make the transition easy. As with any international relocation, whether the accompanying partner is male or female, the mutual support of both partners is essential to protect and develop the relationship and the individual happiness of both those involved.

A relationship that is working well before the relocation stands a much better chance of remaining solid after the move than one that is not doing so well, no matter which partner is the employee. Any problems or conflicts that are already present, whether they are active or dormant, are likely to be magnified by an overseas move. Most family counselors agree that an overseas posting should not be seen as an opportunity to repair a damaged relationship, but more as a chance to temper an already good one.

As a male accompanying partner life can be lonely – not only from a lack of men to socialise with, but because it takes time to adjust to a new role in life. It's not just different from what has gone before, it's often a public reversal of status within the relationship.

There can often be the feeling that people think the male accompanying partner is not fulfilling his role as breadwinner, 'as a man should'. This feeling is likely to come from the man himself, since despite all the politically correct talk that men and women are equal, the reality is that men are still generally conditioned to think of themselves as the breadwinner and protector of their family. They are expected by society to work and 'do their duty', and they expect it of themselves too. Giving up all financial contribution to the household, or even just reducing that input, can be psychologically tough for a man to accept, as it leaves him dependent on a woman. The phrase, 'sponging off your wife' is likely to cross a male accompanying partner's mind a few times, even if it's not used within earshot.

Women are caught somewhere in the middle too. It is supposed to be acceptable for them to have careers and be successful, though they are expected to take care of the family at the same time. For a woman to rise so high in her career that it's economically sensible for her to stay at work, while her partner gives up his career to stay at home and look after the children, can raise eyebrows. When a couple has children the conflicting emotions of needing the mental stimulation of a demanding job and maternal guilt over being away from the children can also cause stress for the woman. Just as men are conditioned to be the provider, many women still have at least a residual conditioning that they should be the one staying at home with the children.

'AND WHAT DO YOU DO?'

Once a couple is abroad, the fact that the spouse is a male accompanying partner becomes an obvious and unavoidable fact. At parties, social gatherings and in daily life, the initial batch of questions asked of newly arrived expatriates always includes, 'So... what do *you* do?' The answer 'nothing' provokes various reactions, and almost always involves some element of surprise – though it can include disapproval or downright derision. Being confident and proud of your answer will increase the likelihood of a positive response – whatever you decide to say.

For a male accompanying partner who previously defined much of his personal sense of worth through his job, this lack of status can be demoralising. Starting from a position where he feels himself in some way to be less than the working men around him, he can then find it hard to integrate himself into the male expatriate community.

This is precisely why it can be very important for a male accompanying partner to have a portable career – especially if there is a likelihood that his partner will continue to move around the world as she progresses in her career, and he wants to go with her.

As Carrie Shearer says, 'Since men seem to more closely align themselves by what they do, it becomes more imperative for them to have meaningful work.'

The True Story Of A Male Accompanying Partner

As mentioned earlier, in 1995, with the approach of the handover of Hong Kong to China, Seonaid and I decided it was time to leave the territory for another part of the world. Ieuan was less than a year old and we were keen to move somewhere closer to the UK, so we both applied for jobs, again with the intention of accepting the first decent one to come along, whoever got the offer.

My wife was offered two jobs before I was offered any at all, so we picked Ankara and headed off to Central Anatolia in Turkey. We ended up in the hills 15km from the city living on a campus that had the dubious ability to seem quiet and secluded sometimes and, at other times remote, isolated and claustrophobic.

It was a joint decision to move to Ankara, and a joint decision that Seonaid would be the salaried employee while I would be a male accompanying partner (before we had even heard of the title), stay at home, look after the family and be a 'writer'.

THE REALITY

One thing became clear from the start: it didn't really matter what I had done before the move, it was what I did now that mattered to most people. The good job I'd left behind in Hong Kong counted for nothing; I was now a househusband and nothing else.

The first year was hard for both of us as we learned to cope with our new roles and I struggled to launch my career as a writer.

I knew I wanted to write a novel, but I also needed to earn some money to contribute to the household finances. I had to do the housework too and my wife and I had very different ideas about when the housework was finished! Writing had seemed to be the perfect choice as a job to do from home, but as most aspiring novelists will tell you, it's not the best way to earn money quickly – plus I had to try and do enough housework to keep Seonaid happy before I sat down to write.

So I made the first adjustment of many in my career aims. I decided to write some non-fiction articles (because they're much quicker to write) and get them published while I was writing the novel. Being an expatriate it seemed like a good idea to write travel pieces and articles about expatriate living.

It was over a year before the first article was published and I only found out because my neighbour brought round the newspaper he was reading to show me that I was in it – they gave a six month subscription as payment for that first article. The second article earned me $25 soon afterwards.

Over the years the expatriate living articles got published fairly regularly, but it takes a lot of effort to sell a travel article on a city that gets visited by less than five per cent of all tourists who visit the country. Mind you, I did sell a few destination pieces on Ankara. Getting published is, however much you are paid, a great way to boost your self esteem and sense of worth. When you feel your status in life has fallen from the heights of a good job in glamorous Hong Kong, to being the domestic drudge in a city not many people can even find on the map, it's amazing what little things make you feel good again!.

Not many people seemed to take my writing career seriously during that first year in Turkey, though with the friends who were supportive, the subject of writing a handbook on expatriate living was also raised quite a lot. Among those who were less supportive it seemed to be a common idea that writing was easy and something that anybody could do, so it was really not that impressive. Somehow, during that first year in Turkey, the idea of writing a handbook on expatriate living stayed little more than an idea.

Then, a year after we arrived in Ankara, a new family arrived and I was no longer the only expatriate with a young child on the campus. When I'd been the only parent of a pre-schooler I had spent a lot of time wandering around the city, shopping in the markets and enjoying the wonderful food of the little restaurants in the narrow streets of the old town. With my blond haired, blue eyed son in a backpack I was never short of people to talk to and the Turks were incredibly hospitable – I spent many happy hours drinking chay and eating kebab while Ieuan was kept entertained by the waiters. However, now I had someone I could talk to in English, my Turkish stopped improving so dramatically as I spent more time on campus to allow the children to play together.

The new spouse, Michelyne Callan, also seemed keen on the idea of writing the handbook for expatriates and we agreed to work on it together. I bought a few books, notably *How to Write A Book Proposal* by Michael Larsen, *The Writer's Handbook* (UK publication) and *The Writers Market* (US publication) – and started to write the outline and book proposal.

That was in 1997 and we didn't sell the book proposal that year.

Being at home with a pre-school child has its good points, but intellectual conversation isn't one of them. So to meet people, I volunteered to edit an orientation handbook for newly arrived expatriates in Ankara, and also participated in orientation programmes every summer as the new expatriates arrived. At the time I offered to take part in this for the benefit of my sanity, but in the long run the volunteering had other benefits too.

I also kept writing articles, especially for the booming number of websites whose publishers did not really care where I was, as long as I had email. I also kept working on the novel. *Mule Train* was about two backpackers who become caught up in a drug smuggling ring, and was based on the three months I had once spent travelling from the far south of Pakistan, through Afghanistan and on into Xinjiang province of China.

During 1998 and 1999 I found quite a few online markets that wanted to publish my articles and some of them paid well too. But it was hard to build up a solid list of publications that took my work regularly, because no sooner had I established a good relationship with the editor, than the publication went bankrupt. I learned a good lesson during that period – never rely on one good client, because you never know when they might disappear.

In 1998, to supplement our household income, I took a job teaching classes at a language school in Ankara. Although it was not the writing I wanted to do, it was another chance to meet people, boost my self-confidence and advertise myself to a new set of people. It worked! A positive result came from this surprising quarter and in the summer of 1998 the boss of the school asked me to write a textbook for him. I had my first big writing commission.

The pay was good and writing a text book was almost what I wanted to do – it was a book sized project, even if it wasn't a novel.

Despite my hard work, it took me three years to feel the majority of people I knew really took me seriously as a writer – mostly because no one I knew ever saw my articles published and so they had no idea it was happening so regularly.

However, at cocktail parties, embassy functions and at every other opportunity, I kept telling anyone who would listen, that I was a writer.

This self-promotion eventually paid off and in 2000 I was offered the chance of working as a consultant for the British Council, to produce a major report for the Education Counselling Service advising UK education providers how best to market their services in Turkey. This extensive document was another book length project that, although it was still not my novel, allowed me to work as a writer and drew on my knowledge of Turkey, a country I had grown to love. It paid well, too.

Shortly after finishing the consultancy job for the British Council the proposal for *Live and Work Abroad: A Guide for Modern Nomads* was finally accepted. It was now three years since I'd started work on it. After sending the proposal off to more than twenty publishers around the world (and hearing back from less than half of them, despite the enclosed SASE) a publisher (Vacation Work Publications, *www.vacationwork.co.uk*) finally accepted the proposal and wanted us to write it in six months.

The whole process of selling our book to the publisher was completed over the Internet. I emailed him with an initial enquiry, he asked for more information by email and I submitted the full proposal the same way.

Six months of intensive hard work saw the manuscript sent off just before Christmas – also by email. The letters on my keyboard were fading and somewhere a small forest of renewable soft wood trees was being replanted. However, email, having sold the book, also allowed the book to be written in the time available. Almost 100 people contributed their experiences, knowledge and advice to it and most of that input came into my computer electronically. Apart from the fact that delivery of the input was quicker by email than snail mail, it also meant the text did not have to be carefully retyped – a quick 'cut and paste' allowed us to do the job in a fraction of the time transcription would have taken.

After a short break over Christmas, the proofs came back early in the New Year and it took three days to read through the 255 pages. *A Guide for Modern Nomads* appeared on the shelves in March 2001 and the feeling of satisfaction was immense.

Almost four years of slog went into that book, but it was well worth it. Labouring through the stress of relocating to Turkey and swapping roles with my wife; the hours spent slogging to write for low-paying markets; teaching late into the evening on cold winter nights in Ankara; writing the textbook; volunteering on the orientation programmes and doing the consultancy work for the British Council – all of those experiences went into that book. Plus the four years in Hong Kong before that. I also had the wonderful opportunity to stay at home with my sons while they were young – our second son, Sean, having been born in an Islamic Foundation hospital in Ankara.

BENEFITS OF HAVING A
SUCCESSFUL PORTABLE CAREER

When *Live and Work Abroad: A Guide for Modern Nomads* came out, people started writing to me with offers of work. The best promotional tool I ever found was that book – and, like most advertising, its creation cost me more money than the publisher was paying for it.

The Internet made marketing and selling the book easier too. I was able to send out press releases via the Internet to businesses, consultants and my friends across the globe. By encouraging people to forward my announcements to their friends as well, it went even further. As the book was available from Amazon.co.uk, Amazon.com, Amazon.fr, Amazon.jp and other online bookstores, expatriates and potential expatriates all round the world could get hold of the book, even though it might not be in their local bookstore.

Since the book's publication, I have been getting paid more for writing articles. I have updated another book (*Live and Work in Italy*, also from Vacation Work) and done a lot more consultancy work with international organisations.

Although I write mostly on the subject of expatriate living, I have found a niche that not many other writers on this subject can fill: I am a male accompanying partner. I don't always write on this subject – but I can offer a different point of view on many aspects of international living.

The novel, *Mule Train*, is finished too – but I'm still trying to find a publisher for that. I've also started on the next novel too.

I have in fact become a writer and consultant, and this won't appeal to every male accompanying partner. But having a 'job' that I find mentally stimulating makes the 'trailing' bit of life much more enjoyable.

The other indispensable part of being a successful male accompanying partner, and having a real portable career, is having a supportive partner willing to listen to my gripes and support me in the work I choose to do. We are a team, and doing our best to support each other as we aim for our career and personal goals is essential for the ongoing health of our relationship and our individual careers.

Carrie Shearer believes that men perceive themselves much more by what they do than by what they are. But I would add that most people find it easier to relate to a male accompanying partner if they can categorise that man as something other than 'just a househusband'.

Back then I was a lot more confident when I told people I was a writer than when I said I was a househusband – mostly, I believe, because I was unsure of my own status. But now that I have been successful with my portable career, I can happily call myself a househusband – though I still get strange looks from people who don't know what else I do. However when Seonaid adds, 'He's a writer and has a book published too,' you can see a lot of people visibly relax because they now have a pigeon hole they can more comfortably (for themselves) put me in.

HINDSIGHT IS 20/20

Hindsight is a wonderful thing, but you don't have the benefit of it when you're just starting out. Looking back over the past six years there are many things I could have done differently – but they are just details within the big picture and I'm glad that I had the chance to be a male accompanying partner.

Overall, I was lucky. I'd never heard of the term male accompanying partner when I became one – and so Seonaid and I went into it without thinking of me as anything but an equal partner with my wife. We just had different roles within the family unit.

We were naïve too. We never realised it would be so tough adjusting to our new roles and the loss of respect accorded by the people around us to someone in my position. Another challenge was adjusting to my isolation at home with a pre-school child and hardly anyone to talk to in English all day – especially other men. The isolation was compounded by the fact that I naturally wanted to catch up on the talking at the end of the day when my wife returned from work, just as she wanted to stop talking – which is what she, as a teacher, did for most of the day.

I was lucky in that I knew what I wanted to do with my life – I wanted to be a writer. Staying at home with the kids and being a househusband was fun – but I also needed an intellectual challenge and a part of my life to claim as my own. To be content I needed a well-rounded life – family, leisure and work (or intellectual challenge). The first two were not a problem but the work aspect easily could have been. As with most people, if one of the those three elements had been missing for too long, the levels of stress would have built up and affected the rest of family as much as myself.

Having a goal to aim for was probably the most important factor in making the whole arrangement successful. The final destination I was heading for developed and changed over the years as I realised some things were not attainable – but I still kept moving forward. I followed a correspondence course, volunteered, wrote, and accepted job offers I never would have considered before.

By doing things for myself – networking, making contacts, working, exploring the host city, studying – I made friends and created an identity for myself (rather than being an extension of my wife). It was an identity that I could feel comfortable with and therefore other people could too, which helped my self-confidence and further increased my sense of satisfaction with my role and position in life.

The majority of non-employed spouses in the area where we lived were female (there has only been one other male accompanying partner living near us in six years) and to a certain extent that made daytime socialising difficult. To counteract that I found socialising at darts nights and playing football much more appealing than I might otherwise have done – but even that became less important as I became more secure with my new role (the househusband and male accompanying partner part) in life.

The most important factor in making my endeavours successful, though, was my wife. Everyone expects the *accompanying* expatriate spouse to be supportive to his or her *working* partner, but it needs to work both ways. Seonaid was very positive about my ambitions and without that support it would have been much harder to create a niche for myself with which I was comfortable. However, if I hadn't had something to aim for, she could not have supported me so effectively – and we both would have found the experience much more difficult to cope with.

Communication is a key aspect in helping both the male accompanying partner and the leading female feel comfortable and secure in their disparate roles.

Options For The Male Accompanying Partner

The options will be different for every man. Some will be able to take salaried employment – but the reality of that option is not as widespread as most people seem to think before they relocate.

Working for yourself is an obvious choice, but one that is not so easy to put into practice. What to do, where to find clients, how to manage the business, how to make sure you get paid? The practical aspects are challenge enough in your own country, but abroad they can seem insurmountable. A good start is to take advice from other expatriates and your embassy that can guide you on local business conditions and services. Though other expatriates are a good source of information, try to make sure you ask people who have actually tried working for themselves (preferably in that location) and not just thought about it – there will be no end of armchair entrepreneurs who will be happy to tell you it is impossible.

No matter what you decide to do, success rarely comes overnight. Developing your product, cultivating clients and making a sale usually take time and a lot of effort. It's all very well being positive as you start out on your new adventure, but the optimism needs to be tempered with realism.

When deciding what you're going to do, you have to expand your thinking to cover concepts you've never considered before – because many opportunities that you have abroad would never have been an option in your home country (private language tuition being an example). However, you need to consider not only what you would like to do, but also how likely it is that you'll succeed – and how important the end result is to you. If success will be measured purely by making money you will need to look at different jobs than if you define it by a sense of satisfaction. Also, you need to measure the negatives of potential failure against the future possibility of regretting never having given the idea a good chance to get off the ground.

You need a product to sell, whether it's a physical object or your own knowledge that other people want. As an expatriate, certain markets will be closed to you, while others are much more open. For example, unless you have good foreign language skills, or the language of your host country is the same as yours, you may find it difficult to market your product to locals – unless the foreign language skills of the locals are much better than yours.

Fortunately, there are some huge markets out there perfect for expatriate entrepreneurs, as is discussed extensively in *Chapter Seven*, 'Working for Yourself' – your home country, other countries where they speak your language, as well as other expatriates. English happens to be the language of international business, so the fact that you're reading this book means you can also market your product to international companies. Identifying a product and a market for it is an important part of any business – and no less so for a male accompanying partner who wants to work for himself.

Whether you decide to become a consultant and offer international companies the benefit of your many years of cross-cultural experience, or to export lace from Belgium to shops in your home country, you need to find potential clients and contact them.

Traditional market sources are still there, but there are now many that are much more convenient (and cheaper) for the novice international entrepreneur.

Locally produced English language newspapers and magazines seem to be available in most countries around the world, produced by the British and American Chambers of Commerce, local investment agencies and expatriate entrepreneurs. These publications can be an excellent source of contacts, clients and ideas – as well as markets in themselves if you want to be a writer.

The Internet has supposedly revolutionised many aspects of our lives, and for expatriate entrepreneurs it certainly makes life much easier. The telephone directories of most countries are now online – both white and yellow pages. There are numerous electronic directories of companies, classified by function, product, nationality, domicile and language, that are accessible from your desktop – use search engines such as *www.yahoo.com* (which has regional versions that can be reached from bottom of the home page), *www.google.com, www.mamma.com* or *www.dogpile.com*.

Email allows quick, convenient and cheap international communication and reduces the psychological impact of being half way round the world from a potential client. It is also possible to use your computer to make cheap international telephone calls with services such as *www.skype.com* and to receive faxes (*www.efax.com*).

Many countries also have development agencies, whose prime role is to encourage international businesses to set up in their country. The agencies usually have an online presence and can provide targeted market information to international enquirers.

Finally, when launching your portable international career, always bear in mind that you might suddenly have to move again to another new country – and unless you can pack everything up and carry on when you next open your suitcase, the frustration and disappointment can be overwhelming. Though remember, if you want to export lace from Belgium but are worried about moving to somewhere they do not make lace, most countries produce some local product that you can export to the same or similar markets as the lace you send from Belgium. The fine art of a successful career in your suitcase doesn't mean having a big bag, but having a big imagination and the enthusiasm to carry it out.

The options for that portable career are many and various and though not all will appeal to every male, having a career goal and going after it can make the experience of being a male accompanying partner much more enjoyable.

60 BRILLIANT IDEAS

All these simple ideas have worked for me or for people I have known. Most of them have become freelance businesses. Remember, listen to complaints of unmet needs and take note of what people say they will pay money for. Maybe one of these projects could be yours.

1. Teach people to do the things you find easy – cooking, typing, sewing, painting or word processing, for example.
2. Write a guidebook about your new town for newcomers, tourists or visiting grandparents.
3. Learn a new skill and turn it into a business. Aromatherapy, reflexology, meditation, yoga, astrology, hypnotherapy, writing, painting, teaching, flower arranging, cooking, stencilling, fitness, interior design and so on.
4. If you can't do anything artistic or creative yourself, then be aware that there are lots of artists out there who are hopeless at marketing. Offer to help them with their business. I knew an artist who teamed up with a marketing person and together they ran successful Christmas card business.
5. Teach other people to teach something that you already teach yourself. After I taught word processing and ran my own computer training company, I taught others how to teach too and run their own training courses. Produce a course outline and sell it to potential teachers.
6. Make your life one long garage sale. Buy things cheaply and sell them at a mark-up.
7. Export local goods back home.
8. Import goods from home to the place you are living.
9. Print tee-shirts or sweatshirts with locally desirable motifs.
10. Offer to act as a guide to other people's visitors.
11. Type from home. People often need their dissertations, curriculum vitae or labels typed or word processed. Small businesses may not be able to afford a secretary of their own.
12. Paint individual greeting cards.
13. Paint Christmas cards, get them printed, and sell them at Christmas bazaars and to friends.
14. Paint a picture or take a photograph, enlarge it at a copy centre, and produce laminated copies to sell as place mats.
15. Offer to paint or photograph people's homes.
16. Make and sell chutney or jams from local ingredients.
17. Offer to make soft furnishings for your friends.
18. Get a wood burning pen and engrave personalised messages on simple boxes, memo holders and other gift items.
19. Make items out of locally available products. Perhaps you could turn shells into jewellery or ornaments.

20. Make special occasion cakes to sell for office birthdays and other celebrations. You could even deliver the cake yourself, with a helium balloon and a personally delivered song or poem.
21. Start a mobile sandwich service selling in local offices.
22. Offer to rewrite any poorly translated English for local companies.
23. Contact food manufacturers and see if they need people to promote items in supermarkets.
24. Contact exhibition organisers to see if stallholders require help.
25. Offer a dog walking or child walking service.
26. Prepare cocktail nibbles for delivery to parties.
27. See if someone you know would like to start a takeaway or ironing service and offer to market these services on a commission basis.
28. Offer to water plants, feed cats or open and close curtains for people who are away on holiday.
29. Offer to look after people's holiday homes off-season. When a British couple based in France thought about this, they decided to help them rent them out too. The idea became a thriving business and franchise for *www.franceonecall.com*
30. Take photographs of local scenes and sell them to photo libraries back home.
31. Rent out baby equipment to visitors, or sell second hand baby equipment.
32. Start a group for other mothers, organising playgroups, support, equipment hire and coffee mornings. Charge for a monthly newsletter.
33. Lead a conversation group, or a book group, in your home in a language you speak well.
34. Join a recruitment agency and offer to do temporary work or holiday cover.
35. Start your own recruitment agency.
36. Create a website covering what's going on in your local community and charge local service companies to advertise.
37. Run a crèche or playgroup close to shops.
38. Offer to do shopping for people and deliver it to their home. This would be really useful to mothers of small children who live in apartments.
39. Make bean bag chairs to order, in fabric chosen by your clients.
40. Grow herbs or plants to sell at garage sales or fundraising events.
41. Make Christmas decorations or handmade crackers and sell them.
42. Offer to take newcomers round the shops and markets on a familiarisation tour.
43. Write travel articles on where you go on holiday and sell them to your local magazines upon return. Take good quality photographs while you are away, and investigate all the travel logistics and prices.

44. Organise children's parties. You could create them according to a theme, arrange games, provide food and perform a puppet show or narrate a story.
45. Teach people how to cook the food from your home country, showing them where to buy the best ingredients locally.
46. Start a newcomers support group and consider selling membership to local companies.
47. Run a curriculum vitae production service.
48. Become proficient in beauty therapy, colour or style analysis and run a business from your home or visit your clients in their homes. Wardrobe weeding and personal shopping are also popular services.
49. Become a counsellor, career advisor or life coach. You should even be able to study online for your certification and work with local clients face to face, and with others by telephone and email.
50. Buy books, videos or audio tapes at discount from small publishing companies and sell them locally.
51. Organise local seminars, plays or concerts from visiting speakers or artists. Often you can identify local sponsors who would be glad to help with funding.
52. Become a qualified Teleclass leader, and run your own seminars by telephone from anywhere to anywhere in the world. Find out more at *www.teleclass.com*.
53. Rent out a room in your home for other people to use to run workshops.
54. Create a free flyer that advertises all the locally run workshops and courses in English.
55. Run a public relations service advertising local expat businesses to expats.
56. Source products that are hard to come by in your new location.
57. Teach others how to garden in their own gardens.
58. Learn to proof-read and be a book editor.
59. Write an interesting journal of your life and experiences and turn it into a book. Write about what you have learned.
60. Learn to be a presenter and travel to groups inspiring others to do something differently by sharing your own stories and learnings,

If you would like to help inspire others please go to:
www.career-in-your-suitcase.com and add your ideas to the list.

MEET THE TEAM

JO PARFITT

www.expatrollercoaster.com

When Jo Parfitt joined her new husband in Dubai and received a stamp in her passport that read 'Not Permitted to Take up Employment' she was devastated.  Since then she has let nothing prevent her from maintaining a professional identity regardless of regular intercontinental moves and the responsibilities of her family. Jo went on to create and sustain a shifting portfolio of portable careers, ranging from making and selling date chutney in Oman through being a successful journalist in Dubai to running seminars and workshops worldwide from her current home in The Netherlands. By the time she was in her third country and tenth year of expatriation Jo realised she had been there, done that and got the tee-shirt and that it was time she wrote a book that would inspire and empower others to develop their own career in a suitcase too. The first and second editions sold out and this, the third, published a decade after the first, has been completely updated. It stands as testament to her work as she begins her third decade overseas and her umpteenth reincarnation.

To book Jo as a keynote speaker for your next conference or event visit *www.expatrollercoaster.com* to find out her availability and request her full speaker profile. To learn more about bulk discounts on all of Jo's books contact her at *www.expatrollercoaster.com*.

GALEN TINDER

www.r-e-a.com

Galen Tinder is a Manager and Senior Career Consultant for Ricklin-Echikson, Associates (REA). Founded in 1981, REA is a global human resources firm specialising in talent management and global mobility support services such as career coaching for accompanying partners of relocating employees and family acclimation assistance. With more than 15 years experience as a counsellor, career coach, trainer and successful writer, Galen currently recruits, trains and supervises some of REA's 2200+ Consultants to ensure service excellence throughout the US and around the globe. Tinder developed REA's comprehensive Career Planning Manual, which provides clients with guidance and practical tools to support all aspects of an effective job search, and to assist those seeking self-employment options as well. He was co-author of the book, A Career in Your Suitcase 2 and has published award-winning articles on careers, the practice of consulting and corporate solutions for supporting expatriates, repatriates and families in global transition. Galen graduated from Brandeis University with a BA in philosophy. He also earned his Master of Divinity degree and later his Doctor of Ministry degree in counseling during his tenure as a Lutheran Minister, serving a congregation in New Jersey, USA. Leaving the ministry after 13 years, Galen has also worked as a government consultant on the mental health issues of senior citizens and as an Employee Assistance Counsellor in private industry.

Galen is solely responsible for the chapters, Talking to a Professional and Coping with Transition. He is a major contributor to Getting a Proper Job, particularly the section called Cyber-Chutzpah and the business plan section and what to charge sections of Working For Yourself.

MARY VAN DER BOON

www.globaltmc.com

Mary is Managing Director of global tmc international management training and consulting. She is a consultant, lecturer, writer, trainer and coach in the areas of organisational behaviour, transcultural management, diversity and inclusiveness and international assignment management to multinational, governmental and non-governmental organisations around the world. Mary is Canadian and has been an expatriate for thirty years. Her work has taken her to four continents and she speaks six languages. Mary studied Anthropology at Padjadjaran University in Indonesia, has an MBA from Leiden University and is a PhD candidate in Organisational Behaviour at the University of Amsterdam. She lectures in Transcultural Management and Diversity for the University of British Columbia and Nipissing University in Canada , as well as TIASNimbas Business School and Leiden University in the Netherlands. She is President of the European Professional Women's Network-Amsterdam and contributing author to the *International Handbook of Women and Small Business Entrepreneurship*.

Mary contributed to the sections called Start at the Beginning, Time for Some New Skills, New Perspectives, Volunteer, Learn the Language and A Woman's World.

GAIL MACINDOE
www.macIndoe.com

Gail is a learning & development manager, specialising in talent management, mentoring and coaching of senior executives. She is master NLP practitioner and holds an MBA and a BA in Psychology. Prior to moving to the UK in 1997, Gail lived over 30 years abroad working in a variety of fields including advertising, public relations and marketing in the USA, Middle East, Africa and Europe. You can contact her at gailMacIndoe@hotmail.com.

Gail contributed to the sections on stress, goal setting, motivation, branding and marketing

HUW FRANCIS
www.huwfrancis.com

Huw Francis lived abroad for ten years until his return to the UK in 2002. He qualified as an engineer in the UK and later gained a post-graduate qualification in International Business Management from the US. After working in the UK for five years he moved to Hong Kong where he became a business manager and consultant and met his Scottish wife. In 1996 he accompanied her on a move from Hong Kong to Turkey and in 2001 to France. In 2002 they returned to Wales. When Huw, his wife and son moved to Turkey, Huw began working as a freelance writer and independent business consultant while also being primary care-giver to the children. Since 1996 Huw's articles have been published in sixteen countries and four languages. He has also co-authored *Live and Work Abroad: A Guide for Modern Nomads* (Vacation Work, £11.95), updated *Live and Work In Italy*, and has worked with organisations and individuals to develop their commercial presence in international markets. In 2002 they returned to Wales, before moving on again to the Western Isles of Scotland in 2007.

Huw wrote the chapter on male accompanying partners.

RESOURCES

Books

FIRST LOOK INSIDE YOURSELF
AND CREATING A CAREER

Parfitt, J *Find Your Passion* Lean Marketing Press
Benziger, K *Thriving in Mind www.benziger.org*
Sher, B *I Could Do Anything I Wanted if Only I Knew What it Was* Hodder and Stoughton
Goldberg , N *Writing Down the Bones* Shambala
Cameron, J *The Artist's Way* Pan Macmillan
Anderson, N *Work with Passion* New World Library
Keirsey, D *Please Understand Me II* Prometheus Nemesis Book Company
Taylor, R *Transform Yourself* Kogan-Page
Sinetar, M *Do What You Love and The Money Follows* Dell Trade Paperback
Nelson Bolles, R *What Color is Your Parachute?* Ten Speed Press
Nelson Bolles, R *What Color Is Your Parachute Workbook: How to Create a Picture of your Ideal Job or Next Career* Ten Speed Press
Clark, J *The Money or Your Life* Century
McGraw, P *Life Strategies* Vermilion
McGraw, P *Self Matters* Simon and Schuster
McConnell, C *Soultrader* Momentum
Longman, S *Choosing a Career* The Times with Kogan-Page
Pyke, G & Neath, S *Be Your Own Careers Consultant* Momentum
Freemantle, D *How to Choose* Momentum
Eikleberry, C *The Career Guide for Creative and Unconventional People* Ten Speed Press
Nelson Bolles, R *How to Find Your Mission in Life, gift edition* Ten Speed Press
Williams, N *The Work We Were Born to Do* Element Books
Buckingham, M & O Clifton, D *Now, Discover your Strengths: How to Develop your Talents and those of the People You Manage* Simon & Schuster
Buckingham, M *Go Put Your Strengths to Work* Free Press
Bryson, DR & Hoge, CM *Portable Identity* Transition Press
Malewski, M *Generation Xpat* Nicholas Brealey
Longman, C *Creating a Career* The Times with Kogan-Page
Handy, C & Handy, E *The New Alchemists* Hutchinson
Sangster, C *Brilliant Future* Momentum
MacKinnon, L *Cosmic Coaching* Ryder
Ibarra, H *Working Identity: unconventional strategies for reinventing your career* Harvard Business School Press

274

JOB HUNTING

Nelson Bolles, R *Job-Hunting on the Internet* Ten Speed Press
The Occupational Outlook Handbook BLS Publications
Yate, M & Dourlain, T *Online Job-Hunting - Great Answers to Tough Questions* Kogan-Page
Semple, A & Haig, M *The Internet Job Search Handbook* How To Books
Krechowiecka, I *Net That Job* The Times with Kogan-Page
Brownfoot, J & Wilks, F *Directory of Volunteering and Employment Opportunities* Director of Social Change Publications
The Voluntary Agencies Directory National Council for Voluntary Organisations (NCVO)
Volunteer Work Central Bureau for Educational Visits and Exchanges
Reily Collins, V *Getting into the Voluntary Sector* Trotman
Adair King, J & Sheldon, B *The Smart Woman's Guide to Resumés and Job Hunting* The Career Press
CEPEC Recruitment Guide: A Directory of Recruitment Agencies and Search Consultants in the United Kingdom CEPEC
Executive Grapevine: the International Directory of Executive Recruitment Consultants Executive Grapevine
Key British Enterprises (Lists the top 30,000 British companies) Dun and Bradstreet
Personnel Managers' Yearbook AP Information Services
Edited by Andrew Stead, A *The Candidate Yearbook (Essays and statistics on job hunting in the UK)* Career Counsel Ltd
Kimeldorf, M *Portfolio Power* Petersons
Thompson, MA *The Global CV and Resumé Guide* Wiley and Sons

TRANSITION

Bridges, W *Transitions: Making Sense of Life's Changes* Perseus
Bridges, W *The Way of Transition: Embracing Life's Most Difficult Moments* Perseus
Marx, E *Breaking Through Culture Shock* Nicholas Brealey
Shepherd, S *Managing Cross-Cultural Transition* Aletheia
Lewis, RD *When Cultures Collide - Managing Successfully across Cultures* Nicholas Brealey Publishing
Dehner, H & Dehner, M *Life on the Outside* Wanderlust
Jeffers, S *Feel the Fear and Do It Anyway* Arrow
Whyte, D *Crossing the Unknown Sea: Work and the Shaping of Identity* Michael Joseph
Palmer, PJ *Let Your Life Speak: Listening for the Voice of Vocation* Jossey Bass Wiley
May, GG *Addiction and Grace* Harper San Francisco

MAKING IT HAPPEN

Seligman, M *Learned Optimism* Pocket Books
Matthews, A *Being Happy* Media Masters

O'Connor, J *NLP: A Practical Guide to Achieving the Results You Want: Workbook* HarperCollins

O'Connor, J *Coaching with NLP - How to be a Master Coach* HarperCollins

O'Connor, J *Free Yourself from Fears* HarperCollins

Charvet, SR *Words that Change Minds* Kendall/Hunt Publishing

O'Connor, J and Ian McDermott, I *Principles of NLP* Thorsons

Shircore, I & McDermott, I *NLP and the New Manager* Orion Business Books

Knight, S *NLP at Work* Nicholas Brealey Publishing

Halsall, I *NLP 4 U* Lloyd West Sdn Bhd

Grant Viagas, B *Stress, Restoring the Balance to Our Lives* The Women's Press

Goleman, D *Emotional Intelligence* Bloomsbury

Matheny, K & McCarthy, CJ *Write Your Own Prescription for Stress* New Harbinger Publications Inc

Orme, G *Emotionally Intelligent Living* Crown House Publishing Ltd.

Peale, NV *The Power of Positive Thinking* Vermilion

Robbins, A *Unlimited Power* Simon & Schuster

Robbins, A *Notes From a Friend* Simon & Schuster

Robbins, A *Awaken the Giant Within* Simon & Schuster

Scala, J *25 Natural Ways to Manage Stress and Burnout* Keats Publishing

Stewart, W *Building Self-Esteem* How To Books

Blakeslee, T *The Attitude Factor* Harper Collins

Covey, SR *The Seven Habits of Highly Effective People* Fireside

Pedrick, C *The Habit Change Workbook: How to Break Bad Habits and Form Good Ones* New Harbinger

Buzan, T *Use Your Head* BBC Consumer Publishing

Buzan, T *The Mind Map* BBC Consumer Publishing

Griffiths, B *Do What You Love for the Rest of your Life: A Practical Guide to Career Change and Personal Renewal* Ballantine

Spillane, M *Branding Yourself* Pan Macmillan

Courtenay, G *How to Write Sales Letters with Clout* Summertime Publishing

Byrne, R *The Secret* Atria Books

The Mind Gym *The Mind Gym: Wake Your Mind Up* Warner Books

Callaghan, RJ with Richard Trubo, R *Tapping the Healer Within: Using Thought Field Therapy to Instantly Conquer Your Fears, Anxieties, and Emotional Distress* McGraw-Hill

Tracy, B *Goals!* Berrett-Koehler Publishers

Foster, TRV *101 Ways to Generate Great Ideas* Kogan Page

Shircore, I & McDermott, I *Manage Yourself, Manage Your Life* Piatkus Publishing

Kazerounian, N *Stepping Up* McGraw-Hill

Kaufman, R *Up Your Service* www.ronkaufman.com

Cranwell-Ward, J & Bacon, A & Mackie, R *Inspiring Leadership* Thomson

Cooper, CL & Lewis, S *Balancing Your Career, Family and Life* The Daily Telegraph with Kogan-Page

Bryan, M with Cameron, J & Allen, C *The Artist's Way at Work: Twelve Weeks to Creative Freedom* Pan Books

Burns, D *The Feeling Good Handbook* Plume
Buzan, T *Head Strong* Thorsons
Chapman, M *The Emotional Intelligence Pocketbook* Management Pocketbooks

WORKING FOR YOURSELF

Parfitt, J *Expat Entrepreneur* Lean Marketing Press
Ferris, T *The Four Hour Workweek* Crown
Barrow, C & Golzen, G & Kogan, H *The Daily Telegraph Guide to Taking Up a Franchise* Kogan-Page
Gerber, M *The Emyth* Harper Business
Chopra, D *Synchrodestiny: Harnessing the infinite power of coincidence to create miracles* Rider Books
Friedman, TL *The World is Flat* Penguin Books
Moore, DP & Buttner, EH *Women Entrepreneurs: moving beyond the glass ceiling* Sage Publications
Perrin Moore, D *Careerpreneurs: lessons from leading women entrepreneurs on building a career without boundaries* Davies-Black Publishing

MAKE YOU THINK

Tapscott, D & Williams, AD *Wikinomics: How mass collaboration changes everything* Penguin Group
Katie, B *Loving What Is* Random House
Wachs Book, E *Why the Best Man for the Job is a Woman: The Unique Female Qualities of Leadership* Harper Collins Business
Helgesen, S *The Female Advantage: Women's Ways of Leadership* Doubleday
Kanter, RM *When Giants Learn to Dance: Mastering the Challenges of Strategy, Management and Careers in the 1990s* Routledge
Austin, L *What's Holding You Back? 8 Critical Choices For Women's Success* Basic Books
Gladwell, M *The Tipping Point* Abacus
Reals Ellig, J & Morin, WJ *What Every Successful Woman Knows: 12 Breakthrough Strategies to Get the Power and Ignite Your Career* McGraw-Hill, New York
Wilen, T *International Business: A Basic Guide for Women* Xlibris
Garratt, S *Women Managing for the Millennium* Harper Collins Business
Salmansohn, K *How to Succeed in Business Without a Penis: Secrets and Strategies for the Working Woman* Random House
Evans, G *Play Like a Man, Win Like a Woman* Broadway Books
Pinkola Estes, C *Women Who Run With the Wolves* Ballantine Books
Rimm, S *See Jane Win: The RIMM Report on How 1,000 Girls Became Successful Women* Crown
Rosener, J *America's Competitive Secret: Utilizing Women as a Management Strategy* Oxford University Press
Rubin, H *The Princessa: Machiavelli for Women* Doubleday

Hansen Shaevitz, M *The Confident Woman: Learn the Rules of the Game* Crown/Random House

Hewlett, SA *Off-Ramps and On-Ramps* Harvard Business School Press

LIVING AND WORKING ABROAD

Edited by Boels, AM *The Insider's Guide to Working in Europe* Benefactum

Going Global Guides www.goinglobal.com

Francis, H & Callan, M *Live and Work Abroad* Vacation Work *www.vacationwork.co.uk*

Golzen, G & Reuvid, J *Working Abroad 23rd Edition* Kogan-Page *www.kogan-page.co.uk*

Health Professional Abroad, The Good Cook's Guide to Working Worldwide, Working with the Environment, Working with Animals, and many other career specific titles Vacation Work *www.vacationwork.co.uk*

Living and Working in Britain, Living and Working in America, Living and Working in France, Living and Working in Spain, and many other country specific titles Survival Books *www.survivalbooks.net*

Culture Shock! Culture Shock! Venezuela, Culture Shock! Austria, Culture Shock! Japan, Culture Shock! Norway, How to Succeed in Business in Thailand, How to Succeed in Business in India, Global Customs and Etiquette guides, and many other country specific titles Kuperard *www.cultureshockconsulting.com/books*

Foster, D *The Global Etiquette Guide to Asia, The Global Etiquette Guide to Europe, and other country specific titles* John Wiley and Sons

Aletheia Publications Inc, *numerous books on expat issues www.members.aol.com/alethpub*

Landes, M *The Back Door Guide to Short-Term Job Adventures* Ten Speed Press

Griffith, S *Work Your Way Around the World* Vacation Work

Mole, J *Mind Your Manners* Nicholas Brealey Publishing

Trompenaars, F *Riding the Waves of Culture* Nicholas Brealey Publishing *and many other titles from Nicholas Brealey and Intercultural Press www.interculturalpress.com*

Kruempelmann, E *The Global Citizen* Ten Speed Press

Home Away From Home, Relocation 101, Let's Make a Move, and other books from BR Anchor www.branchor.com

PRESENTATION SKILLS

Kurtz, P *The Global Speaker* Amacom

Searancke, C *How to Write Winning Presentations* Be Clear

NETWORKING

Parfitt, J & Tillyard, J *Grow Your Own Networks* Summertime Publishing

Lopata, A & Roper, P *And Death Came Third* Lean Marketing Press

Darling, D *The Networking Survival Guide* McGraw Hill

Power, T *Networking for Life* Ecademy Press

Boothman, N *How to Make Someone Like You in 90 Seconds or Less* Workman Publishing

Boothman, N *How to Connect in Business in 90 Seconds or Less* Workman Publishing

Ward, S *No Sweat Networking - Simple Solutions to Overcome Networking Obstacles (ebook) www.fireflycoaching.com*

Schalks, E *Networking - a tool to achieve your goals (ebook) www.ande.nl*

Websites

Learn to teach online at:

www.elearningprofessional.com
www.sheffcolac.uk/lettol/
www.teleclass.com
www.anysubject.com

Learn about being a virtual assistant at:

www.ivaa.org
www.assistu.com
www.allianceofvirtualassistants.org.uk

Learn about becoming a coach at:

www.coachfederation.com
www.coachville.com

Learn about online trading at:

www.tradingday.com

Franchises can be found at:

www.floridaservicenet.com

Find out more about teleclasses at:

www.teleclass.com
www.raindance.com

Skills

www.lsc.gov.uk Central London Learning and Skills Council, Work based training and qualifications for EU citizens, Centre Point, London

www.beclear.co.uk
www.professionalspeakers.org
www.nsaspeaker.org
www.toastmasters.org

Networks

www.europeanpwn.net
www.belgiumstuds.com
www.londstuds.org
www.ecademy.com
www.linkedin.com
www.fawco.org
www.newcomersclub.com
www.brxnet.co.uk
www.bni.com
www.connectingwomen.nl
www.winconference.net
www.auroravoice.com
www.hightech-women.com
www.womeninenterprise.com
www.wireuk.org
www.advancingwomen.com
www.t-i-a.com
www.iwt.org
www.webgrrls.com
www.expatwomen.com
www.paguro.net
www.global-connection.info
www.expatica.com
www.british-expats.com
www.transitionsabroad.com
www.work-lifeforum.com
www.parentsatwork.org.uk
www.xpatsreunited.com
www.expats-abroad.com
www.expatsreunite.com
www.witi.com
www.womenconnect.org.uk
www.aafsw.org
www.sietarinternational.org
www.wowwomen.com
www.ecademy.com
www.slowlane.com
www.trailingspouse.net
www.expatexchange.com
www.globalnetwork.co.uk

Other websites

www.skype.com
www.teleclass.com
www.happiness.co.uk

www.anincomeofherown.com
www.enterweb.org
www.mmmonthly.com
www.aentrepreneur.com
www.sbaonline.sba.gov/womeninbusiness
www.bizoffice.com
www.homebasedbusiness.com
www.hbba.com.au
www.talesmag.com
www.expatexchange.com
www.theamericanhour.com
www.writersnews.co.uk
www.bllc.co.uk
www.businessadviceonline.org
www.workingchallenged.com
www.transitionsabroad.com

Organisations

www.cbimobility.org
www.tckinteract.net
www.knowyourtype.com

Working abroad

www.permitsfoundation.com
www.dejanews.com
www.fortune.com
www.clearinghouse.net
www.dnb.com
www.vault.com
http://hoovers.com
www.websense.com
www.financials.com
www.focus-info.org
http://fragomen.com
www.h1visajobs.com
www.y-axis.com
www.us-immigration.org
www.smarterwork.com
www.freelancersintheuk.co.uk
www.freelance.com
www.gofreelance.com
www.quintessential.com
www.careerbuilder.com
www.careerpath.com
www.monster.com
www.hotjobs.com

www.fish4jobs.co.uk
www.jobbankinfo.org
www.netlondon.com/employment/agencies/index.html
http://dbm.com/jobguide
www.partnerjob.com
http://fragomen.com
http://thomas.loc.gov
www.jobhunt.com

and, to give you an idea of what else is available and to inspire you to start surfing ...

www.monster.co.uk
www.reed.co.uk
www.gojobsite.co.uk
www.charityjob.co.uk
www.bigbluedog.com
www.londonjobs.com
www.newmonday.co.uk
www.jobserve.com
www.ftcareerpoint.com
www.thetimes-appointments.co.uk
www.iht.com
www.appointments-plus.com
www.jobs.guardian.co.uk
www.londoncareers.net

Transition

www.transition-dynamics.com
www.sietar-europa.org

People mentioned in this book

www.antion.com
www.infoselling.com
www.connectuscanada.com
www.businesstree.com
www.businesswomancanada.com
www.benziger.org
www.going-beyond.dk
www.lopata.co.uk
www.kintish.co.uk
www.gwenrhys.com
www.dianedarling.com
www.whereonearthgroup.com
www.expatexpert.com
www.r-e-a.com

INDEX

"One of the best books there is for expatriates who want a career adventure. This book is packed with examples, tips and, of course, lots of inspiration. Don't forget to pack it before you set off on your new life."
Robin Pascoe, www.expatexpert.com

ENTREPRENEUR

How To Create and Maintain Your Own
Portable Career Anywhere In The World

JO PARFITT

Claim your FREE special report at
www.expatentrepreneurs.com

find your
passion

second edition

*20 tips and 20 tasks
for finding work that
makes your spirit soar*

jo parfitt

expat writer

RELEASE THE BOOK WITHIN

Jo Parfitt

For more of Jo Parfitt and her work please go to
www.**expatrollercoaster**.com and www.**bookcooks**.com

Printed in the United States
122717LV00001B/137/P